1-2-3® Release 2.3
Made Easy

Mary Campbell

Osborne McGraw-Hill

Berkeley New York St. Louis San Francisco
Auckland Bogotá Hamburg London Madrid
Mexico City Milan Montreal New Delhi Panama City
Paris São Paulo Singapore Sydney
Tokyo Toronto

Osborne **McGraw-Hill**
2600 Tenth Street
Berkeley, California 94710
U.S.A.

For information on translations and book distributors outside of the
U.S.A., please write to Osborne **McGraw-Hill** at the above address.

1-2-3® Release 2.3 Made Easy

1234567890 DOC 9987654321

ISBN 0-07-881732-3

Acquisitions Editor: Elizabeth Fisher
Technical Reviewer: Campbell & Associates
Project Editor: Janis Paris
Copy Editors: Dana Dubrinsky, Valerie Haynes-Perry
Proofreading Coordinator: Nancy Pechonis
Design: Patricia Jani Beckwith, Stefany Otis

Contents

Acknowledgments

This book is the result of the efforts of many individuals. I would like to extend my special thanks to the following individuals:

Gabrielle Lawrence, who helped with every phase of the book. Eriks Usis, who created all the screens and checked each exercise to ensure it produces the correct results.

At Osborne McGraw-Hill, Liz Fisher, who managed the entire process of making this a book and helped in many ways to produce a quality product. Wendy Goss, who prepared all of our chapters for editorial. Janis Paris, who did a fine job as project editor; and Judy Wohlfrom and her department, who did their usual wonderful job with the production of this book.

To all of those at Lotus who were such an immense help through the beta process for Release 2.3, including Susan Erabino, Steve Ormsby, Mary Beth Rettger, and Alexandra Trevelyan.

Introduction

1-2-3 has become such an important business tool that it seems difficult to remember what it was like to perform financial analyses without it. Although there have been many spreadsheet products from which to select, 1-2-3 has continued to offer the speed and functionality to meet the needs of the majority of spreadsheet users.

Release 2.2 introduced many new features that extended the usefulness of the product; for example, the Settings Sheets that provide a look at the overall selections within a given area of 1-2-3. Now Release 2.3 presents a WYSIWYG feature that allows you to view text and graphs together, change fonts and look at the effect; and this release allows you to use a mouse for your selections.

Why 1-2-3 Release 2.3 Is for You

There are many spreadsheet products on the market today, and these offerings include several versions of 1-2-3, such as 1-2-3 3.1 and 1-2-3/G.

The various 1-2-3 products have a larger installed base than any other product available. This means that you will be able to find more users of this spreadsheet product than any other, and the knowledge gained in working with the product is transportable from company to company. The reason you would choose 1-2-3 2.3 over other 1-2-3 releases relates to the hardware that you are using.

- 1-2-3 Release 2.3 will run on an older model XT system with a minimum of 320K of memory.

- 1-2-3 Release 3.1 requires a 286 or 386 machine and at least 1MB of memory and can take full advantage of the extended and expanded memory in a PS/2 machine.

- 1-2-3/G requires that you use OS/2 as your operating system rather than DOS and requires even more memory.

Although you can continue to use older releases of 1-2-3, such as 1-2-3 2.01 and 2.2, you will not have access to all the new features of 1-2-3 Release 2.3.

1-2-3 Release 2.3 offers many new features, including full mouse support, the WYSIWYG add-in that provides a "what you see is what you get" approach to spreadsheet design, dialog boxes for quick selection of features, a viewer add-in that can "look" inside files, and new graph types.

About This Book

This book is designed to present 1-2-3's features, including the new Release 2.3 options, in an easy-to-learn format. You will use these new features as you create practical application examples. Because you are introduced to these commands in the context of application examples, you not only will see the keystrokes used to make things happen but will learn what capabilities these features offer.

The exercises within the book are presented in a step-by-step tutorial format to guarantee your success. Knowing when to use a command is not left to chance, since you are offered detailed instructions throughout the model-building process. With the building block approach presented in this book you will find your 1-2-3 skills increasing rapidly as you move from chapter to chapter.

How This Book Is Organized

This book is divided into 12 chapters. In most cases, each chapter contains just the right number of new features to cover in a single session. The first few chapters provide the building blocks for your first model. After you have mastered these topics, you will probably want to progress through the remaining topics sequentially, leading gradually to more advanced topics. Because the models in the later chapters are self-contained, you can also work with them without first becoming familiar with the examples in earlier chapters.

Chapter 1 will get you started with the package. It explains the important features of 1-2-3's display and introduces the new help structure for the package. It also introduces the entry of numbers and labels on the worksheet. You will learn how to use the Undo feature to protect your worksheet investment.

Chapter 2 provides an introduction to the use of formulas on the worksheet. You will learn how formulas add power to the worksheet through What-if capabilities.

Chapter 3 provides information to tailor the format of your entries to your needs. You will learn how to select currency, fixed, percent, scientific notation, date, or other cell formats on the worksheet. You will also learn how to change the width of columns to display the new formats and to use Release 2.3's efficient Column-Range option.

Chapter 4 shows you how to protect your investment in model building through the use of files that can be stored on your disk permanently. You will learn about Release 2.3's ability to create backup files, as you learn how easy it is to store and retrieve data on your disk.

Chapter 5 covers everything you need to know to copy entries that you have already made to other locations on the worksheet. In this chapter you will learn techniques for rearranging worksheet data to change models. You will also learn to use Release 2.3's Range Search feature to locate cell entries quickly.

Chapter 6 provides explanations and examples of 1-2-3's print features. You will learn how to do everything from printing a draft of your worksheet to adding headers and other sophisticated options. Later, in Chapter 12, you will supplement the basics learned in this chapter with the spreadsheet publishing options offered by the Allways or new WYSIWYG add-ins that ship with every copy of the Release 2.2 and 2.3 software.

Chapter 7 introduces you to the different categories of 1-2-3's built-in functions. These are formulas that are prerecorded and stored within the package for instant access. You will learn about the different categories of functions that 1-2-3 offers and learn to select those that meet your needs. All of 1-2-3's functions are listed in this chapter.

Chapter 8 introduces 1-2-3's graphic features, which provide tools for presenting numeric data in an understandable fashion. You will learn how to create a variety of graph types. In Chapter 12 you will learn how to supplement 1-2-3's basic graph printing features with WYSIWYG or Allways, which can print graphs without exiting from 1-2-3.

Chapter 9 covers the data-management features of the package. You can use these to create a simple database. You will also find examples that show you how to sort information in the database and selectively copy information to create a quick report.

Chapter 10 expands on the basic file-management features introduced in Chapter 4. The chapter teaches you how to combine several files and how to link cells between worksheets to access data. You can use these features to create consolidations for your business.

Chapter 11 examines the basics of 1-2-3 macros, including the Learn features which make macro creation easy. You will learn how to record keystrokes for execution at a later time.

Chapter 12 introduces the powerful spreadsheet publishing add-ins WYSIWYG and Allways. These add-ins allow you to use the full capabilities of your print device and to integrate text and graphics on the page. You will also have an opportunity to try the Auditor add-in for a close up look at your model.

The appendix provides detailed installation instructions.

Conventions Used in This Book

Throughout this book you will be instructed to make entries in 1-2-3 models. Each of these entries will be shown in boldface. If you are already somewhat familiar with the technique being presented, scan the instructions quickly and enter only the information in boldface to perform the exercise.

The full menu command is shown in each instruction requiring a menu selection. You can choose to type the first letter of each menu option or highlight the desired option and press ENTER.

1

Worksheet Basics

You are about to enter the world of 1-2-3. This journey will give you a new way of working with everyday business problems—a way that is both efficient and flexible. Traditionally, business problems have been worked out on green-bar columnar pads, commonly used by accountants and business managers to evaluate financial decisions. 1-2-3 replaces the paper versions of these worksheets by turning your computer into a large electronic version of this columnar pad.

You will learn to use 1-2-3's worksheet features to handle the same types of problems previously solved on columnar pads. Applications such as budgeting, financial planning, project cost projections, break-even analysis, and cost planning are some of the applications you might consider. You also will learn to pattern calculations after real-world situations and lay out models representing the problem to be solved on the electronic worksheet.

The electronic sheet of paper that 1-2-3 places into your computer's memory has a structure organized to help you construct these models. The electronic worksheet is arranged into rows and columns, allowing you to enter numbers, labels, and formulas. Making these entries on 1-2-3's worksheet offers significant advantages over making them on paper. For example, once you have entered a calculation on paper, it is difficult to make a change. However, 1-2-3 provides a number of features that facilitate change. On a paper worksheet, you must update calculations every time you change a number; however, because 1-2-3 can remember calculations, it recalculates the worksheet automatically when you update a number.

In this chapter you will look at beginning and ending a worksheet session, worksheet organization, entering numbers and labels on the worksheet, correcting data-entry errors, using the new Undo feature, and accessing 1-2-3's Help features. Since the material in this chapter covers some of the basic building blocks of worksheet-model construction, you will want to master it completely before progressing to more advanced topics. Although you probably are eager to start using 1-2-3's features, you may have to complete some preliminary work first in order to get maximum knowledge from this chapter. Before you begin, assess your current knowledge of the PC and whether your copy of 1-2-3 is ready to use. If you are a new PC user, read Appendix A, "Installing 1-2-3 and WYSIWYG," before proceeding. If 1-2-3 has not yet been installed on your system, complete this step from the instructions in Appendix A. Then, once you have filled in the gaps, continue reading and working with this chapter.

Loading and Quitting 1-2-3

You cannot begin to use 1-2-3 until you have loaded it into the memory of your computer system. The procedure depends on whether you are using a floppy disk or hard disk system. Network users follow different procedures depending on where 1-2-3 has been installed and need to follow the specific instructions supplied by the network administrator for activating 1-2-3.

Starting 1-2-3 from a Hard Disk

To start 1-2-3 from a hard disk, you need to activate the directory that contains the 1-2-3 files. If you have installed the files in a directory on drive C named 123, you need to follow these steps.

1. Activate the C drive by starting (*booting*) the system from drive C.
   If your system is already on with DOS loaded but another drive is active, you can activate drive C by typing **C:**. Once drive C is active, the DOS prompt displays as C>.

2. Activate the subdirectory containing the 1-2-3 files. To activate the directory 123, type **CD\123** and press ENTER.
   If your files are in another directory, substitute the name of your directory for 123 in the entry.

3. Type **123** and press ENTER to start the 1-2-3 program.
   A Lotus copyright screen will display and after a brief delay it will be replaced by an empty worksheet screen.

Starting 1-2-3 from a Floppy Disk

To start 1-2-3 on a floppy disk system, follow these steps:

1. Place the operating system disk in drive A and turn on the system.
   The operating system will boot and is likely to respond with a prompt for the date.

2. Enter the current date in the format mm-dd-yy and press ENTER.

3. Enter the current time in the format hh:mm and press ENTER.

4. Remove the operating system disk and replace it with the 1-2-3 System disk.

5. Type **123** and press ENTER.
   The copyright screen appears briefly, followed by an empty worksheet display.

Quitting 1-2-3

When you have finished all your 1-2-3 tasks for the day, you will want to return to the operating system to work with other programs. To end your 1-2-3 session and return to the operating system, you can type **/**, which activates 1-2-3's menu, and then type **/QYY** to select the Quit and Yes commands. 1-2-3 understands your entry as a request to clear memory and end the program unless there is data in memory that has not been saved. 1-2-3 keeps track of whether you have changed any cells on the worksheet and whether you have saved the worksheet after making changes. If you have not saved the changes, 1-2-3 prompts you with the message "WORKSHEET CHANGES NOT SAVED! End 1-2-3 anyway?"

and expects you to respond with **Y** or **N**. Typing **Y** causes 1-2-3 to end immediately. Once you are back at the operating system, you can run another program or enter direct operating system requests. You can start 1-2-3 again by typing **123** and pressing ENTER. If you elect to stay in 1-2-3 in response to the prompt, type **N**. 1-2-3 does not end, allowing you to save the data in memory if you wish. Also in this chapter you will learn the procedure for saving entries in the worksheet.

Worksheet Organization

When you load 1-2-3 into the memory of your computer, you will see only the upper left corner of your worksheet. Your display should match the one shown in Figure 1-1. This initial display lets you glimpse the 8 leftmost columns and the first 20 rows of the worksheet. The worksheet is much larger than it first appears. There are 256 columns in the worksheet, named A to IV. Single alphabetic letters are used first; then AA to AZ, BA to BZ, and so on until reaching the limit of IV. Rows are named with numbers rather than letters. Release 1A of the package has 2048 rows; Release 2 and higher releases have 8192 rows. Figure 1-2 shows the entire worksheet, compared with the small portion that is visible when you first load the package.

The Cell Pointer

Each location on the worksheet is referred to as a *cell*. Each cell is uniquely identified by its column and row location. The column is always specified first to create cell locations such as A1, C10, IV8192, Z1025, and IJ850. A *cell pointer* always marks the current location with a small highlighted bar. In a new worksheet, such as the one in Figure 1-1, the cell pointer is located in cell A1. The location of the cell pointer is extremely important: It marks the location of the active cell, the only cell into which you can make an entry without first moving the cell pointer.

Elements of Your Screen

The top three lines of the screen are called the *control panel*. You can see this panel in Figure 1-1; it is used to monitor most of your 1-2-3 activities. As you make entries on the worksheet, these entries will appear

Figure 1-1.   *Left corner of worksheet visible on the screen*

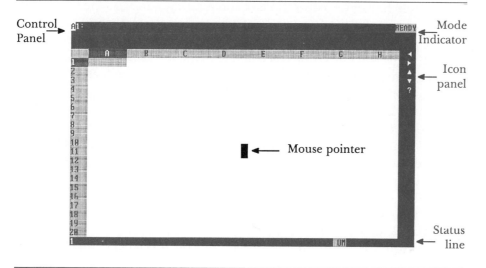

in the control panel. The panel also monitors 1-2-3's activities and tells you when 1-2-3 is ready to proceed with new activities. In addition, the control panel functions as a place keeper, letting you know your current location on the worksheet and specifics about that location.

Figure 1-2.   *Worksheet layout*

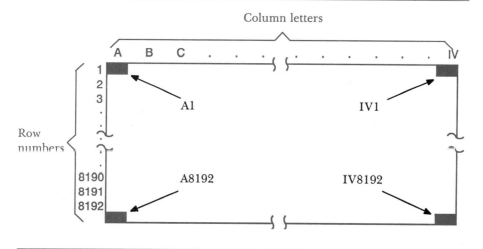

The Top Line

The top line of the control panel almost always displays the location of the cell pointer in the left corner. This location is referred to as the *cell address;* it always matches the location of the cell pointer in the lower portion of the worksheet. As you begin to make worksheet entries, you will find that this location also displays the contents of the cell, as well as any width or formatting changes that you have applied to this cell.

Figure 1-3 shows a 1-2-3 screen with $5 in cell C6. Here, the control panel tells you that the cell pointer is in C6, a format of currency with zero decimal places is used for the format (C0), and the column has been assigned a width of three [W3]. The last piece of information is the *contents* of the cell, represented by the 5. All these special entries will be discussed in detail in other chapters.

The Mode Indicator

The right corner of the top line of the control panel contains a *mode indicator.* When you first load 1-2-3 this indicator will display READY, indicating that 1-2-3 is ready to respond to whatever you enter. The mode indicator can tell you either that 1-2-3 is busy with your previous request or that it is ready to do something new. It can also tell you to correct an error, point to a worksheet location, or select a menu choice. Once 1-2-3's mode indicator changes from READY to another mode, you must either follow along with 1-2-3's plans or change the indicator. Many new users become frustrated at this point, but you can avoid frustration by watching the mode indicator and staying in sync with its current mode. Table 1-1 lists all the modes you can encounter, along with their meanings. They will also be pointed out in later chapters, as new activities cause mode changes.

Figure 1-3.   *Control panel entries for cell format, width, and contents*

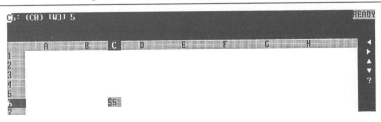

Table 1-1. *Mode Indicators*

Indicator	Meaning
EDIT	The cell entry is being edited. EDIT can be generated by 1-2-3 when your cell entry contains an error. It can also be generated by pressing F2 (EDIT) to change a cell entry.
ERROR	1-2-3 has encountered an error. The problem will be noted in the middle or bottom of the screen. Press ESC to clear the Error Message and correct the problem specified in the Error Message.
FILES	1-2-3 wants you to select a filename to proceed. This message is also shown when you request a list of the files on your disk.
FIND	The Data Query Find command is active.
FRMT	A format line is being edited after you selected Data Parse Format-Line Edit.
HELP	A Help display is active.
LABEL	1-2-3 has decided that you are making a label entry.
MENU	1-2-3 is waiting for you to make a selection from the menu.
NAMES	1-2-3 is displaying a menu of range or graph names.
POINT	1-2-3 is waiting for you to point to a cell or a range. As soon as you begin to type, the POINT mode will change to the EDIT mode.
READY	1-2-3 is currently idle and is waiting for you to make a new request.
SETTINGS	1-2-3 is letting you make entries in a dialog box.
STAT	Worksheet status information is displayed.
VALUE	1-2-3 has decided that you are making a value entry.
WAIT	1-2-3 is processing your last command and cannot begin a new task until the flashing WAIT indicator changes to READY.

Other Control Panel Lines

Lines two and three of the control panel will take on special significance as you begin to alter cell entries and use 1-2-3's features. When you use 1-2-3 commands, line two lists all your options at any point. Line three gives an explanation of each choice. The use of these lines to alter cell entries will be covered elsewhere in this chapter, and displaying options in this area is discussed in Chapter 3, "Changing the Worksheet Appearance."

The Status Line

The status line can also provide a variety of information. In Release 2.3, the lower left corner displays the date and time unless you ask 1-2-3 to display the filename in this area. The date and time are updated constantly. If you choose to display the filename, the date and time will still display until a file is assigned a name and saved on disk. You will learn how to change Release 2.3's display for this area in Chapter 3. In releases prior to Release 2.3, if an error occurs it is temporarily replaced with an Error Message, such as "Disk Full," "Printer Error," or "Disk Drive Not Ready." Release 2.3, displays the Error Message in a box in the middle of the screen. Whenever an Error Message displays, the mode indicator displays ERROR in the upper right corner. The ERROR indicator will blink and your computer will sound a warning beep. You cannot proceed until you press the escape (ESC) key to acknowledge the error.

The area to the right of the date and time informs you when certain keys have been pressed. It also tells you if 1-2-3 has encountered a special situation. Six of these indicators are designed to inform you that a certain key or key sequence has been pressed. These indicators are

CAPS	This indicates that the CAPS LOCK key has been pressed. Pressing this key causes the alphabetic keys to produce capital letters.
END	This indicates that the END key has been pressed. The END key is used to move the cell pointer to the end of entries in a given direction or to the end of a group of blank cells in a given direction. After using the END key, you must use an arrow key to indicate the direction. The END indicator reminds you to press an arrow key.
LEARN	This indicates that ALT-F5 (LEARN) has been pressed and that 1-2-3 is recording your keystrokes in a worksheet range.

NUM   This indicates that the NUM LOCK key has been pressed and that you can enter numbers from the numeric keypad as an alternative to using the top row of keys.

OVR   OVR indicates that the INS (INSERT) key has been pressed. When editing cell entries, you will sometimes want to use the overstrike. This feature lets you enter characters that replace the characters in the original entry, rather than adding them to the original entry.

SCROLL This indicates that the SCROLL LOCK key has been pressed. Without SCROLL LOCK, information scrolls off your screen one row or column at a time. With SCROLL LOCK, the entire window shifts each time you press an arrow key.

There are also eight other indicators that monitor advanced features and have broader meanings. These indicators will be covered as they occur elsewhere in this book. They are CALC, CIRC, CMD, MEM, RO, SST, STEP, and UNDO.

Moving Around the Worksheet

Now you are ready to learn to navigate your way around 1-2-3's worksheet in preparation for constructing models with entries in worksheet cells. You will look at the basic features as well as the more advanced options that let you travel long distances quickly.

Basic Options

You can accomplish 1-2-3's basic pointer movements with the *arrow keys*. These may be located directly on the numeric keypad keys or they may reside on separate keys, depending on the age and model of your computer system. Figure 1-4 shows one popular keyboard configuration, with the arrow keys highlighted. Even if your keyboard is slightly different, you should find it relatively easy to locate the keys with the arrows on them. If the arrow keys on your keyboard also house other functions, be careful that the keys are set for the arrow key function. For example, on keyboards where the arrow keys reside on the numeric

Figure 1-4. *IBM's enhanced keyboard*

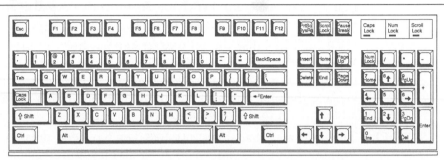

keypad keys, pressing NUM LOCK causes these keys to enter numbers rather than move the cell pointer. You can tell that NUM LOCK has been pressed by the NUM indicator in the status line; in that case, press NUM LOCK a second time to remove the indicator from the screen before using the arrow keys to move the cell pointer.

Using the Arrow Keys

Each of the arrow keys moves the cell pointer one cell in the direction indicated by the arrow. Your computer's keyboard will record multiple presses if you hold down a key. So if you need to use the arrow key, be careful to press it only once and release your finger if you want to move the cell pointer only one cell at a time. Try the following exercise with these keys to become expert in their use.

1. With your cell pointer in the starting A1 location, press the RIGHT ARROW once.

   Your cell pointer should now be in B1, as follows:

2. Press RIGHT ARROW a second time to move your cell pointer to C1.
3. Press DOWN ARROW twice to move your cell pointer to C3.

1

4. Press DOWN ARROW a few more times until your cell pointer reaches C20.

   If you depress DOWN ARROW and move too far down the screen, row 1 will scroll off the screen. You can move your cell pointer back to line 20, but line 1 will not reappear until you move your cell pointer all the way to the top.

5. Press RIGHT ARROW until your cell pointer is in H20; then press it again to scroll a column off the screen as you move to I20.

6. Press UP ARROW until your cell pointer is in I1; then press the LEFT ARROW until the cell pointer returns to A1.

7. Press LEFT ARROW again.

Unless someone has disabled 1-2-3's beep feature, you will hear a beep informing you that the cell pointer cannot be moved. You may want to practice with these keys a little more to ensure that you are comfortable with their use. You can use them to move to any worksheet location. Clearly, however, some shortcuts will be required. The arrow key method would take too long to move you to cell IV200, for example, and return to A1.

There is a variety of methods for moving the cell pointer more quickly. Some use special keys to make the move to a new location; others use a combination of keys. The HOME key is the quickest way to return to A1, the home position or beginning location on a worksheet. As soon as you press this key, the cell pointer moves from its current location to A1. If you have only one key labeled HOME, you will want to be certain NUM is not shown at the bottom of the screen before pressing HOME.

Moving with the Mouse

If you are using a mouse, you will see the *icon panel* on the right edge of the screen and a small rectangle that represents the cell pointer. You can use the icon panel to move within the worksheet or you can use the mouse to point to the cell you want. The ◀, ▶, ▲, and ▼ icons on the icon panel represent the LEFT, RIGHT, UP, and DOWN arrow keys. By pointing to one of them and pressing the left mouse button, you will move the cell pointer one cell in the direction you select. Pressing the left mouse button once is called *clicking* the mouse. During 1-2-3 installation, you had the option to change the mouse button you use to make selections. Most users choose the left mouse button. That way, when the mouse is in your right hand, your index finger is conveniently resting on the mouse button. The left mouse button was selected for examples in this book. If you selected the right mouse button during installation, you will need to substitute "right" for "left," and "left" for "right" for all mouse button instructions. If your mouse has three buttons, you will not use the middle one.

Another way you can use the mouse to move to a cell is by pointing to the cell and clicking on the *mouse pointer*. If the cell is not displayed on the worksheet, you will need to use the arrows in the icon panel to access it.

You can use either the mouse or the other keys described in this chapter to move through your worksheets. You can switch between using the keys and using the mouse for your own convenience. When the step-by-step instructions direct you to move to a cell, your results will be the same whether you use your keyboard or your mouse. You can practice using a mouse to move around in the worksheet by following these steps:

1. Move the mouse pointer to G1 and press the left mouse button.

2. Point to F15 and click on the cell.

3. Hold down the ▶ until the cell pointer moves to M15.

4. Point to M1 and click on the cell.

5. Hold down the ◀ until the cell pointer returns to A1.

PGUP and PGDN

PGUP moves the cell pointer up 20 rows without moving it from its current column. Of course, this key works effectively only when the cell pointer is in row 21 or greater. If the cell pointer is in B1 and you press PGUP, 1-2-3 will beep at you and will not move the cell pointer at all, since the cell pointer is already at the top of the worksheet. If the cell pointer is in B5, PGUP will move it to B1; if the cell pointer is in B26, PGUP will move it up 20 rows to B6. PGDN does the exact opposite: It moves the cell pointer down by 20 rows. However, if you are fewer than 20 rows from the bottom edge of the sheet, then it will take you to the bottom.

The END Key

The END key can be used in combination with the arrow keys to move you to the end of the worksheet in the direction specified. When a worksheet contains data, END functions differently and moves you to the last blank cell, or to the last cell containing data in the direction you specify. END will stop at the last cell with an entry or the last blank cell, depending on whether it was resting on a blank cell or a cell containing data when you pressed it.

To use the END key and arrow combination, follow these steps:

1. Move the cell pointer to A1, then press the END key.
   Verify that the END indicator has appeared in the status line. Next, press the arrow key that specifies the direction in which you wish to move.

2. Press the RIGHT ARROW key.
   The cell pointer will move to the last cell on the right, IV1.

3. Press END followed by the DOWN ARROW key.
   The cell pointer is now in IV2048 or IV8192, depending on whether you are using Release 1A or a higher release of 1-2-3.

Once you have placed entries on the worksheet, the END key can take on a different function. It will move the cell pointer to the last entry in the direction you indicate. Figure 1-5 shows a worksheet containing data with the cell pointer originally located in A2.

In the example shown in Figure 1-5, if you press the END key and then the DOWN ARROW key, the cell pointer will be relocated to A10, the last cell in column A that contains data. 1-2-3 places the cell pointer in this location since it is searching for the first blank cell in the specified direction. It is

Figure 1-5. *Entries for monitoring the effect of the END key*

	A	B	C	D	E	F	G	H
A2: 'Part_No								READY
1								
2	Part_No	Price	Quantity		Bin	Warehouse		
3	AX-8976	4.67	100		7	15		
4	BY-8761	8.90	75		6	1		
5	CD-7865	7.75	100		8	6		
6	ER-5412	6.68	50		2	3		
7	FG-6611	12.98	65		1	4		
8	GT-8811	15.89	76		7	1		
9	NB-6512	3.56	150		5	15		
10	RT-8976	10.95	100		4	4		
11								

important that your data be entered in contiguous cells for this feature to work effectively. If you press the END key again and then the RIGHT ARROW key, the cell pointer will be relocated to E10, the last cell in row 10 that contains data.

Press the HOME key to move to A1 again, then try a quick approach to move to E10. First press the END key, then press HOME. When this sequence is used, 1-2-3 moves the cell pointer to E10, the last worksheet cell that contains an entry.

The CTRL KEY

The CTRL key can be used with the arrow keys to move a width of the screen to the right or left. Unlike the END key, CTRL is not pressed before the arrow key, but simultaneously. To move the cell pointer from A1 to I1, press CTRL and hold it down while pressing the RIGHT ARROW key. To move the cell pointer back to A1 again, press CTRL with the LEFT ARROW key.

The GOTO Key

Your last option for moving the cell pointer quickly is the GOTO option provided by the F5 key. To use this direct cell pointer movement, follow these steps:

1. Press F5 (GOTO).

2. Type **Z10** and press ENTER.
     1-2-3 immediately positions your cell pointer in Z10, regardless of the pointer's beginning location.

Using Basic Cell Pointer Options

The following comprehensive example uses a variety of the quick pointer movement features. It should help to reinforce your understanding of the various options. First press HOME to position your cell pointer in A1. Then follow this sequence of entries:

1. Press PGDN twice to position the cell pointer in A41.

2. Press END, followed by RIGHT ARROW, to position your cell pointer in IV41.

3. Press CTRL-LEFT ARROW twice to move two screens to the left and position your cell pointer in HY41.

1

4. Press END, followed by LEFT ARROW, to position the cell pointer in A41.

5. Press END, followed by UP ARROW, to position your cell pointer in A1.

6. Press F5 (GOTO), enter **S2**, and press ENTER to place your cell pointer in S2.

7. Press HOME to return your cell pointer to A1.

Correcting Errors

You may wonder why you are already learning about error correction when you have not yet made a single cell entry. The reason is that everyone makes at least a few mistakes, and it is impossible to predict when you will make your first one. Therefore, it is best to be prepared before you begin to explore cell entries. There are several error-correction methods. The one you use depends on whether you are still entering the entry you want to correct, or whether you have already finalized the entry by pressing ENTER or moving the cell pointer to a new location.

Fixing an Entry Before It Is Finalized

To correct an error while making an entry into a cell, you can press BACKSPACE to delete the last character you entered. Suppose that you intend to enter "SALES" but that you omit the "E". To correct this error, try this option with the following steps:

1. Move your cell pointer to A1.

2. Type **SALS**, then press BACKSPACE to delete the last "S".

3. Type **ES**.

Do not press any additional keys. You will use this partially completed entry in the next example.

ESC is a more dramatic way to eliminate characters. It eliminates all the characters you have typed in a cell as long as you have not finalized the entry. Try this method: Press ESC or click the right mouse button. The right mouse button is equivalent to pressing ESC, so you can use it any time you would press the ESC key. The entire entry, SALES, will disappear and 1-2-3 will be ready to accept a new entry.

There is one more error-correction method that allows you to edit an entry while you are making it. Since it functions the same whether or not the cell entry has been finalized, it will be discussed in the next section on finalized entry-correction methods.

Fixing a Finalized Entry

You can finalize and display entries in the cells in which you want to enter them by pressing ENTER or moving the cell pointer to a new location. Once the entry is finalized in this way, you must use other methods for correcting mistakes.

Retyping Entries

One way to change a cell entry that has been finalized is to retype it. Follow these steps to create and correct finalized entries:

1. Type **SALS** in A1 and press ENTER.

    This time you will find that neither BACKSPACE nor ESC will affect the entry. One method of changing the contents of A1 is to retype your entry.

2. With the cell pointer in A1, type **SALES** and press ENTER to make the correction.

    This method gets the job done but requires a considerable amount of unnecessary typing.

Editing a Finalized Entry

A better method, especially for longer entries, is to edit the entry and change only the mistakes. You must be in the EDIT mode to make this type of change. To place yourself in EDIT mode, press F2 (EDIT). (Later you will find that 1-2-3 sometimes automatically places you in EDIT mode when it is not happy with the cell entry you are trying to finalize.) Regardless of how you get there, once you are in EDIT mode, the entry in the cell will be placed in the second line of the control panel, just as it was when you originally entered it.

Within the EDIT mode, the special keys that you used to move the cell pointer around on the worksheet function differently. Now the RIGHT and LEFT ARROW keys move you a character to the right or left each time you press them. This allows you to position your small flashing cell pointer on a letter that you want to delete, or to move it where you want to make an insertion.

The HOME key also takes on a new function within the EDIT mode: It moves you to the front of the entry. If the correction you need to make occurs at the beginning of the entry, HOME moves you to that location quickly. The END key moves in the opposite direction. It places the flashing cell pointer at the end of the entry.

Within the entry, two different keys can be used to remove characters. You can press BACKSPACE to delete the character to the left of the flashing cell pointer, or you can press DEL to delete the character above this cell pointer. If you type a character from the keyboard, it will be added to the right of this cell pointer location unless you first press INS to start the *overstrike* setting (overstrike replaces characters already in the entry). Let's try an example using each of these keys.

1. Type the characters **SELRS** in B2 and press ENTER. The screen looks like this:

2. With the cell pointer still in B2, press F2 (EDIT).

   1-2-3 will display the entry in the cell in the second line of the control panel with a small blinking cell pointer at the end, like this:

3. Press BACKSPACE to move the cell pointer one position to the left to delete the "S". Then type **Y**.

4. Press the LEFT ARROW twice to position the cell pointer under the "R"; then type **A**.

    Since 1-2-3 was in its default insert mode, the "A" was added to the left of the "R".

5. Move the cell pointer until it is under the "E" and press INS once to go into overstrike mode. Then type **A**. 1-2-3 will replace the "E", with the following result:

6. Press ENTER.

    The entry will be finalized in the cell and INS will disappear from the edit line of the control panel. You can press INS again to toggle back to INSERT, as the opposite feature is activated each time you press it.

The New Undo Feature

Releases 2.2 and 2.3 offer the new Undo feature. This new feature allows you to reverse the effect of the last menu command in most cases and can reverse the last entry you finalized. The secret to using Undo effectively is to make sure you invoke it before taking any other actions, since it can change only the last action performed.

The actual effect of Undo is to reverse the effect of the actions taken since the last time 1-2-3 was in READY mode. If you just made an entry in a cell, using Undo would reverse this entry. If you just performed an action requiring multiple steps and 1-2-3 did not return to READY mode between steps, using Undo would reverse all the steps.

In Chapter 4, "Working with Files," you will learn about the use of Undo for reversing menu commands. For now, you can use it to eliminate your last cell entry if you see UNDO at the bottom of the screen. All that is required is pressing the ALT-F4 (UNDO) key. If you do not see UNDO at the bottom of your screen, it is disabled. To enable the feature, you must first clear the worksheet from memory since Undo cannot be enabled with worksheet data in memory. If the worksheet has not been saved, you would enter **/FS**, type a 1- to 8-character name for the worksheet, and press ENTER to save it. You would then enter **/WEYY** to clear memory. With the preliminary work completed, you can enter **/WGDOUEQ** and the UNDO indicator should appear. You would then put the worksheet back in memory by entering **/FR**, typing the name you used when saving it, and pressing ENTER. Note that earlier releases of 1-2-3 do not have the Undo feature unless you installed the Lotus HAL program.

Types of Worksheet Entries

1-2-3 has two basic types of entries for worksheet cells: *labels* and *values*. Labels are text characters that can be used to describe numeric data you plan to place on the worksheet or to store character information. Label data can never be used in arithmetic calculations, even if it contains numbers. Value data, on the other hand, consists of either numbers or *formulas*. Formulas result in numbers but are entered as a series of calculations to be performed. The numeric digits, cell addresses, and a limited set of special symbols are the only entries that can be made in those cells categorized as value entries.

1-2-3 attempts to distinguish label entries from value entries by the first character you enter into a worksheet cell. As long as this first character is not one of the numeric digits or characters that 1-2-3 considers numeric, it will be treated as a label.

1-2-3 will generate a default label prefix for any entry it considers to be a label. If you were to enter **Sales** in a cell, 1-2-3 would treat the entry as a label because the first character in the entry is an alphabetic character. Since 1-2-3 always makes its determination from the first character, entering **15 Johnson St.** causes 1-2-3 to reject your entry when you attempt to finalize it; the first character is numeric and 1-2-3 attempts to treat the entire entry as a value. 1-2-3 is also very stubborn once it determines the type of entry it thinks you planned for a cell. The only way you can change its mind is by editing the cell contents or pressing ESC to start over. After a little practice with the label entries in your first few models, however, you will know all the tricks to put you in command of how your entries are interpreted.

Entering Labels

Label entries in 1-2-3 cells usually begin with one of the three acceptable *label prefixes*. These are an apostrophe ('), a double quotation mark ("), or a caret (^). Each of these three symbols causes 1-2-3 to align the contents of the cell differently.

Beginning with a ' is the default option and causes the label entry to be left aligned in the cell. 1-2-3 will even generate this label prefix for you if your entry begins with an alphabetic character or a special symbol that is not considered part of the value entry options. Using the " causes the entry to be right aligned in the cell, and using the ^ symbol causes the entry to be centered. If you choose right or center justification, begin your label entry with the special symbol and follow it immediately with the text that you wish the cell to contain. If you choose to begin a label entry with a character that 1-2-3 considers to be a value, you may start your entry with one of the three label prefixes to trick the package into treating it like a label. Before starting an actual model, try the following exercises.

1. Move your cell pointer to A1, type **AT**, and press ENTER.

   AT appears in the display of the worksheet. However, when you observe the entry in the top line of the control panel, you will notice that it reads 'AT. The reason is that 1-2-3 generated the label prefix for you. Because of this prefix, your entry should also appear as left aligned within cell A1 and will match this:

1

2. Use DOWN ARROW or click A2 to move the cell pointer to A2. Type
   "AT and press ENTER. Your entry should be right aligned in the cell
   display.

3. Use DOWN ARROW to move to A3. Type **^AT** and press ENTER.
   The entry should be centered in the cell, as follows:

4. Use DOWN ARROW and move to A4. Type **3AT** and press ENTER.
   Notice that 1-2-3 beeps at you, will not accept this entry, and
   places you in EDIT mode.

5. Press HOME and add the apostrophe at the front of the entry. Then
   press ENTER again.
   This time 1-2-3 accepts the entry. This is because you have
   asked it to treat the entry as a label, even though the first
   character is a number, by placing a label prefix at the front of the
   entry. Your worksheet should now appear like this:

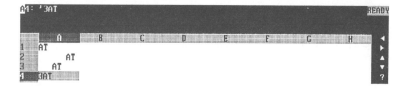

6. To have a blank screen displayed, select Worksheet Erase Yes
   typing the slash (/) and the first letter of each word. Next, select
   Yes a second time since 1-2-3 requests an additional confirmation
   that you want to erase a worksheet that has unsaved entries. This
   was just a practice exercise, so you can clear everything you have
   entered. You will find the commands required to erase an entire

worksheet on 1-2-3's menus. For now you need to take the required key sequence on faith, but you will learn all the details in a subsequent chapter.

Now you will put your newly acquired label entry techniques to work to build the model shown in Figure 1-6. This model compares two investment properties. You could easily modify the model to compare two potential stock or bond investments, two departments, or two sales managers. All you need is information pertinent to the subjects being compared. All the entries you make in this section of the chapter will be entered as labels. These labels can be used to describe the data the model will contain and the calculations the model will perform, as well as to provide an overall description of the model's purpose so that you can see the versatility of label entries. You will continue to build this model by adding numeric entries in the next section of this chapter; you will complete it in Chapter 2 ("Defining Your Calculations") by adding formulas. Follow these steps to create the model shell shown in Figure 1-7.

1. Move the cell pointer to A5 with the arrow keys or mouse, and type **Cost**.

Figure 1-6.   *Real estate investment model*

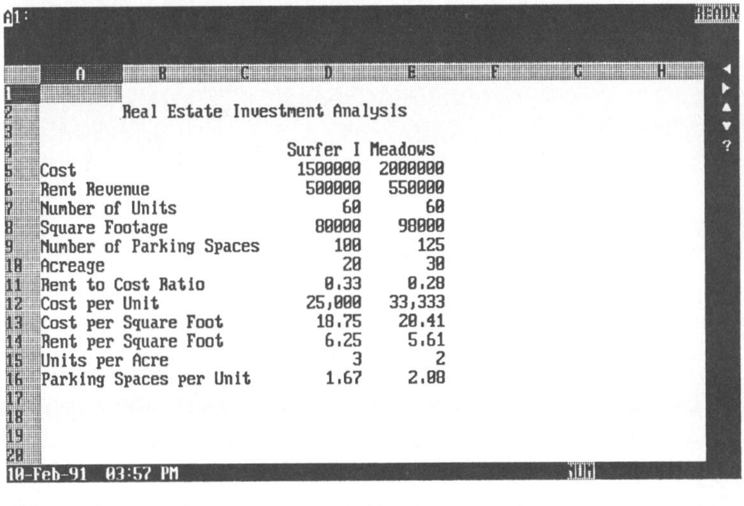

Figure 1-7. *Label entries that build the shell*

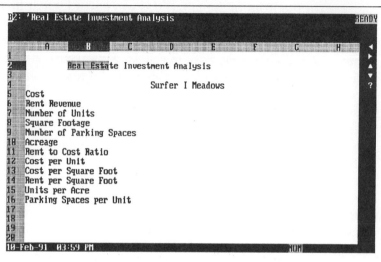

This step enters a label that describes the detail entries that will be placed in row 5. You may wonder why you are not entering the title or heading line first. Often it is easier to choose an appropriate location for titles and headings after you have positioned the detail below it. A few rows are skipped to allow for the eventual addition of a heading and entries, which is why you begin in row 5 rather than row 1.

2. Press DOWN ARROW to move to A6 and finalize your entry in cell A5.

   There are two methods for finalizing cell entries. You can use the arrow keys to move to a new location, or you can press ENTER. To finalize your entries with a mouse, you can either click on the control panel, or click on the cell that you want to move to, which is A6. The DOWN ARROW is a better method: You need to position your cell pointer for the next entry anyway, and this approach lets you both finalize and position with a single keystroke.

3. With your cell pointer in A6, type **Rent Revenue** and press ENTER or click on the control panel.

   This time you are using ENTER rather than the DOWN ARROW so that you can examine the label entry in the cell in which you

entered it. Notice the label prefix that is automatically generated
for you at the front of the entry; this was also added at the front
of your last entry. This label entry is different from the last one:
It is longer than the default cell width of nine characters, which
means that it is too long to fit in cell A6. However, 1-2-3 borrows
display space from cell B6 rather than shortening the label entry
to fit in A6. Had B6 contained data, its space would not have been
available; 1-2-3 then would have truncated the display to fit
within the nine-character width for column A. But even though
the label entry may be truncated when displayed, 1-2-3 will
always retain the complete entry in memory.

   This approach means that complete label entries are always
available for display in the event that the cell width is increased or
the cell to the right no longer contains an entry. Remember that
these long label entries are always stored in the original cell
where you entered them. If you choose to go back and edit the
entry, you must edit this cell regardless of where the entry is
displayed.

4. Move to A7 with the DOWN ARROW or the mouse. Type **Number of
   Units** and press the DOWN ARROW again or click on A8.

5. Complete the remainder of these vertical label entries by making
   sure that your cell pointer is in the cell specified and typing the
   entry shown here:

A8:	Square Footage
A9:	Number of Parking Spaces
A10:	Acreage
A11:	Rent to Cost Ratio
A12:	Cost per Unit
A13:	Cost per Square Foot
A14:	Rent per Square Foot
A15:	Units per Acre
A16:	Parking Spaces per Unit

6. Press F5 (GOTO), type **D4,** and press ENTER. Type **Surfer I** and
   finalize by pressing the RIGHT ARROW or clicking on E4.

This step added a column heading, which represents the name of the first apartment house you are evaluating.

7. Type **Meadows** and press ENTER.

8. Use the UP ARROW and the LEFT ARROW or the mouse to move to B2.

9. Type **Real Estate Investment Analysis** and press ENTER.

    The heading is a little too far to the left. Using C1 for the entry would not work, since it would be too far to the right. A useful method is to add a few spaces at the front of the entry to position the heading exactly as you wish.

10. With your cell pointer in B2, press F2 (EDIT). Then press HOME to move to the front of the entry.

11. Press the RIGHT ARROW once to move the cell pointer to the right of the label prefix. Press the SPACEBAR twice to add two spaces at the front. Then press ENTER.

    These extra spaces make your model look better by moving the heading toward the center.

The entry of the title should complete the label entries and lay the groundwork for the numeric data, which you will add in the next step.

Entering Numbers

Numbers are one of the two types of value entries that 1-2-3 permits. As value entries, they follow much more rigid rules than label entries. Like labels, numbers are constant; they do not change as the result of arithmetic calculations. They are placed in a cell and will remain as you enter them unless you take some direct action to change them. Numbers can contain any of the numeric digits from 0 through 9. The other characters that are allowable in regular numeric entries are . and + and −. The . is used to separate the whole-number portion of the entry from the decimal digits; + indicates a positive number, and − indicates a negative number.

Several characters can be part of a numeric entry in special situations. A **%** sign can be used at the end of a numeric entry to indicate a percentage, but it is not allowed in other positions within the entry. Spaces, commas, and other characters cannot be added to numeric entries except by using the formatting options. Formatting options will be covered in Chapter 3, "Changing the Worksheet Appearance." The only exception to this rule is for the letter "e" (either "E" or "e"), which can be used to represent numbers in powers of 10 (referred to as *scientific notation*). For example, 3.86E−5 is .0000386. This number can also be represented as (3.86*10^−5) or 3.86E−5. The caret symbol represents exponentiation, or the power of 10 that this number is raised to. Entering 3.86*10^−5 would be considered a formula. Although it is still a value entry, it requires operations that are not needed when entering numeric digits.

You will enter only the numbers for the constant numeric data on the worksheet. Even though numeric entries are considered constants, there is nothing to prevent you from updating any of these numbers, once they are entered, by typing a new number or editing the existing entry. For this model, the numbers you will enter are the first six entries in the column. The other entries will be the result of formulas added in the next chapter; these cells will remain blank initially. As you enter the first numeric digit in each cell, you will notice that the READY mode indicator is replaced by VALUE. The first character is all that 1-2-3 needs to determine the type of cell entry. Follow these steps:

1. Move the cell pointer to D5 with the arrow keys or the mouse. Type **1500000** and press ENTER or click on the control panel.

   Notice that you did not enter any commas or other characters. You can have 1-2-3 add them at a later time as a formatting option, if you wish. Also, notice that 1-2-3 did not add a label prefix in front of this number since it considers it a value.

2. Move the cell pointer to D6 with DOWN ARROW or by clicking on it. Type **500000**, then press DOWN ARROW or click on D7.

3. Type **60**, then press DOWN ARROW or click on D8.

4. Type **80000**, then press DOWN ARROW or click on D9.

5. Type **100**, then press DOWN ARROW or click on D10.

6. Type **20**, then use UP ARROW and RIGHT ARROW or click on E5 to move to E5.

7. Complete these same entries for the Meadows building with the following entries:

1

```
E5:    2000000
E6:    550000
E7:    60
E8:    95000
E9:    125
E10:   30
```

Figure 1-8 shows the result of entering each number. Remember that it is easy to change any of the entries. You can type a new number or edit a cell. Try a few changes, following these steps:

1. Move to E8 and press F2 (EDIT).

2. Press LEFT ARROW to move your cell pointer under the 5.

3. Press DEL to remove 5.

4. Type **8**.

5. Finalize your entry by pressing ENTER.

Figure 1-8.   *Adding numbers to the shell*

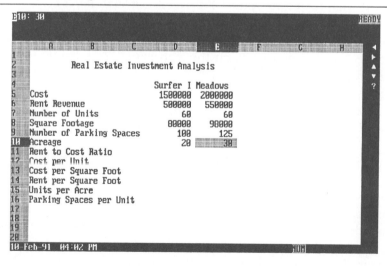

You also could have finalized with the UP or DOWN ARROW key. However, the RIGHT and LEFT ARROW keys are not options for finalizing while you are editing, since they take on the new function of moving within the cell entry. Since this is the last entry that you will make in the model, save a copy of the model to disk. The commands that handle saving files are covered in Chapter 4 in detail. For now, all you need to know is that you need a menu command in order to save a file. You must select File Save and enter the name of the file you wish to save. If the file is already stored on the disk, you must confirm your desire to save by entering **R** for Replace. You can select each of these commands by typing the first letter of the command, but you must enter the filename in full. Select File Save, type **REALEST**, and press ENTER.

Getting Help

Navigating your way around the worksheet and entering numbers and labels in worksheet cells probably has seemed quite simple. That is because you have taken everything a step at a time. As you begin to add more skills to your toolkit of 1-2-3 options, you may find that you need a quick refresher on an earlier topic. Although you can always look back to the particular chapter or to your 1-2-3 reference manual, 1-2-3's onscreen *Help facility* will often provide just the hints you need to complete your planned task. Accessing the Help feature is as easy as pressing F1 (HELP) or clicking the question mark on the icon panel. You can do this even if you are in the middle of a task, such as entering a label in a cell. 1-2-3 will not disrupt the in-progress task; instead, it will set the task aside temporarily to let you review help information on the screen. Assuming that you are in READY mode, try this right now and press F1.

If you are using Release 2.3, your screen should match the one in Figure 1-9. The HELP screens for other releases are similar but not always exactly the same. To select information on any topic, just place your highlighted bar on the desired topic and press ENTER. If you choose 1-2-3 commands, additional information will be presented on selecting menu commands. There may be additional levels of help that you can select in the same manner, depending on the topic. The topics you can select appear in a different color or intensity on the HELP screen. When you have finished, leave HELP mode by pressing ESC. This returns you to the

1-2-3 task where you left off. If you request help with F1 after beginning a task, 1-2-3 provides context-sensitive help. This is 1-2-3's best guess as to the type of help you need, based on the entries you have made so far. Assuming that you were entering a label and wanted additional information on 1-2-3's label-entering rules, you could press F1 before finalizing. Try this by entering the label **Salaries** in a worksheet cell and pressing F1 before finalizing your entry. 1-2-3 shows the HELP screen for entering labels. You can return to the help index by pressing F1 again in Release 2.3, or by choosing the Help Index at the bottom of the screen in other releases. Figure 1-9 shows some typical topics provided by this index.

In Release 2.3, you can also use other keys while a help screen is displayed. Since many topics may provide more information than 1-2-3 can fit in the window, you can press PGUP or PGDN to scroll up and down one screen at a time. You can move from one highlighted topic to the next by pressing the arrow keys or TAB and SHIFT-TAB. If no other help topics are displayed on the HELP screen, pressing these keys will scroll the help information up and down. You can also press HOME and END to quickly move to the first and last help topic displayed. To return to the previous help topic, press F8. To display a list of keys you can use press F3.

Figure 1-9.   *HELP screen presented from READY mode*

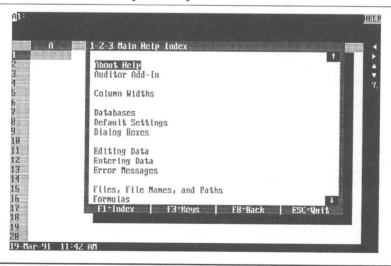

If you are using a mouse, you can use the arrow keys on the right side of the HELP screen to scroll, or move, around the screen. With a mouse, you can select a help topic by clicking on it. You can select the ESC, F1, F3, and F8 features just described by clicking on them. They are located at the bottom of the HELP screen.

When you have finished using the Help feature, you can press ESC again to return to the worksheet. Everything will be exactly as you left it. 1-2-3 effectively places a marker in your current location and records your actions up to that point before displaying the HELP screen so that it can put things back exactly as you left them. Even the partially completed label entry will be waiting for you to finalize it. Since you actually do not wish to make another entry at this time, you can press ESC again to eliminate it.

In Release 2.3, 1-2-3 remembers the last help topic it displayed. When you press CTRL-F1, 1-2-3 displays the HELP screen you saw last before you pressed ESC to leave Help.

1-2-3 can assist you when you encounter an error message. Just press F1 (HELP) and 1-2-3 will display explanations as to what might have triggered the message. In prior releases, you can select the Help Index, and choose Error Message to see an explanation of each message, as well as actions that you can take to correct the error.

Review

- To start 1-2-3, you must first load the operating system into the memory of your computer. With a hard disk system, all you need to do is turn the system on with drive A empty. Next activate the 1-2-3 directory. For example, if 1-2-3 is stored in the 123 directory, you would type **CD\123** and press ENTER, then type **123** and press ENTER to begin the program. On a floppy disk system, you must place the operating system disk in drive A before turning the system on. After the operating system starts, respond to its prompts for date and time entries, remove the operating system disk, put the 1-2-3 system disk in the drive, type **123**, and press ENTER.

- The highlight that marks your place on the worksheet is called the cell pointer. Use the keys in the following section, "Commands and Keys," to move it around. The control panel at the top of the screen provides valuable information about 1-2-3. Look at the upper right corner of the screen to determine 1-2-3's current mode. Look at the upper left of the screen to see the current cell's contents, format, and width.

- In Release 2.3, you can use a mouse to point to items on the screen and select them. You can point to a cell and press (click) the left mouse button to move to that cell. Later you will learn how you can use the mouse to complete other tasks.

- The status line displays the date and time or filename. It also displays indicators for several keys and other options that can tell you what to expect from 1-2-3.

- Correcting worksheet entries will depend on whether or not they were finalized. One set of techniques works for active entries and another set is most useful for the ones that were not finalized. The Undo feature can eliminate an entry just finalized or reverse the result of a 1-2-3 command if Undo is enabled. Just press ALT-F4 (UNDO) to use it.

- Cells can be empty or contain labels or values. Labels are treated as characters by 1-2-3. Depending on the label prefix, they may be left aligned ('), right aligned ("), or centered (^). One type of value is a number. You can use the digits 0 through 9 or special symbols like **.** or **+** and **−** in number entries.

- To save the current worksheet, enter **/FS**, type a name of not more than eight characters with no spaces, and press ENTER. If there is a file with that name on the disk, you can type **R** if you wish to replace the existing file with the current worksheet.

Commands and Keys

Entry	Action
UP ARROW	Moves the cell pointer up one cell.
DOWN ARROW	Moves the cell pointer down one cell.

Entry	Action
RIGHT ARROW	Moves the cell pointer one cell to the right in READY mode. In EDIT mode, moves one character to the right.
LEFT ARROW	Moves the cell pointer one cell to the left. In EDIT mode, moves the cell pointer one character to the left.
CTRL-LEFT ARROW	Moves one screen to the left.
CTRL-RIGHT ARROW	Moves one screen to the right.
PGUP	Moves up one screen.
PGDN	Moves down one screen.
END	Causes the arrow key pressed next to move the cell pointer to the last blank cell or the cell containing the last contiguous entry in the direction specified. When pressed with EDIT mode in effect, takes you to the end of the entry.
HOME	Moves the cell pointer to A1. When EDIT mode is in effect, places the cell pointer at the front of your entry. When pressed following END, moves the cell pointer to the last cell on the spreadsheet that contains an entry.
ESC	Eliminates an entry that is not finalized. Exits from the 1-2-3 Help feature. When pressed repeatedly allows you to escape from a menu selection made in error.
F1 (HELP)	Activates the 1-2-3 Help feature.
F2 (EDIT)	Places you in EDIT mode to allow the correction of entries without retyping. The arrow keys, HOME, and END all function differently when EDIT mode is in effect.
ALT-F4 (UNDO)	When no intervening actions have occurred, eliminates the last cell entry finalized. Can also eliminate the effect of most menu commands.
F5 (GOTO)	When followed by typing a cell address and pressing ENTER, moves the cell pointer to the address specified.

1

Entry	Action
/FS	File Save saves a worksheet in a disk file.
/QYY	Quit Yes Yes leaves 1-2-3 and returns to the operating system.
/WEYY	Worksheet Erase Yes Yes erases the current worksheet.
/WGDOUEQ	Worksheet Global Default Other Undo Enable Quit turns on the Undo feature.

2

Defining Your Calculations

Calculations are an important part of many of the business tasks that you perform. Some calculations are simple. If you get a 10% discount when you purchase from a given vendor, it takes no great effort to calculate your savings. And it is simple to calculate the total number of employees in your group if the headcount increases by five. In fact, these calculations are so easy that you can compute them without even writing them down.

However, not all computations are this simple. For example, if you want to determine the most economic quantity to order for each item in your inventory, you will need to perform a much more complex calculation, one that is difficult to compute without writing it down. Even when you do write complex computations on paper, mistakes are easy to make. And if conditions change slightly, the numbers in your computations are likely to change as well, requiring you to redo the calculations. Evaluating a *series* of conditions could cause you to spend a considerable amount of time redoing calculations.

1-2-3 provides an easy-to-use solution, one that eliminates the need for you to perform calculations yourself. You simply define for 1-2-3 the calculations you wish to perform, and it handles the computations. To do this you must determine each step in the computational process and record these instructions in a cell on 1-2-3's worksheet. These recorded instructions for handling calculations are known as formulas. Once these formulas are entered, 1-2-3 will handle all the work required for computing your results.

The process of entering these formulas is really quite simple and not too different from the way you entered numbers and labels in Chapter 1. These formulas will tell 1-2-3 what data to operate on and which of the operators will be used. A sample formula for profit might be Sales −Cost of Goods Sold; a sample formula for net payable on an invoice might be Amount −(Amount*Purchase Discount).

This chapter will show you how to enter any of these formulas, using references to the worksheet cells that contain your data. This feature is very powerful; it allows you to reuse applications even when significant changes occur. This flexibility makes formulas a valuable addition to your worksheet models.

In this chapter, you will look at all the features provided by 1-2-3 to handle your calculations. You will find that they have wide applicability: The same methods are used to calculate interest expense, budget projections, salary increases, and any other calculation. In addition to the basics, you will also explore 1-2-3's full set of features for building more complex formulas, including the string formulas (which manipulate text data rather than numeric values).

Formula Basics

Formulas, like the numbers you entered in Chapter 1, are value entries. Unlike numbers, however, they produce results that vary, depending on the entries they reference. This variability makes formulas the backbone of spreadsheet features: It allows you to make *what-if projections* based on changing entries on your worksheet. You can update the formula results without changing the formula itself. The only requirement is new entries for the variables referenced by the formula.

Entry Rules

To enter a formula in a cell, you must define for 1-2-3 the location of the variables involved and the operations you wish performed on them. 1-2-3 supports three types of formulas: arithmetic formulas, logical formulas, and in Release 2 and higher, text or string formulas. A few general rules apply to all formulas and some special conventions will be observed for the special types of formulas. The special rules will be discussed when each type of formula is discussed, but the general guidelines will be given here.

- The first and perhaps most important rule is that the first character in a formula entry must always come from the following list of value characters:

    + − (@ # $. 0 1 2 3 4 5 6 7 8 9

- The second rule is that formulas cannot contain extraneous spaces except within names or text. As you type the examples presented, be especially careful not to separate the formula components with spaces.

- The third and last rule pertains to the length limitation for a formula: As with other cell entries, it cannot exceed 240 characters in Release 2.3. Unless you are building some really complex calculations, this last rule is not likely to impose a restriction.

Arithmetic Formulas

Arithmetic formulas are nothing more than instructions for certain operations: addition (+); subtraction (−); multiplication (*); division (/); and exponentiation (^), which represents raising a number to a specific power, such as 3 cubed or 2 squared. These are the same types of operations you can compute by hand or with a calculator. When you record these formulas on the worksheet, you can build the formula with the arithmetic operators and references to the numbers contained in other worksheet cells. The result of the calculation will be determined by the current value of the worksheet cell referenced. You can see the advantage of recording these formulas on a worksheet more clearly when you wish to change one of the numbers. All you need to do is change the number in the referenced cell. Since the formula has already been entered and tested, it will be available on a permanent basis. Any time you wish the same set of calculations to be performed, you can enter the numbers involved without having to reenter the formula; the sequence of required calculations will be stored on the worksheet in the cell that contains the formula.

1-2-3's formulas can be entered with numeric constants, as in 4*5 or 3+2. However, numeric constants within formulas are limiting: You would have to change formulas as conditions change. A better method is to store these constants in a worksheet cell. When you wish to use this value in a formula, you can use its cell address within the formula. Then, if the value changes, you need only enter a new number where it is stored; the formula will use it automatically. Using cell addresses in formulas requires one additional rule: Since cell addresses begin with non-numeric characters, an entry's initial alphabetic character (for example, A2+B3) will cause it to be treated as a label entry.

This means that an entry like this would appear in the worksheet cell just as you typed it, rather than performing any calculations. Try this with the following entries.

1. Move the cell pointer to A2, type **3**, and press ENTER.

2. Move the cell pointer to B3, type **2**, and press ENTER.

3. Move the cell pointer to D2, type **A2+B3**, and press ENTER.

   No calculation is performed for you. 1-2-3 decided that the cell entry was a label, since its first character was alphabetic. This approach, which does not perform any calculations, produces the following display:

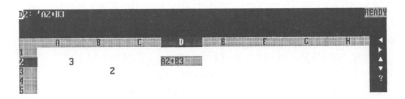

Several of the numeric characters can be used to begin a formula. The + is a logical choice as a character to add to the front of the formula: It requires only one keystroke and will not affect the contents of A2. Try this new entry to see the results: Type **+A2+B3** in D2.

This time, 1-2-3 interpreted your entry as a formula and computed the result of adding the current contents of A2 to the current contents of B3. Since A2 contains a 3 and B2 contains a 2, the formula you entered displays a 5 in D2, as follows:

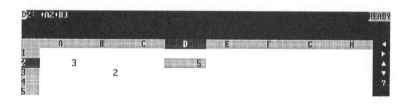

When you point to D2, you still see the formula you entered in the control panel. If, later on, you decided to change the value in A2 to 10, the result displayed in D2 would change to a 12 as evidence that the formula was still doing its assigned task.

When you enter formulas using their cell addresses, 1-2-3 is not fussy and will accept either upper- or lowercase. The formula +A2*AB3 is equivalent to +a2*ab3 or +a2*Ab3 and computes the same results.

Adding Formulas to the Real Estate Model

You will use your new formula techniques to add the formulas to the real estate investment model that you started in Chapter 1. If the model is still in the memory of your computer, you are ready to begin. If you have just started a new 1-2-3 session and wish to recall your copy of the model from your disk, type **/FRREALEST** and press ENTER. The model shown in Figure 2-1 should display on your screen before adding the formulas.

The first formula you need to enter is the *rent-to-cost ratio.* You compute this ratio by dividing the rent by the cost. Each investment will be evaluated separately; you will enter the computations for Surfer I first. Follow these instructions to add the formulas:

1. Move the cell pointer to D11.
    This is an appropriate location for the first calculation.

Figure 2-1.   *Real estate model from Chapter 1*

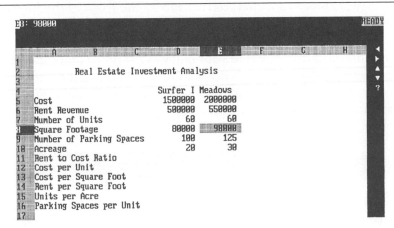

2. Type **+D6/D5** and press ENTER.

    Since the rent revenue for this property is stored in D6 and the cost is in D5, the formula will calculate the ratio you need. Your result should appear like the one in Figure 2-2, with the formula you entered displayed in the control panel and the result of the calculation shown in the cell.

    The next computation is *cost per unit*. This calculation splits the total cost evenly across all units to give you an estimate of what one unit costs.

3. Move the cell pointer to D12 with the mouse or DOWN ARROW key. Type **+D5/D7**. This formula divides the cost by the number of units. The next formula will allocate the cost on a square-footage basis.

4. Move the cell pointer to D13 with the mouse or DOWN ARROW key. Note that moving down a cell after typing the formula finalizes your entry and positions you for your next entry. Then type **+D5/D8** and press the DOWN ARROW key or click on D14.

Figure 2-2.   *Formula entered in D11*

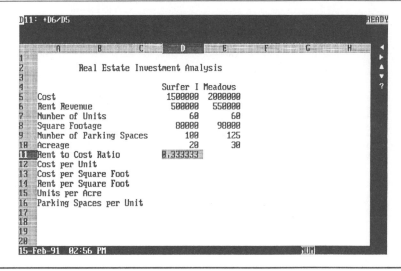

The remaining three formulas for Surfer I follow the same pattern.

5. Type **+D6/D8** and press DOWN ARROW or click on D15.

6. Type **+D7/D10** and press DOWN ARROW or click on D16.

7. Type **+D9/D7** and press ENTER.

This completes the entries for Surfer I and produces the results shown in Figure 2-3.

Subsequently, you will learn techniques for copying formulas like these to other locations rather than reentering a set of similar formulas for the Meadows property. For now you need practice with formula entry, and the second set of formulas lets you look at another formula-entry method.

Entering Arithmetic Formulas with the Point Method

The formulas in the last section were all built by typing both the arithmetic operators and the cell addresses they referenced. This method works fine if you are an average typist and if all the referenced cells are

Figure 2-3.   *All of the formulas entered for Surfer I*

```
D16: +D9/D7                                                           READY

          A        B        C         D        E        F        G       H
   1
   2                    Real Estate Investment Analysis
   3
   4                                       Surfer I Meadows
   5    Cost                               1500000  2000000
   6    Rent Revenue                        500000   550000
   7    Number of Units                         60       60
   8    Square Footage                       80000    98000
   9    Number of Parking Spaces               100      125
  10    Acreage                                 20       30
  11    Rent to Cost Ratio                0.333333
  12    Cost per Unit                        25000
  13    Cost per Square Foot                 18.75
  14    Rent per Square Foot                  6.25
  15    Units per Acre                           3
  16    Parking Spaces per Unit           1.666666
  17
```

within view on the worksheet. However, if neither of these conditions is true, typing the formulas may lead to a higher error rate than necessary. 1-2-3 provides a second method of formula entry, which can reduce the error rate. With this method, you type only the arithmetic operators, and you select the cell references by using the arrow keys to position the cell pointer on the cell you wish to reference. 1-2-3 adds the cell address to the formula being built in the control panel and changes the mode indicator from VALUE to POINT. This method provides visual verification that you are selecting the correct cell and eliminates the problems of typing mistakes. Follow these steps to add the first formula for the Meadows property using the pointing method of formula entry.

1. Move your cell pointer to E11, then type **+**.

   You can use the + on the key next to the pointer movement keys or the one over the **=**.

2. Next move your cell pointer to E6 by using the arrow keys or clicking on the cell.

2

This will cause the cell address to appear in your control panel like this:

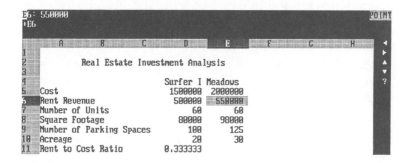

Note that the indicator in the upper right corner of the screen has changed to POINT.

3. Type /.

   Notice that the cell pointer returns to the cell where the formula is being recorded.

4. Move your cell pointer to E5 by using the arrow keys or clicking on the cell. Your control panel will now contain the complete formula, +E6/E5.

5. Press ENTER to finalize the formula.

   The result of .275 will appear in the worksheet cell and +E6/E5 displays in the control panel.

Completing the Meadows Formulas

The remaining Meadows formulas can be completed by using the pointing method, following these steps.

1. Move your cell pointer to E12 and type +. Then point to E5 with the UP ARROW or mouse and type /. Next point to E7 and press ENTER.

2. Move your cell pointer to E13 and type +. Point to E5 with the UP ARROW or mouse and type /. Point to E8 and press ENTER.

3. To enter the formula for rent per square foot, begin by moving the cell pointer to E14 and typing +. Use the UP ARROW or mouse to move to E6. Then type /, move to E8, and press ENTER.

4. Move the cell pointer to E15 and type +. Use the UP ARROW or mouse to move to E7. Type /, then move to E10 and press ENTER.

5. Move the cell pointer to E16 and type +. Use the UP ARROW to point to the number of parking spaces in E9. Then type /, move to the number of units in E7, and press ENTER or click on the control panel. The completed model is shown in Figure 2-4.

You will notice that ENTER was used to finalize each of the formulas. If you had attempted to finalize by pressing an arrow key, the last reference in the cell would have been changed by this movement of the cell pointer. With the pointing method of formula construction, pressing ENTER or clicking on the control panel will always be your only way of finalizing a formula.

Figure 2-4.   *Remaining formulas entered for Meadows*

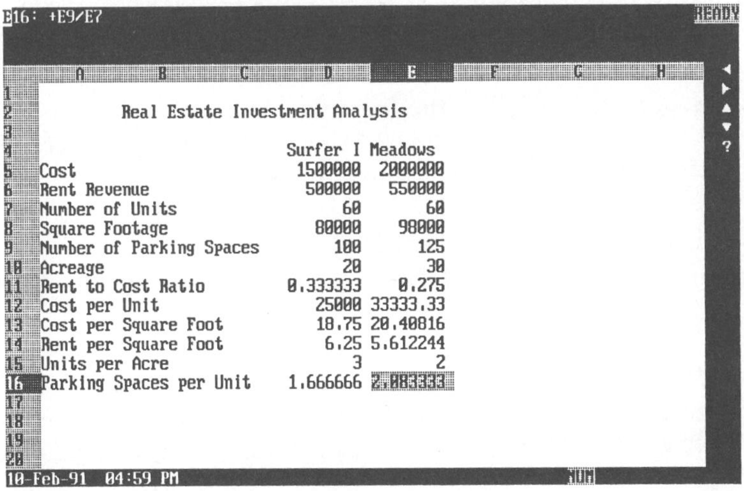

Other than the differences in the entry method, these two sets of formulas will perform identically. Once a formula has been entered, it is not possible to determine which entry method was chosen since the results are the same.

2

Performing a What-If Analysis

Now that you have entered the basic formulas, your investment analysis model is complete. This kind of model will help you compare the two properties; in addition, it can assist you in your negotiations. You might feel that the price of one unit has more flexibility than the other; or perhaps the seller might be willing to add additional parking spaces or to include vacant land that is adjacent to the apartment complex. All these factors can change your evaluation of the properties. If you were perform-ing your computations manually, each of the possibilities would require a new set of calculations and be time-consuming. But now that you have automated the calculations, each option requires only that you enter a new number on the worksheet to have the package perform a new comparison immediately.

Let's look at how easy it is to evaluate each change in conditions. Suppose that you were able to negotiate a new price of $1,600,000 for the Meadows building. To add the updated data to your model, follow these steps.

1. Move the cell pointer to E5.
2. Press F2 (EDIT) to enter EDIT mode.
3. Press HOME to move to the beginning of the entry.
4. Delete the first two digits by pressing DEL twice.
5. Type **16** to replace the digits you just eliminated.
6. Press ENTER to finalize your entry.

After entering these new entries, you will find that the results of formula calculations have been updated. They indicate that the rent-to-cost ratio and the cost per unit for the two properties are much closer than you might have thought.

Use the same process to add the updates for the Surfer I building. If you feel that the owners will agree to add 50 more parking spaces and include another 15 acres of land at the same purchase price, you will want to make the following changes.

1. Move the cell pointer to D9.
2. Type **150** and press ENTER.
3. Move the cell pointer to D10.
4. Type **35** and press ENTER.

Rather than editing the original entries, you retyped the new figures this time. You will have to evaluate each situation to see which is the quickest method. For very short entries like these last two, it is often just as easy to type the new entries.

As these last entries show, what-if analysis is quite simple once you have the formulas entered. The results of the most recent changes are shown in Figure 2-5. You could easily use these techniques to evaluate potential changes in purchase price or other options with only a minimal investment in time.

Now that you have updated your model with formulas and the results of what-if analysis, you will want to save the updated copy on disk to reflect the current status of the worksheet. Enter **/FS** and press ENTER. You did not have to type the filename this time, since it was saved previously. To ensure that the copy on disk is replaced with the current copy in memory, take one additional step: When 1-2-3's prompt message asks if you wish to cancel the request, replace the copy on disk, or back up the file saving the old copy with a .BAK extension and the current model with a .WK1 extension, then enter **R** to replace the file.

Logical Formulas

Logical formulas   are used to compare two or more worksheet values. They use the logical operators = for equal, < > for not equal, > for greater than, > = for greater than or equal to, < for less than, and < = for less than or equal to. Logical formulas can be entered with

Figure 2-5. *Changing the acreage to see the formula results updated*

```
D10: 35                                                              READY

       A         B        C         D        E        F       G      H    ◄
1                                                                          ►
2                  Real Estate Investment Analysis                        ▲
3                                                                         ▼
4                                   Surfer I Meadows                      ?
5     Cost                          1500000  1600000
6     Rent Revenue                   500000   550000
7     Number of Units                    60       60
8     Square Footage                  80000    98000
9     Number of Parking Spaces          150      125
10    Acreage                            35       30
11    Rent to Cost Ratio           0.333333  0.34375
12    Cost per Unit                   25000 26666.66
13    Cost per Square Foot            18.75 16.32653
14    Rent per Square Foot             6.25 5.612244
15    Units per Acre               1.714285        2
16    Parking Spaces per Unit          2.5 2.083333
17
18
19
20
10-Feb-91  05:20 PM                                          NUM
```

the same methods used for arithmetic formulas, but unlike arithmetic formulas, they do not calculate numeric results. Instead, they produce a result of either a zero or a one, depending on whether the condition that was evaluated is true or false. If the condition is true, 1 will be returned; if the condition is false, 0 will be returned. For example, if D4 contains a 5, the logical expression +D4<3 will return 0, since the condition is false. This capability can be used to evaluate a series of complex decisions or influence results in other parts of the worksheet.

If an expression contains both logical operators and arithmetic operators, the expression containing the arithmetic operators will be evaluated first. For example, the logical expression +D4*2>50 will be evaluated by first multiplying the current value in D4 by 2 and then performing the comparison.

Creating a Model to Calculate Commissions

One application of logical operators in a spreadsheet might be the calculation of a commission bonus. In your example, sales personnel are paid a quarterly bonus, which includes a regular sales commission and a bonus paid for meeting sales quotas. The regular commission is computed as 10% of total sales. The bonus is calculated by product. A bonus of $1000 is paid for each product for which the sales quota is met. A salesperson could thus gain $3000 by meeting quotas for three products.

Look at the steps required to build the commission model shown in Figure 2-6. First, follow these directions to add the labels that are required.

1. Move the cell pointer to B1, type **Commission Calculation**, and press ENTER.

2. Move the cell pointer to A4, type **Employee:**, and press the DOWN ARROW key or click on B5.

3. Type **Sales Product 1:** and press the DOWN ARROW key or click on A7.

4. Type **Sales Product 2:** and press the DOWN ARROW key or click on A7.

Figure 2-6.   *Commission model*

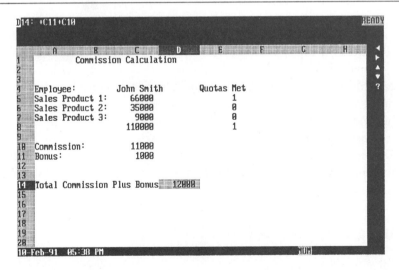

5. Type **Sales Product 3:** and press the DOWN ARROW key or use the mouse to place the cell pointer in A10.

6. Type **Commission:** and press the DOWN ARROW key or click on A11.

7. Type **Bonus:** and press the DOWN ARROW key or use the mouse to place the cell pointer in A14.

8. Type **Total Commission Plus Bonus** and press ENTER.

    Notice that a colon (:) has not been added at the end. This is for convenience since you do not wish the entry to display beyond column C. It means you do not have to widen the column to show more than the default of nine characters.

9. Use F5 (GOTO), type **C4**, and press ENTER or click on C4. Type **John Smith** and press the DOWN ARROW key or click on C5 to finalize the entry of the name of the employee for whom you will be calculating commissions.

10. Type **66000** and press the DOWN ARROW key or click on C6. Type **35000** and press the DOWN ARROW key or click on C7. Type **9000** and press ENTER or click on the control panel .

11. Position the cell pointer in E4 and type **Quotas Met**. Then press the DOWN ARROW key or click on E5.

Adding Formulas to the Commission Model

The number and label entries for this model are now complete. At this point, it is time to add the formulas for calculating the regular and bonus commission. For the purpose of computing the bonus, assume that the quota is $50,000 per product. Use the following steps to enter the logical formulas for determining whether the sales quota in each category was met.

1. Type **+C5 > 50000** and move to E6.

    This formula will produce a 1 if the Product 1 quota is met and a 0 if it is not.

2. Type **+C6 > 50000** and move to E7.

3. Type **+C7 > 50000** and move to E8.

4. Total the number of quotas met by adding the result of each of the logical formulas; type **+E5 + E6 + E7** and press ENTER.

In Chapter 7, "Worksheet Functions," you will learn a short-cut method for summing entries, but for now you will use simple addition.

5. Total the sales of all three products in the same fashion: move the cell pointer to C8, type **+C5+C6+C7**, and move to C10.

6. Enter the formula for commission in C10 by typing **+C8*.1** and pressing DOWN ARROW.

7. Type **+E8*1000** and press ENTER.
   This lets you calculate the bonus commission by multiplying the number of quotas met by 1000.

8. Position the cell pointer in D14, type **+C10+C11**, and press ENTER.

Your completed model should now match the one shown in Figure 2-6 at the beginning of this section. The logical formulas it contains will respond to changes in the model's data. Let's try a few.

1. Move the cell pointer to C7.

2. Type **73000** and press ENTER.
   You will find that a new commission plus the bonus figure of $19,400 is calculated immediately. The result does not display the dollar sign or comma; you will learn how to make 1-2-3 add them in Chapter 3, "Changing the Worksheet Appearance."

Using Compound Operators

1-2-3 also has three *compound operators* that can be used with logical formulas. These operators are either used to negate an expression or to join two different expressions. The negation operator #NOT# has priority over the two compound operators, #AND# and #OR#. When the compound operator #AND# is used to join two logical expressions, both expressions must be true for the compound formula to return a *true value*. If the two expressions are joined by #OR#, either one can be true for the condition to return a true value.

You can add a second condition to your commission calculation by using the compound operators. Let's say that bonus commissions require a minimum of six months of service in addition to the minimum sales level for a product. Revise the model to allow for this new condition by following these steps.

1. Move the cell pointer to A9, type **Months in Job:**, and move to C9.

2. Type **4** and press ENTER.

3. Move the cell pointer to E5.

4. Press F2 (EDIT), type **#AND#C9>6**, and then press the DOWN ARROW key.

5. Use the same procedure outlined in step 4 to revise the formulas in E6 and E7.

    You will find that the bonus commission in Figure 2-7 is now zero, since the employee has been on the job fewer than six months.

Figure 2-7. *Using a complex logical formula to test two conditions*

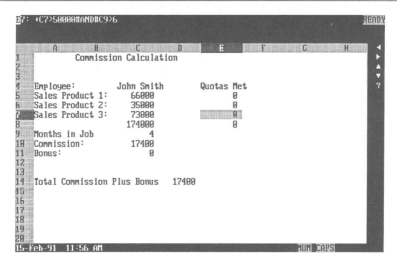

6. Move the cell pointer to C9 and type **8**. Then press ENTER to see the bonus commission calculated again.

7. Enter **/FSCOMM** and press ENTER to save this worksheet to disk.

8. Enter **/WEY** to erase memory.

String Formulas

String formulas were added to 1-2-3 with the introduction of Release 2. Although they do not perform formula calculations as arithmetic formulas do, they enable character strings to be joined together to create headings or other data elements for the worksheet. String formulas use only one operator, the ampersand (**&**). This operator can be used to join variables containing character strings or string constants. For example, +"John"&"Smith" will result in JohnSmith; +"John"&" "&"Smith" will result in John Smith; and +A1&A2&A3 will result in abc if A1 contains an "a," A2 contains a "b," and A3 contains a "c." As with the other types of formulas, with string formulas you can either type the complete formula or point to the cell addresses referenced and have 1-2-3 place them in the formula for you.

Use the string formula feature to build a part number. In this model, separate data elements provide all the different components of the All Parts, Inc. part number structure. The warehouse location, bin number, product type, and vendor are all combined to create a part number. Follow these steps to enter the data for the model.

1. Enter the worksheet heading by moving the cell pointer to B3, then typing **All Parts, Inc. Inventory Listing**, and pressing ENTER.

2. Move the cell pointer to A5, type **Location**, and move to B5.

3. Type **Bin** and move to C5.

4. Type **Type** and move to D5.

5. Type **Vendor** and move to E5.

6. Type **Part No** and press ENTER.

7. Move the cell pointer to A6, type **'5,** and press the RIGHT ARROW.

2

The apostrophe is required since string formulas can only join label entries. Using the apostrophe ensures that the 5 is stored as a label.

8. Type **'12** and press RIGHT ARROW.

9. Type **AX** and press RIGHT ARROW.

10. Type **CN** and press RIGHT ARROW.

11. Verify that the cell pointer is in E6, type the formula **+C6&"—"&D6&A6&B6**, and press ENTER.

   The part number for the first item will appear as follows:

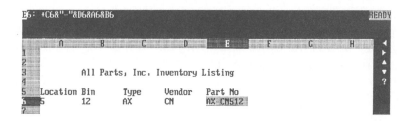

For practice, you may wish to enter the data and the required string formula to build the several additional part numbers. Like the other formula types, changing the values for any of the variables will immediately change the results produced by the string formula. Once you have completed your entries, you can save the model by entering **/FS** from the menu, typing **PARTNO**, and pressing ENTER. To clear the screen enter **/WEY**.

The advantage of the part number display in the last example would occur if the model contained information on additional parts as well as fields to the right that were also important to view. Using the string formula to build the part number, you could move the cell pointer to the right and view the other data without losing track of the part number.

The full power of 1-2-3's string formulas will be realized when you learn to combine the string concatenation features with special string functions that can extract a portion of a string entry. These special string functions can be used for complex combinations and are an excellent tool for correcting data-entry errors. String functions will be covered in Chapter 7.

When more than one operator is used in a formula, it is important to know which operation 1-2-3 will perform first. Table 2-1 shows the priority order for each operation that 1-2-3 can perform. If more than one operator has the same priority, they will be evaluated from left to right.

More Complex Calculations

When 1-2-3 encounters more than one operator in a formula, it does not use a left-to-right order to compute the result. Instead, it evaluates the formula based on a set priority order for each of the operators. As you begin to build more complex formulas, you will see how important it is to understand 1-2-3's priorities in order to achieve the desired effects.

Table 2-1 shows the order of priority for each of the operators. You will notice that the parentheses are at the top of the list. This indicates that any expression enclosed within them will be evaluated first. The other operators that may cause confusion are the + and − symbols shown in levels 6 and 4. The first set represents the positive or negative sign of a value. For instance, −5*3 indicates that the five is a negative number,

Table 2-1.   *Operation Priorities*

Priority	Operator	Operation Performed
8	( )	Parentheses to override priorities
7	^	Exponentiation
6	+ −	Positive and negative indicators
5	/ *	Division and multiplication
4	+ −	Addition and subtraction
3	= < >	Logical operators
	< >	
	<= >=	
2	#NOT#	Complex not indicator
1	#AND#	Complex and
	#OR#	Complex or
	&	String operator

2

which should be multiplied by a positive three. On the other hand, in the expression $5 - 4*2$ the minus symbol represents subtraction and has a lower priority than the multiplication operation, which will be carried out first.

A short example will demonstrate this clearly. Suppose you wish to project an 8 percent sales increase you will have next year. To get the correct result, you must add this year's sales plus an additional eight percent of this year's sales. The formula is this year's sales multiplied by the sum of 1 (for 100 percent of this year's sales) plus the percentage the sales will grow. To create a worksheet that uses this example, follow these steps:

1. Type the following entries in the worksheet cells specified using the arrow keys or the mouse to move between worksheet cells:

   A1: This year's sales
   A2: Percentage growth
   A3: Next year's sales
   C1: 150000
   C2: 8%

2. Create the formula to calculate the growth in sales. Move to C3 and type **+**. Point to C1 and type ***(1+**. Point to C2, type **)**, and press ENTER or click on the control panel. At this point your worksheet looks like this:

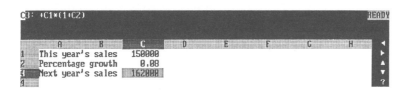

You must use parentheses when you want to select the order in which 1-2-3 will calculate different parts of the formula. If you do not include the parentheses, 1-2-3 will multiply this year's sales by 1 and then *add* .08 rather than calculate 8 percent. The result would be 150000.08 rather than 162000, which is the correct result.

Using Names in Formulas

Meaningful names are often easier to remember than cell addresses. If you have sales stored in B10 and a discount rate in Z2, it will be easier to remember the name of the type of information you have stored than the cell addresses, especially when you have a model with many items of data. 1-2-3 provides a way for you to name the data stored in worksheet cells. Although you will not want to make this extra effort for every model, it can be especially helpful in some situations. Before learning how to assign names to your data, you will need to learn about 1-2-3 ranges.

Range Basics

In 1-2-3, a *range* is a group of one or more cells that form a contiguous rectangle. You can use ranges in 1-2-3 to tell the package to take the same action on each of the cells in the group. When used in this way, they can provide a substantial time-savings over making separate requests to change each cell in the group. You will see more in Chapter 3 about using ranges this way. For now, you will want to learn the essentials that allow you to use ranges to assign names to individual worksheet cells.

Cell references are expressed by stating the column location followed by the row location, as in A10 or C4. Since a range can include a rectangular area of cells, a range address is always expressed as two separate cell addresses set apart by a period. The typical method used to describe a range is to state first the upper left cell in the range, then use a period as a separator and supply the lower right cell in the range as in A1.B10 or C3.G20. Although you need to type only one period as a separator, 1-2-3 always converts it to two and would show these ranges as A1..B10 and C3..G20. You can assign a name to any range so that you can refer to the range by the name rather than by its cell addresses.

Elsewhere in the book, you will look at applications for applying names to ranges that include more than one cell. For now, you will assign range names only to individual cells, since the formulas you have used thus far operate on only one cell at a time. Even though you are interested in naming one cell, you still need to refer to that cell as a range rather than attempt to use its individual cell address. This is because the command that you are using is designed to accept range addresses rather than cell addresses. The proper way of expressing a range consisting of one cell is to use the cell address for both the beginning and the end of the range. When A1 is treated as a range, the range address is expressed as A1..A1.

Naming a Range

You need to use a command from 1-2-3's menu in order to name the range. You will learn more about the various menu options in Chapter 3, but for now all you need to do is use a slash whenever you need to invoke the menu and type the first letter of the commands that you need to execute. The sales formula entered in the previous section is a good place to try out the benefits of *range names*.

As you name each of the cells in the model, you are limited to 15 characters for your range name. Each range name must be unique and can refer to only one cell if you want to use it in the types of formulas entered thus far. 1-2-3 does not distinguish between upper- and lowercase, and displays all range names in uppercase when you see them in formulas.

To name the three values used in the previous section, follow these steps:

1. Move the cell pointer to B1.

2. Type **/** to invoke the menu. Type **R** to select the Range command. Type **N** to select the Name option from the Range menu. Type **C** to select Create from the Name menu. 1-2-3 will prompt for a name.

3. Type **this_year's** and press ENTER.

4. Press ENTER a second time to accept 1-2-3's suggested range designation of the current cell.

    If you forget to position the cell pointer before requesting the Range Name Create command, 1-2-3 suggests a different range address. You can replace its suggestion by typing your own in the format B3.B3.

5. Move the cell pointer to C2, enter **/RNC** followed by **percent_growth**, and press ENTER twice.

    Again, the keystrokes /RNC are requesting an action through 1-2-3's menus. You will learn more about these menus in Chapter 3.

6. Move the cell pointer to C3, enter **/RNC** followed by **next_year's,** and press ENTER twice.

Your formula should now display like this:

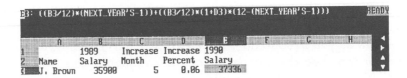

This formula is easier to understand since you do not need to make the mental comparison between cell address and cell contents for each entry in the formula. If you want the range names available the next time you use a model, you must save it after assigning the range names. When you edit a cell with the F2 (EDIT) key that contains range names in the formula, the edit line displays the cell addresses rather than the range names shown in the top line. Your display will look like this:

Press ENTER to finalize the entry and return to READY mode.

Although the range names are practical in this small example, they are not a good solution in all models. If you expand this model to have 100 computations, range names for each calculation would be impractical. In this situation, it is best to continue to use cell addresses in your formulas. On the other hand, a model containing a financial statement that is to be used in the preparation of ratios would be a good application for the assignment of range names, as similar data items are not repeated and the use of the range names would make the formulas much more readable. In a worksheet with many calculations, you may only be interested in naming a few important cells.

Building Formulas with Range Names

The last example showed you how a formula changes to display range addresses once they have been assigned. You can also assign a name to a cell before you reference it in a formula. This will allow you to specify the name with the F3 (NAME) key when building a formula. Follow these steps to try the new approach.

1. Move to A4, type **Difference in sales** and move to C4.

2. Type **+**, then press the F3 (NAME) key. Your display will look like this:

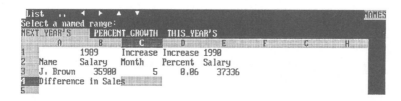

3. Press ENTER with the highlight on NEXT_YEAR'S. With a mouse, you can select this range name by clicking on it.

4. Type **−**, then press F3 (NAME). Move the highlight to THIS_YEAR'S and press ENTER or click on this range name to add it to the formula. Your display will use the range names instead of the cell addresses.

5. Press ENTER to finalize the formula entry. Your display will look like this:

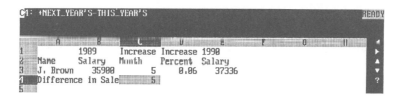

Deleting Range Names

You can delete range names that you no longer need. The command to eliminate them is also on the Range Name menu that you have been using to create them. When you eliminate a range name, you do not eliminate the worksheet data with the range name. The formulas with references to the deleted range names revert to displaying the cell address rather than its name. To delete the range name NEXT_YEAR'S from the previous example, follow these steps.

1. Select /Range Name Delete.

2. Highlight NEXT_YEAR'S and press ENTER.

   The formula will no longer display the deleted range name and will look like this:

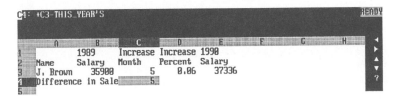

Review

- Formulas allow you to define computations that you want 1-2-3 to perform with the contents of worksheet cells.

- Formulas must always start with a value character and cannot exceed 240 characters.

- Arithmetic formulas are the most popular type of 1-2-3 formulas since they support typical business calculations like computing purchase discounts, invoice extensions, and sales projections. They use operators for addition (+), subtraction (−), multiplication (*), division (/), and exponentiation (^).

- String formulas use only one operator, the ampersand (&), which allows you to join two character strings.

- Logical formulas use the logical operators equal to (=), not equal to (<>), less than (<), less than or equal to (<=), greater than (>), and greater than or equal to (>=).

- All formula operators do not have the same priority. You can use parentheses to raise the priority of an operation since 1-2-3 evaluates entries in parentheses first. Table 2-1 lists the normal priority sequence of the operators.

- A range name can be assigned to any cell on the worksheet. Formulas referencing this cell automatically display the range name in the formula. To access an existing range name when building a formula, use the F3 (NAME) key and select it from the list presented.

- A range name that is no longer needed can be deleted without deleting the data in the referenced cell. After the range name is deleted, the formula displays the cell address rather than the range name.

Commands and Keys

Entry	Action
/FR	Accesses File Retrieve to allow you to read a file from disk into memory
/RNC	Names a worksheet cell with Range Name Create
/RND	Deletes a range name with Range Name Delete
/WEYY	Invokes Worksheet Erase and responds with Yes, Yes to clear memory
F3 (NAME)	Allows you to access a list of range names

3

Changing the
Worksheet
Appearance

Up to this point, you have accepted 1-2-3's choices for how to present your
entries. You have used the package's *default* for the format in which the
data has been displayed. It is great to have this default available; it lets you
build a model that produces completely accurate results without having to
concern yourself with how your entries should be displayed. But it is also
great to know that 1-2-3 provides a set of powerful formatting options and
other commands that let you change the default settings affecting the
display of your entries. There are commands that let you select a new
display format for all the values on the worksheet, or change the format
for the value entries in a small section of the worksheet. Other 1-2-3
commands allow you to affect the alignment of labels, either before or after
you enter them. Still other commands let you change the number of
characters that can be displayed in a column or hide certain columns from
view. In this chapter, you will look at examples using each of these
techniques. You will find that each of these 1-2-3 commands is easy to use

and provides significant improvements in the appearance of your worksheet models. First, let's address how you access these commands, since
they can be accessed only when 1-2-3's menu is on the screen.

1-2-3's Menu Structure

1-2-3's menu system is designed to make 1-2-3's commands easy to
access and remember. Only one keystroke is needed to access the menu
system, and Lotus has chosen words that represent their function in
building the menu. Each menu option also includes a description of the
tasks that it can accomplish for you. This descriptive information will make
it easier for you to select the correct command as you are learning.

Activating the Menu

1-2-3's menu is activated by pressing the slash key (/) from READY
mode or by moving the mouse into the control panel. The / key is located
on the lower right side of your keyboard near the SHIFT key. If the mode
indicator currently reads WAIT, POINT, ERROR, or something other
than READY, it means that 1-2-3 will not be ready to accept your request.
If you type a slash or move the mouse into the control panel when 1-2-3
is not ready to respond, the menu will not appear onscreen. If 1-2-3 is in
EDIT mode when you type a slash, 1-2-3 adds the slash to the current
entry. You must take an action to return the indicator to READY before
activating the menu. This action may be completing the entry you have
already started, waiting for 1-2-3 to finish its current task, or pressing ESC
to acknowledge that you saw an Error Message.

Note

*For the rest of this book, when the steps direct you to select a menu command, you
will want to type **/** or point to the control panel with the mouse.*

The Main Menu

Type **/** or move the mouse into the control panel to activate the main
menu and produce this display:

This is called the *main menu* because all commands must start at this point. By selecting one of the options in this display, you often are shown a submenu of choices. These allow you to refine your command. You may be given as many as six levels of menus to select from before you get to your final choice. You need not be concerned with the complexity of the menus, however. The options are organized logically; with a little practice, it is easy to decide which path to select at any point.

Notice that the mode indicator also changes to MENU. (It will remain this way as long as one of 1-2-3's menus is displayed on the screen.) The second and third lines in the control panel are devoted to the menu display. (The second line in the control panel shows the various menu choices; the line beneath it provides an explanation of the types of tasks performable by the currently highlighted selection in the top row.)

The third line of the control panel, describing each of the menu choices onscreen, is to help guide you in making a selection. And if you make an inappropriate choice, there is an easy way to retreat with ESC and start fresh down the path to the exact command you are seeking. Again, do not be discouraged by the complexity; you will not need to learn all the menu commands. You can accomplish 90% of your work using only a small percentage of the total menu. The other commands are there to provide sophisticated options for 1-2-3's power users.

Before you examine any one particular menu choice in further detail, take a quick look at each of the main menu selections to get an overview of the types of features each of them provides. Each main menu choice and the category of tasks it performs is listed here.

Menu Selection	Type of Task Handled
Worksheet	The Worksheet commands make changes to the entire worksheet. Options include globally setting the format of value entries in the worksheet cells, inserting and deleting worksheet rows or columns, and erasing the entire worksheet.

Menu Selection	Type of Task Handled
Range	The Range commands make changes that are less extensive and affect only a section of the worksheet. Options in the Range menu include formatting a section of the worksheet, assigning a name to a group of worksheet cells, and erasing a section of the worksheet.
Copy	Use the Copy selection whenever you wish to duplicate the information from one group of worksheet cells to another group of cells. With this menu choice, you do not have to select from additional submenus. You need only specify which cells you need to copy and where you want them copied to.
Move	Move is similar to Copy, but it relocates data rather than copying it. As with Copy, Move requires you to respond to its prompts rather than select from additional submenus.
File	The File commands are used whenever you wish to perform tasks that relate to saving or retrieving data stored on the disk. Options include saving a file, retrieving a file, and listing the files in the current directory.
Print	Use the Print selection whenever you wish to obtain a printed copy of the worksheet that is currently in memory.
Graph	The Graph commands create a graphic representation of data stored on the worksheet. Some of the options include defining the type of graph you wish to create, defining the data to be shown on the graph, and viewing the graph that is currently defined.

Menu Selection	Type of Task Handled
Data	The Data commands are a special category that provides data-management features along with some special arithmetic features. The two most frequently used options under Data are the Sort option, which allows you to resequence your data, and the Query option, which allows you to locate and extract specific information from your model.
System	The System option provides access to the basic DOS operating system commands without having to exit to 1-2-3.
Add-In	The Add-In menu options make it easy to work with add-in programs. With the submenu options presented with this selection, you can attach, detach, and invoke add-in programs.
Quit	Quit exits 1-2-3 without saving the worksheet currently in memory. Use this selection only when you have completed your 1-2-3 session and already saved your work.

Each of these main menu selections will be discussed in more detail as you proceed through this book. Next, you will look at how you can select the options from 1-2-3's menus.

Making Menu Selections

You can select an option in any menu that is displayed by typing the first letter of the menu selection, using either upper- or lowercase. In other words, to select the first option, Worksheet, you can type **w** or **W**. If you type a letter that is not used on the menu, 1-2-3 will beep at you and will not respond until you enter a valid menu selection.

3

A second way to make your selection is to use the LEFT or RIGHT ARROW key to move the highlighted bar (cell pointer) to the item you want, then press ENTER. This latter approach is preferred while you are learning the menu, since it causes 1-2-3 to display a description of the command you are about to choose in the third line of the control panel. If after reading this description you decide it is not the correct selection, you can continue to move to new selections until the desired description is displayed. No action will be taken until you activate a menu choice by pressing ENTER.

In Release 2.3, a third way to make a selection from the menu is to point to the text with the mouse and press the left mouse button. You can use any of these three methods to make selections and the results will be the same. Once you make a selection, 1-2-3 will either execute the command, prompt you to enter information, or make an additional selection from another menu.

Often a series of menu selections is needed to complete a task with 1-2-3. After making your first selection, you may need to refine your request by choosing from a submenu of additional choices. A selection from the submenu may complete the process, or it may invoke yet another submenu, taking you one step lower in 1-2-3's menu hierarchy. You can think of making these selections as creating a command sentence, with each word representing a more specific level of the menu structure than the word before it.

Some of 1-2-3's submenu selections display a dialog box showing the current entries and selections for each option in the menu. In the next section of this chapter, you will learn how you can use the dialog box to change the settings for 2.3 instead of using the equivalent menu commands. (This is a new feature; Release 2.2 displayed settings sheets that showed you the current settings but did not allow you to change them.)

If you think of the process as building a command sentence, you might choose File from the main menu to tell 1-2-3 that the command you want to enter involves files. You might choose Save from the File submenu to refine the file operation. Finally, you might enter **REALEST** to complete your command sentence by supplying the name under which 1-2-3 should save the file.

Try a few selections so you can see how the process works.

   1. Type **/** (or point to the control panel) to activate the menu.

2. Select Worksheet by typing **W**, clicking on Worksheet, or pressing ENTER, since the cell pointer is already positioned on that selection.

   1-2-3 will display a menu that includes Global, Insert, Delete, Column, Erase, Titles, Window, Status, Page, and Learn.

3. Press ENTER or click on Global to select Global from the submenu that is presented.

When you select Global, a third-level menu is presented, which should match the top of Figure 3-1. You will notice that Release 2.3 displays a dialog box in the worksheet area as soon as you select Global. This sheet shows you the current setting for each Global option. Any changes made through options in the Global menu will be reflected in this sheet immediately.

Note

As you become more familiar with menu selections, you will be given only the names of the commands you should choose for each exercise; you will no longer be told which keys to press to make these selections. Remember, you can make menu selections by typing the first letter, by using the arrow keys and ENTER, or by clicking on them

Figure 3-1. *The Global menu and Global Settings dialog box*

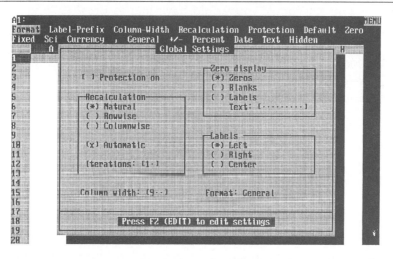

with the mouse. It does not matter which of the three methods you use to make menu selections—use whatever method you prefer. Also remember that when you are instructed to press ENTER *to finalize an entry, you can click on the control panel in place of pressing* ENTER.

Canceling a Selection

Since you are just examining the menu structure, do not make any additional selections at this time. Instead, examine the methods for backing out of menu selections to return to the previous menu and eventually to the READY mode. This is useful when you accidentally make an incorrect menu selection and want to back out of it to make a new choice.

The ESC key is used to back out of one level of menu selection. With a mouse, you can select ESC by pressing the right mouse button. Try this to see how it works.

1. Press ESC once or press the right mouse button.
   The menu of worksheet selections returns to the screen.

2. Press ESC or press the right mouse button again.
   The main menu appears with this second press.

3. Press ESC or press the right mouse button a third time.
   The READY mode indicator appears. If you had made four menu selections, you would have had to press ESC four times to return to READY mode. An easier way to return to READY mode is to press the CTRL-BREAK key combination. That is, hold down the CTRL key while you press the BREAK or SCROLL LOCK key and then release both keys. Regardless of the number of menu selections you have made, you will immediately be taken out of the MENU mode and placed back in the READY mode.

Using Dialog Boxes

Release 2.3 uses dialog boxes as an alternative to using other 1-2-3 commands. You have seen earlier in the chapter that as you make selections with 1-2-3 commands, Release 2.3 updates the information displayed in the dialog box. You can also use dialog boxes to enter commands. To use the Global Settings dialog box that you have seen with several Worksheet Global commands, you would select Worksheet Global to display the Global Settings dialog box and press F2 (EDIT), or click on any part of the dialog box.

When you activate a dialog box, the menu disappears until you are finished. You select options by typing the letter indicated on the screen. When a dialog box is active, each selected option is either highlighted or is distinguished by a different color.

Dialog boxes contain various components that allow you to make different types of entries. Dialog boxes are manipulated by using the following features:

- **Option buttons**   Option buttons are used to select from a group of exclusive choices. The option buttons that make up an exclusive set are grouped together like the option buttons under Labels in Figure 3-2.

- **Check boxes**   Check boxes are used to add or remove features or commands. They appear as brackets that either contain an X indicating that they are marked, or a space indicating that they are not marked, as in Automatic in Figure 3-2.

Figure 3-2.   *Options in an active dialog box*

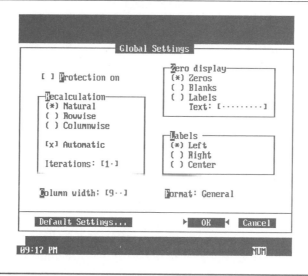

- **Text boxes**   Text boxes are used to accommodate entries that are longer than 1-2-3 can normally handle, making an appropriate entry for the type of information the text box prompt requests. Text box prompts are indicated by square brackets that contain the current entry or dots if no entry is made.

- **Pop-up dialog boxes**   Pop-up dialog boxes are additional dialog boxes that are displayed when you select certain items from the dialog box. When these appear, you can make your selections and then select OK to return to the original dialog box. The Format option in the dialog box shown in Figure 3-2 will display a pop-up dialog box when selected.

- **Command buttons**   Command buttons perform an action such as closing a dialog box and switching to another. All dialog boxes contain OK on the menu to finalize selections. Select Cancel to return to the 1-2-3 menu without retaining any of the changes you made to the dialog box.

- **List boxes**   List boxes (not shown in the preceding figure) supplement selections used with option buttons. A list box is shown here:

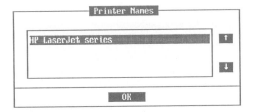

To try using these options, follow these steps:

1. Select Worksheet Global and press F2 (EDIT) to display and activate the Global Settings dialog box.

2. Type **L** for Labels and **R** for Right.
   You can select a component from the dialog box by typing the highlighted letter. You can also move the highlight around the dialog box using the HOME, END, and TAB arrow keys. With dialog

box options, you must select the text listed at the top of the box before you can select one of the items in the box. If you are using a mouse, you can just point to the option you want in the box and click on it.

3. Select Column Width by typing the highlighted letter or clicking on it. Type **15** and press ENTER.

   Since this is another method of selecting the global column width, you must enter a valid column width in the text box.

4. Select Format.

   1-2-3 displays a pop-up dialog box that contains option buttons for the different formats you can select.

5. Select Currency.

6. Type **0** and press ENTER to have no digits display after the decimal point and return to the Global Settings dialog box.

7. Select the Default command button.

8. Select Undo On to enable the UNDO feature.

9. Select Undo On again to remove the mark and disable the UNDO feature.

10. Press SHIFT-ENTER to select the OK command button.

    SHIFT-ENTER always selects the OK command button even when the highlight is not on the OK command button.

11. Select the OK command button to return to the 1-2-3 menu.

12. Press ESC twice to return to READY mode.

    Your changes in the dialog box are still retained.

13. Select Worksheet Erase Yes Yes to erase the worksheet.

    In later chapters you will learn about other commands that are also included in the dialog boxes. You can use either commands or dialog boxes to achieve the same results.

Changing the Display Format

The default format that 1-2-3 uses for all value entries is called the *General format*. It is somewhat unusual in that it does not provide consistent formats for all entries. The display it provides is affected by the size of the number that is entered in the cell. Some numbers display as they are entered, while others are altered to have a leading zero added or so they can be rounded to a number of decimal digits that will fit in the cell width you have selected. The General format also suppresses trailing zeros after the decimal point; if you enter them, they will not appear in the display.

Very large and very small numbers are displayed in *Scientific format*, which means that exponential notation will be used. (*Exponential notation* is a method of representing a number in abbreviated form by including the power of 10 that the number should be raised to.) If 100550000 is entered in a cell when the General format is in effect, 1-2-3 will use scientific notation to display it as $1.0E+8$.

General format handles a wide variety of formats but often results in a display whose results have varying numbers of decimal places. This makes it less than desirable for many business models because of the inconsistencies in the display of decimal numbers. You encountered the inconsistencies in its decimal display with the real estate investment model in Chapter 2, "Defining Your Calculations." However, this inconsistency does not mean that General format is useless; it provides an ideal format in many situations.

General format is useful when you want to minimize the space used to display very large or very small numbers. Scientific notation ensures that these numbers will be shown in a minimum of space and that the conversion will be handled for you automatically if required. It simply is not the display to use when you need to control the number of decimal places shown.

Formatting Options

There are many alternatives to the General display format. 1-2-3 provides a wide range of formatting options that allow you to display your data with everything from dollar signs and commas to percent symbols. You can even specify the number of decimal places for most of the formats. The specific formats supported by 1-2-3 and their effect on worksheet entries are shown in Table 3-1. You will apply some of these formats to models you have already created.

Scope of the Formatting Change

You can also choose how extensive an impact you want a particular format command to have by formatting the entire worksheet or a range of

Table 3-1. *1-2-3's Format Options*

Format	Cell Entry	Display
Fixed	5678	5678.00
2 decimal places	−123.45	−123.45
Scientific	5678	5.68E+03
2 decimal places	−123.45	−1.23E+02
Currency	5678	$5,678.00
2 decimal places	−123.45	($123.45)
,(Comma)	5678	5,678
2 decimal places	−123.45	(123.45)
General	5678	5678
	−123.45	−123.45
+/−	4	++++
	3	−−−
	0	.
Percent	5	500%
	.1	10%
Date (D1)	31679	24-Sep-86
Time (T1)	.5	12:00:00 PM
Text	+A2*A3	+A2*A3
Hidden	35000	

cells in one area of the worksheet. First, you will examine the procedure for changing the default format for a section of the worksheet.

Using a Range of Cells

Everything you have accomplished with 1-2-3 so far has focused on individual cells. However, 1-2-3 also allows you to work with any contiguous rectangle of cells, called a range, to accomplish tasks such as formatting. You were introduced to ranges in Chapter 2 when you assigned names to ranges consisting of single cell references. Figure 3-3 shows groups of cells that are valid ranges as well as some groups that are not. The groups on the left are invalid ranges because they do not form contiguous rectangles. The cell groups on the right are valid ranges because each one forms a contiguous group. As long as this rule is met, the range can be as large as you wish or as small as one cell.

Figure 3-3.   *Invalid and valid ranges*

You can use several methods to specify cell ranges. You can type them in like a cell address or highlight them with the cell pointer. Any two diagonally opposite corners can be used to specify the range as long as they are separated by one or more decimal points. For example, the bottom valid range shown in Figure 3-2 can be specified as E11.H15, E11..H15, E15.H11, E15..H11, H15.E11, H15..E11, H11.E15, or H11..E15.

The most common way to specify a range is to use the upper leftmost cell first and the lower rightmost cell last. Also, since 1-2-3 will supply the second period, you might as well save a keystroke and just type **B4.C8**. If you plan to specify a range by highlighting it, you can save yourself some time by positioning the cell pointer in the upper leftmost corner of the range before beginning.

In earlier releases, you selected a range *after* selecting a command to use the range. However, with Release 2.3, you can select the range *before* you select the command. This is especially useful if you are using the same range for more than one command. To select a range to be used by commands starting from the READY mode, press F4 (ABS). 1-2-3 changes from READY to POINT mode. This is the POINT mode you saw in

Chapter 2 when 1-2-3 was prompting you for a range of cells to name. You may access POINT mode either by pressing F4 (ABS) or by entering a command that prompts for a range. Any cells you select will remain highlighted until you press ENTER.

You can also select a range with a mouse by clicking the first cell that you want to select and *dragging* the mouse to cover all of the cells that you want to include in the range. Dragging a mouse means holding down the left mouse button while you move it to the opposite corner. When you select a range from READY mode with a mouse, you do not have to press F4 (ABS) to access the POINT mode. In Release 2.3, you can try selecting a range from READY mode by following these steps:

1. Move to E11.

2. Press F4 (ABS).

3. Press the arrow keys until E11..H15 is selected and the control panel looks like this:

```
H15:                                                        POINT
Range: E11..H15
```

4. Press ENTER.

   1-2-3 returns to READY mode but the selected range is still highlighted, so 1-2-3 will use this selected range for the commands you want to execute. If you are using a mouse, you would click E11 and then drag the mouse to H15.

When you select a range from READY mode, the range remains selected until you select another range, or until you either press ESC on the keyboard or press the right mouse button. When you select a command, 1-2-3 will automatically use the range you have selected; 1-2-3 will not prompt you for it.

If a command uses more than one range, like the commands to move and copy cells, 1-2-3 will use the selected range for the first range. This means that if you are moving cells, for example, 1-2-3 will first use the selected range for the cells you are moving. Next it will prompt you for a second range — *where* you want to move these cells. While you can select ranges for all commands described in this book *before* you activate the menu, most of the examples will select the range *after* selecting a command.

Changing the Format for a Range of Cells

Remember that when you want to change how values in a range of worksheet cells appear, you can assign one of 1-2-3's formats to the range; as you learned in Chapter 2, changing the format of a range only affects values that are part of the range.

Now retrieve your investment model by typing **/FRREALEST** and pressing ENTER. The model should match the one shown in Figure 3-4. To try out the range specifications as you add some formats to this model, follow these steps:

1. Move the cell pointer to D13, the upper leftmost cell in the range you will format.

2. Activate the menu (type **/** or move the mouse to the control panel).

Figure 3-4.   *The real estate investment model created in Chapter 2*

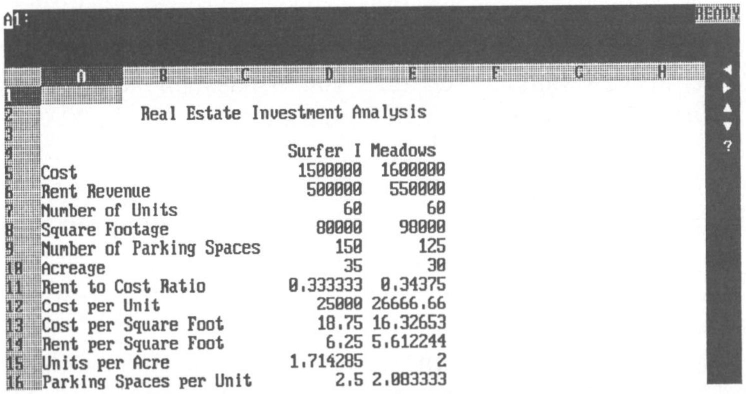

3. Use RIGHT ARROW to move the cell pointer to the menu option Range and press ENTER, or point to it and click on it.

4. Press ENTER or click on Format, which is currently highlighted.

5. Select the Fixed format option by typing **F** or pointing to Fixed and clicking on it.

6. Press ENTER to select the default of two decimal places.

7. Use RIGHT ARROW and DOWN ARROW to position the cell pointer in E16, highlighting the entire area to be formatted. With a mouse, point to D13 and drag the mouse to cover D13..E16. Then press ENTER or click on the control panel.

    The format should immediately change to two decimal places for each of the entries in this section and match the display in Figure 3-5. The other range that needs to be formatted is D11..E11. This time you will not position the cell pointer first so that you can experience the extra steps involved.

8. Select Range Format Fixed and press ENTER.

Figure 3-5. *Worksheet after formatting changes to range D13..E16*

```
D13: (F2) +D5/D8                                          READY

        A           B         C         D        E      F     G     H    ◄
 1                                                                        ▶  ▲
 2                     Real Estate Investment Analysis                       ▼
 3                                                                        ?
 4                                    Surfer I  Meadows
 5     Cost                           1500000   1600000
 6     Rent Revenue                    500000    550000
 7     Number of Units                     60        60
 8     Square Footage                   80000     98000
 9     Number of Parking Spaces           150       125
10     Acreage                             35        30
11     Rent to Cost Ratio            0.333333   0.34375
12     Cost per Unit                    25000  26666.66
13     Cost per Square Foot             18.75     16.33
14     Rent per Square Foot              6.25      5.61
15     Units per Acre                    1.71      2.00
16     Parking Spaces per Unit           2.50      2.00
17
```

This command sequence will accept the default of two decimal places. You cannot expand the range at this point, as it has the incorrect beginning location. You must first free the beginning of the range.

Note that here you have been asked to make menu selections without being told which key to press. If you would like a review of the different methods, reread the section "Making Menu Selections" earlier in this chapter.

9. Press ESC. Now you will find that you can move the cell pointer to D11 without altering a range specification.

10. Type . (period).

This will anchor the beginning of the range again.

11. Expand the range by moving the cell pointer to E11, and then press ENTER to finalize the range selection.

If you want to use the mouse for the last three steps, you would point to D11 and drag the mouse to E11 before you click on the control panel to finalize the command. 1-2-3 will automatically replace the range address in the control panel with the range you select with the mouse.

If you move the cell pointer to any cell that has been formatted with a Range command, you can tell the format that has been assigned to the cell, even if it is empty. This information is displayed as a single character representing the format type in the control panel. Table 3-2 presents examples of some of the commonly used format abbreviations. These format specifications are enclosed within parentheses and placed immediately after the cell address.

For formats that allow you to specify the number of decimal places, a numeric digit follows, as shown here in the (C2) in the control panel.

The real estate model still is not presented in the optimal format. The numbers in the cells at the top would be easier to read if they had commas inserted after the thousands position. There are two formats that will add

Table 3-2. *Examples of Format Abbreviations*

Abbreviation	Format in Effect
(P2)	Percent with two decimal places
(T)	Text to display formulas as they are entered
(G)	General
(C0)	Currency with zero decimal places
(,2)	Comma with two decimal places
(D1)	Date format 1
(D6)	Time format 1
(H)	Hidden format

these commas. One is referred to as the *Comma format* (,); the other is the *Currency format*. The only difference between the two is whether a dollar sign is inserted at the front of the entry. Either of these two formats could be added with another range request, but since the cells that you wish to change include all the remaining value entries on the worksheet, you will use the Global formatting option covered in the next section.

Making a Global Format Change

When you wish to alter the format of the entire worksheet or even most of it, a *global format* change is the ideal solution. A global format change alters the default format for every cell on the worksheet, including both cells with entries and cells that are currently empty. As long as the worksheet cells have not had their formats altered with Range Format commands, the new default format will take effect. For an empty cell, this format will be used as soon as a value entry is placed in the cell. Global formatting is especially useful when most of the worksheet is formatted with the same option. You can choose a global format that meets the requirement for most of the cells, and then go back and format the exceptions with a Range Format command.

To alter the global format for the model, follow these steps:

1. Select Worksheet Global Format.

2. Type **,** to select the Comma format.

3. Type **0** to specify zero decimal places, and press ENTER.

Everything looks fine except that the two cost figures in row 5 are now displayed as asterisks. The values that were stored there are still in memory and are only replaced by the asterisks to indicate that once the new formats are used, the numeric values in these cells require more space than the column width allows. You can correct this quickly by increasing the global width. This command will be explained later in the chapter; for now, the command will be entered as shown.

4. Type **/WGC10** and press ENTER.

The columns will be widened to ten characters, producing the display shown in Figure 3-6. The columns are now wide enough to display the cost figures with commas.

Checking a Format Setting

If you move the cell pointer to one of the cells that has been formatted with the Global option, you will notice that there is no format code in the control panel. Only range formats will display in the control panel. To check the global format setting, you have to check the worksheet's status. With Release 2.2 and 2.3, the global format is displayed in the dialog box or settings sheet (depending on which release you have) that appears

Figure 3-6.   *Worksheet with new global format and column width*

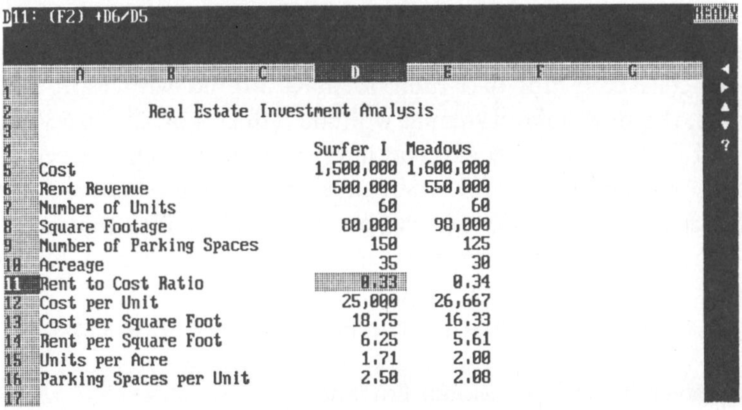

when you select Worksheet Global. In Releases 2.2 and below, the Worksheet Status screen provides information on all the worksheet default settings. In all releases, the Worksheet Status screen displays information about the available conventional and expanded memory, any math coprocessor, and the first cell in the worksheet that is part of a circular reference if the worksheet has one. Check it now by following these directions:

1. Select Worksheet Status.

    If you are using Release 2.2, your screen will look like the one in Figure 3-7. Notice that the indicator has changed to STAT. If you are using Release 2.3, you will see only a few of these options on the Worksheet Status screen; to see all of these options, call up the Global Settings dialog box.

2. Press any key.

    This last step will return you to the worksheet and READY mode. With Release 2.3, you will see the worksheet default settings when you select Worksheet Global to display the Global

Figure 3-7. *Worksheet Status screen*

```
A1:                                                                      STAT
Press any key to continue...

                          ┌──────────── Global Settings ────────────┐
                          │ Conventional memory:  262992 of 287072 Bytes (91%)
                          │ Expanded memory:      1735856 of 2096128 Bytes (82%)
                          │
                          │ Math coprocessor:     (None)
                          │
                          │ Recalculation:
                          │   Method             Automatic
                          │   Order              Natural
                          │   Iterations         1
                          │
                          │ Circular reference:   (None)
                          │
                          │ Cell display:
                          │   Format             (0)
                          │   Label prefix       ' (left align)
                          │   Column width       9
                          │   Zero suppression   No
                          │
                          │ Global protection:    Disabled
                          └──────────────────────────────────────────┘
24-Mar-91  01:44 PM                                              NUM
```

Settings dialog box. By using either Worksheet Global or Work-sheet Status, you will be able to see that the global format is fixed with no digits after the decimal point.

You can use the Format option to look at the formulas within worksheet cells by using a display format of Text. This means that you can review all the formulas at once rather than having to move the cell pointer to each cell and view the control panel to see the formula. The *Text format* displays formulas in the cells where you entered them rather than showing the results of the formulas within the cells. To make this change, you must use both the Global format change and a Range Format change. The global change will alter the default setting for all worksheet cells, but, since range formats take priority, some of the cells will ignore the default. This means that you must reset the format of these cells with the Range Format command before the cells use the default setting.

Before beginning, replace the copy of the investment model on disk with the formatted copy now in memory.

1. Select File Save and press ENTER.

2. A prompt message will display. Select Replace in response. This will replace the file on disk.

Note

It is important to save the file at this time because the reformatting process used to view the formulas will eliminate the Fixed and Comma formats that you wish to retain permanently.

3. Select Worksheet Global Format.

4. Select Text as the format option.

5. Move the cell pointer to D11 and select Range Format Reset to reset the range format to the global default.

6. Move the cell pointer to E16 and press ENTER to view a display of the formulas like the one in Figure 3-8.

Figure 3-8. *Worksheet with new global format applied to range D11..E16*

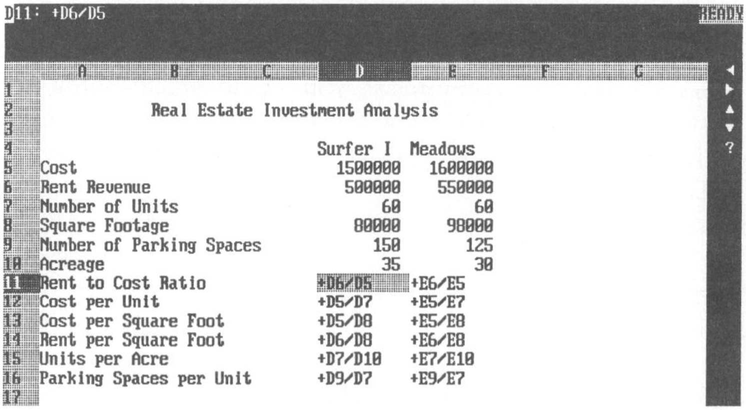

Since the formulas in this particular model are short, you can view the complete formula within each cell. If the formulas were longer, you would need to widen the columns to see the entire formula. In the next section, you will learn all about tailoring the column width to meet your particular needs.

Changing Worksheet Columns

You have examined some of the changes you can make to the appearance of individual entries in cells. There are also several commands that allow you to make changes to one or more columns at one time. 1-2-3 provides options that let you determine the width you wish to use for columns. In Releases 2.2 and 2.3 you can change the width of a range of columns with one command. If you have Release 2 or higher, you can also hide or display columns on your worksheet.

Altering Column Widths

The default width of columns is nine when you begin a new 1-2-3 worksheet. This is adequate for values displayed with the General format; often, however, it is not wide enough when you want to display numbers with commas, dollar signs, and decimal places or some labels and most of the formulas you wish to display with the Text format option. At other times, the opposite might be true. Even though you may have a column that never contains more than one character, the full width of nine is always reserved for the column. If you could make some columns narrower, you might be able to view a few more columns on the screen. 1-2-3 will let you handle both types of changes by altering the column width. In fact, it even lets you choose whether to change the width of all the columns at once or alter the width of a single column.

Changing the Width of One Column

The ability to alter the width of individual columns lets you tailor your display to meet your exact needs. This is the preferred approach when you only have a few columns to change, since columns are neither wider nor narrower than the requirements of your data. Any change you make for a single column will take precedence over the global column width setting that you establish. This means that you can make both types of changes to your worksheet.

The real estate model provides an opportunity for changing a column width. Follow these steps for making the changes:

1. Select File Retrieve REALEST.

    Release 2.3 will display an additional prompt to confirm that you want to retrieve the file over the current worksheet, which has unsaved changes. If you see this prompt, select Yes to continue.

2. Move the cell pointer to column A.

    Notice the list of long label entries in that column. It extends beyond the boundaries of column A and borrows space from column B. You can widen column A so that the entries will completely fit within the column.

3. Select Worksheet Column Set-Width.

4. Press the RIGHT ARROW until column A is wide enough to display the entire entry, as in Figure 3-9. A width of 25 is a good selection.

5. Press ENTER.

    This finalizes the width change. Column A will remain at a width of 25 unless you make another change. Adjusting the width

Figure 3-9. *Column A widened to 25*

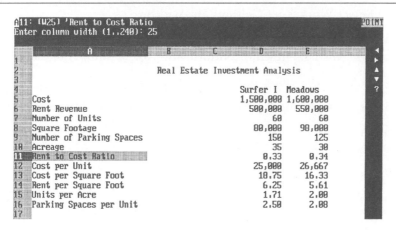

of this column makes it clear where the data is entered. Adjusting the column width can also be important when you print the worksheet. 1-2-3 will print data displayed in the range you select.

Changing the Width of a Range of Columns

Releases 2.2 and 2.3 allow you to alter the width of a range of columns. 1-2-3 changes the width of the range of columns with a single command, but the changes are applied to the individual columns just as if you had changed each one individually with the Worksheet Column Set-Width command. This means that these settings will override any changes made with the Worksheet Global Column-Width command.

You can enter the data in Figure 3-10 prior to trying this command. Note that the heading in row 1 is actually entered as a long label in B1. Also note that the name entries in column A will appear truncated on your screen when you originally enter them. The full names will appear again later when the column width is altered. The labels in B3..D3 are right justified by using the " label indicator. Later in this chapter you will learn how you can have 1-2-3 change the label alignment for you.

After completing the entries, follow these steps:

1. Move the cell pointer to column A.

2. Select Worksheet Column Set-Width.

3. Type **20** and press ENTER.
   This changes the column width for column A to 20.

4. Position the cell pointer in column B.

5. Select Worksheet Column Column-Range Set-Width.

6. Press the RIGHT ARROW key twice to expand the range to include columns C and D, and press ENTER.

7. Press the LEFT ARROW twice to shrink the width to 7.

8. Press ENTER.
   The result of steps 4 through 8 is to change the width of the three columns with one command sequence. Your revised model now matches Figure 3-10.

9. Save this model as VEHICLES by selecting File Save, typing **VEHICLES**, and pressing ENTER.

Changing the Width of All the Columns

For certain models, all the column widths need to be altered. One possibility is using the Worksheet Column Column-Range command, but this command covers only the range you define, whereas the Global option changes the entire worksheet, making model expansion for similar entries

Figure 3-10.   *Model after width adjustment to column range B through D*

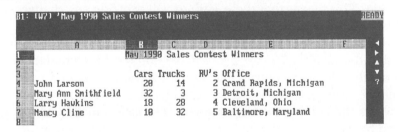

Figure 3-11. *Columns of equal width*

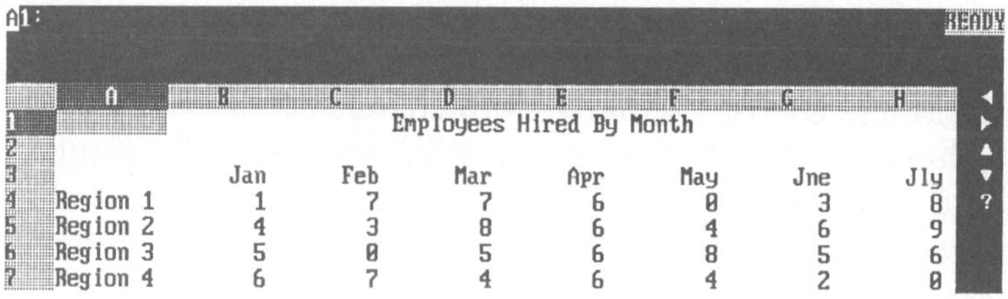

A1: READY

	A	B	C	D	E	F	G	H
1				Employees Hired By Month				
2								
3		Jan	Feb	Mar	Apr	May	Jne	Jly
4	Region 1	1	7	7	6	8	3	8
5	Region 2	4	3	8	6	4	6	9
6	Region 3	5	8	5	6	8	5	6
7	Region 4	6	7	4	6	4	2	8

easy. If you have a model like the one in Figure 3-11 and wish to narrow the column width, it is also tedious to make this change a column at a time, making the Worksheet Global Column-Width option the method of choice.

Since each entry under the "Month" heading is so small, it is better to narrow the columns and view all the months on the screen at once. The Worksheet Global Column-Width command can make this change for you easily: Only one command is required to change all the columns. After entering the command sequence, you can type the new width or use the LEFT ARROW key to make the width narrower by one each time you press it. When you have adjusted the default to the desired width, you need only press ENTER to finalize the current selection. These entries will alter the preceding report so that all the months can be viewed. Follow these steps to make this change.

1. Select Worksheet Global Column-Width.
2. Enter **5** for the width. Press ENTER.

Now all of the worksheet columns are five characters wide. The only problem with this display is that column A has also become smaller and will not display the region numbers. To fix this problem, do the following:

1. Move the cell pointer to column A.
2. Select Worksheet Column Set-Width, type **9**, and press ENTER.

This change to an individual column width fixes the problem and produces the result shown in Figure 3-12.

A Worksheet Global Column-Width change can also be used to make all the columns wider. This is often useful when you are displaying the model as text to view its formulas. If all the formulas are approximately the same length, you may want to widen the column width to accommodate the longest formula entry.

If you want to check the default column width, you cannot point to one of the cells and see it displayed. The width is displayed in the control panel only when the change has been made to a single column with the Worksheet Column Set-Width command. You must give the same status instruction used to check the format by selecting Worksheet Status or Worksheet Global. Remember that you can always change this default; or, if you prefer, you can use the Worksheet Column command to alter the width of one column.

Inserting and Deleting Columns

No matter how thoroughly you plan your worksheet applications, sometimes you need to make substantial changes to a worksheet model. You might need to add an employee to a model, delete accounts that are

Figure 3-12.   *Individual column change overrides global change*

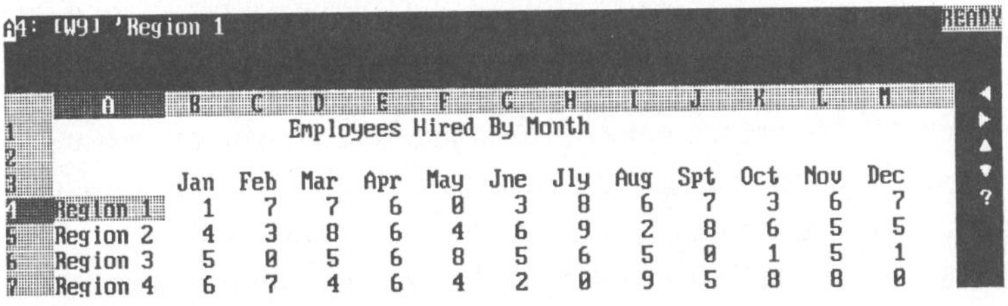

no longer used, or add some blank space to make the worksheet more readable. 1-2-3 will accommodate each of these needs by means of commands that let you insert or delete blank rows or columns in the worksheet.

Inserting Rows and Columns

You can insert blank rows and columns at any location you choose in the worksheet. Before beginning your request, tell 1-2-3 where to place the blank rows or columns by positioning the cell pointer. If you will be adding rows to the worksheet, they will be placed above the cell pointer's location. If you will be adding columns, they will be placed to the left of the cell pointer. Once you make the request to insert rows or columns, you cannot alter the site where they will be placed. If you realize that you forgot to position the cell pointer, your only option is to press ESC to return to READY mode, move the cell pointer, and start the process over again.

When 1-2-3 inserts rows into a worksheet, the cell addresses of the data below this location are changed. It is as though 1-2-3 pushes the data down on the worksheet to make room for the new blank rows. Under normal circumstances, 1-2-3 automatically adjusts all the formulas that reference this data. The same is true for data that resides to the right of the location where columns were inserted.

The insert command is invoked by selecting Worksheet Insert Row. 1-2-3 prompts you for the number of rows to insert but does not use a straightforward question such as "How many rows would you like to add?" Instead, it asks for the range where you want the insertion to occur. It does not use this range to control the placement of the insertion, only to control the number of rows to insert. If you specify a range that includes three rows, three rows will be inserted. If you specify a range of one row, only one row will be inserted. Seeing this in action will clarify the way it works.

Let's add a few blank rows to the commission calculations you created in Chapter 2. Follow these steps to complete the changes:

1. Select File Retrieve.

2. Type **COMM** and press ENTER or click on it in the file list.

3. Move the cell pointer to C8.

Notice that the formula for total sales is entered as +C5+C6+C7. Look at this formula again after inserting a column, and notice how 1-2-3 has automatically adjusted it for you.

4. Position the cell pointer in A9 (anywhere in column A would work just as well).

5. Select Worksheet Insert Column to produce the display in Figure 3-13.

6. Press ENTER to insert one column.

     If you move the cell pointer to D8, you will find that the formula has been changed and the formula for summing sales now reads +D5+D6+D7 to reflect its new location in the worksheet.

Inserting rows is just as easy. Let's insert two blank rows above the section that begins with Months in Job, to separate the sections of the model.

Figure 3-13.   *Inserting a column*

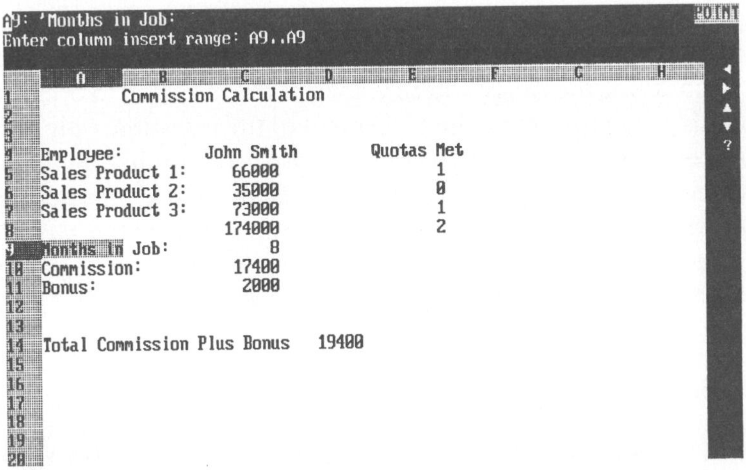

1. Move the cell pointer to D9 (any place in row 9 would work just as well).

2. Select Worksheet Insert Rows and expand the range to include two rows.

3. Press ENTER.

    You will find that two blank rows have been added, producing the results shown in Figure 3-14. Notice that the addition of some blank space on the side and between the two sections makes the model more appealing.

4. Save these changes by selecting File Save, pressing ENTER, and selecting Replace.

Hiding and Displaying Columns

Release 2 added a new feature to 1-2-3 that allows you to conceal columns from view on the display screen temporarily. The data in these columns is not altered in any way and can be displayed again at any time

Figure 3-14.   Two new rows added

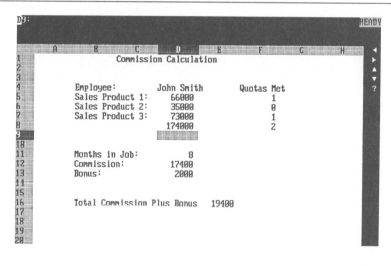

with the entry of another command. This feature is particularly useful if you are working with sensitive information such as salary data and do not wish it to be visible onscreen, in plain view of anyone who walks by your PC.

You can hide the logical formulas in column F by following these steps:

1. Select Worksheet Column Hide.

2. Point to column F and press ENTER.

    The result is a worksheet with the entries in column F hidden as shown in Figure 3-15. To bring these columns back into view, another set of menu entries is required.

3. Move to D13.

    Notice how the formula still uses values in column F. When a column is hidden, it is only removed from the display and not from the worksheet. Formulas can continue to refer to the hidden entries.

4. Move to E13, type **+** and press an arrow key to change 1-2-3 from VALUE to POINT mode.

    When 1-2-3 is in POINT mode, hidden columns temporarily appear with an asterisk to the left of the column letter.

Figure 3-15.   *Column F hidden*

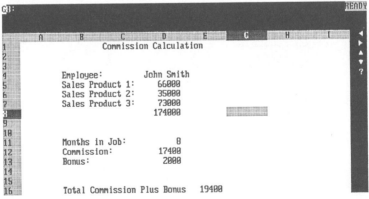

5. Press ESC until 1-2-3 returns to READY mode.

6. Select Worksheet Column Display.

7. Point to column F and press ENTER.

   If you have multiple columns hidden, you can either use separate commands to display each of the hidden columns, or you can select a range with the Worksheet Column Display command that contains cells from the hidden columns you want to display.

Changing Label Entry Alignment

You already learned one method for changing the alignment for a label in Chapter 1, "Worksheet Basics," when you entered a few of the labels by beginning them with a " or ^ symbol. This method works; but if you have a large number of labels to enter, it is time-consuming. It also requires you to edit the entries and replace the label indicator at the front of the label if you want to change its alignment. Fortunately, there are several alternatives that can be real timesavers. One option allows you to change the alignment of labels that are currently on the worksheet; the other changes the default for the current worksheet so that any new labels you enter will use the new alignment setting.

Changing Previously Entered Labels

1-2-3 has two methods for altering the alignment of labels already recorded on the worksheet. You can use the EDIT method, or you can use a Range command that alters the label alignment of the rows in the range. The EDIT method follows these simple rules for editing the entry in any cell.

1. Move the cell pointer to the cell whose alignment you wish to change.

2. Press F2 (EDIT), followed by HOME, to move to the front of the entry.

3. Press the DEL key to eliminate this label indicator. Then type the indicator that corresponds to the type of alignment you want to use and press ENTER.

The second method requires less work; many cell indicators can be changed with a single command. In this case, the command is Range Label. When you select this command, it presents a menu containing Left, Right and Center.

You can choose the type of alignment you want and specify the range of entries that is affected. The major differences between this approach and a Global change are the scope of the change and the fact that the Range Label command affects only the cells that contain entries. Empty cells do not retain this information. If you subsequently place entries in these empty cells, the entries will be aligned in accordance with the default label prefix. To check this default, select Worksheet Status or Worksheet Global to view the by-now-quite-familiar display screen.

Look at the effect of altering the alignment of the labels in this example:

1. Move your cell pointer to A1.

2. Type **Jan** and move to B1.

3. Type **Feb** and move to C1.

4. Type **Mar** and move to D1.

5. Continue making these entries until you enter **Aug** in H1.

6. Move the cell pointer to A1.
   Your display should look like this:

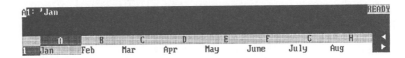

The labels are currently left aligned in accordance with the default.

7. Select Range Label Right.

8. Use the RIGHT ARROW key to move to H1 and press ENTER.

Each of the entries in row 1 is now right aligned in its cell, although subsequent entries in these cells would not be affected.

9. Select Worksheet Erase Yes to erase this example.

Changing Alignment Globally
Before Making Entries

If you change the default label alignment, any new entries you make on the spreadsheet will use this setting. Existing entries will not be affected. This option is especially useful when you wish to enter a series of column headings or other information with a different alignment. You can alter the default alignment without concern for the data already on the worksheet, then make your entries and change the alignment back to its original setting, if you wish.

Let's enter some month names as column headings, using center alignment to see how this might work.

1. Select Worksheet Global Label-Prefix Center.

2. Move the cell pointer to B2 and type **Jan**. Then move to C2.

3. Enter **Feb** and move to D2.

4. Continue entering the month abbreviations across until you have entered **July** in H2.

   Each of your entries will be center aligned in its cell, as follows:

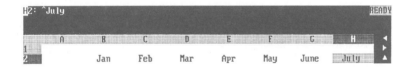

Each entry has a caret symbol at the front of the entry, automatically generated by 1-2-3.

Erasing Worksheet Data

You have learned how to change worksheet entries and completely replace them with other data. However, there are times when you will want to eliminate the entries completely; they may be mistakes or old data that is no longer required. Whatever your reason for wanting to eliminate them, 1-2-3 provides a quick solution. 1-2-3 does not even care what type of entry the cell contains; it erases labels, numbers, and formulas with equal ease. The most common way to eliminate data is to erase a range of cells. This will eliminate all their contents. A second approach is more extensive and thus more dangerous, since it eliminates all the entries on the entire worksheet.

To erase a range of cell entries, the easiest approach is to move the cell pointer to the upper leftmost cell you wish to erase and select Range Erase. In response to the prompt, move the cell pointer to the lower right corner of the range you wish to erase and then press ENTER. This eliminates not only the cell entry but also any label prefix assigned to the cell with a Range command. Formats assigned with a Range command are retained when the cell contents are erased and will be applied to any new entries placed in the cell. In Release 2.3, you have an additional choice. You can delete single cells by moving the cell pointer to the cell and pressing the DEL key. This is the same as using the Range Erase command for a single cell. In Release 2.3, you have an additional choice. You can delete single cells by moving the cell pointer to the cell and pressing the DEL key. This is the same as using the Range Erase command for a single cell.

The following data shows two entries that were made on the worksheet and finalized.

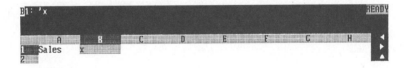

Pressing ESC will not help you eliminate either entry; both have been finalized. To eliminate the "x" that was entered in error, do the following:

1. Place the cell pointer in B1.

2. Select Range Erase.

3. Press ENTER to erase the single cell entry.

A Worksheet Erase command packs much more destructive capability, since it eliminates everything from the worksheet. It is useful mainly if you make a complete mess and want to erase it. In that case, you can select Worksheet Erase Yes Yes to effectively remove the entire worksheet from memory and start over with your entries on a blank worksheet.

3

Undoing Menu Commands

You have looked at 1-2-3's Undo feature for eliminating an entry from a worksheet cell, but Undo has even more power than the ability to eliminate an entry. When the Undo feature is enabled, 1-2-3 keeps track of all the activities that occur from the time that 1-2-3 is in READY mode until the next time it is in READY mode. As long as these activities involve only the current worksheet or its settings, it can be undone. External activities like printing or writing a file to a disk cannot be undone. If you retrieve a file, format a range, or alter the width of a range of columns, 1-2-3 will be able to undo these actions as long as the Undo feature is enabled and you invoke it before performing any new activities. Once you invoke another command or make a new entry, that action is the latest action and is the work that will be undone when you press the ALT-F4 (UNDO) key.

If you press the ALT-F4 (UNDO) key repeatedly, it will toggle the effect of your last action, first eliminating it and then restoring it again. If you change the width of a column and press ALT-F4 (UNDO), 1-2-3 will eliminate the change in the column width. Pressing it again restores the column width change just completed. Pressing it again removes it, and so on for an unlimited number of iterations. You can use this feature to toggle the effect of a number in a cell as you evaluate the results from two different possibilities.

To see how the Undo feature can help you, first check to make sure it is enabled with Worksheet Global Default Other Undo Enable, and then follow these steps:

1. Retrieve the VEHICLES file created earlier in the chapter by selecting File Retrieve, typing **VEHICLES**, and pressing ENTER.

2. Move the cell pointer to column B. Select Worksheet Column Column-Range Set-Width, highlight columns B through D by using the RIGHT ARROW, and press ENTER; then type **20** and press ENTER.

   Notice that the columns become much wider.

3. Press ALT-F4 (UNDO).

   The columns return to the width they had before you executed the last command.

4. Select Worksheet Erase Yes.

   1-2-3 clears the screen and the model is removed from memory.

5. Press the ALT-F4 (UNDO) key to have 1-2-3 restore the worksheet in memory.

6. Press ALT-F4 (UNDO) again to have 1-2-3 erase the worksheet again.

   The Undo feature functions as a toggle switch, alternately removing the effect of your last action and then restoring it again.

Review

- Other than basic entries and function key options, all 1-2-3 features can be accessed with selections from a series of menus. The main menu is invoked with the **/** key or by moving the mouse to the control panel.

- You can select an option from any menu by highlighting your selection and pressing ENTER. Typing the first letter of the menu selection functions the same way. With a mouse, you can select an option by pointing to it and clicking on it.

- When 1-2-3 displays a dialog box, you can use the dialog box to make changes instead of using the commands that appear above it. Press F2 (EDIT) or click on the dialog box to make menu changes.

- You can use the ESC key to back out of the menu by one level.

- You can format numeric entries to match your needs. The Range Format command will format a contiguous group of cells. The Worksheet Global Format command sets the default format and will format any numeric entry not formatted with the Range Format command. Formats established with the Range command are shown in the top line of the control panel.

- You can change the column width of one or more worksheet cells. Use the Worksheet Global Column-Width command to change the width of any cells for which an individual width is not set. Use the Worksheet Column command to change the width of the current column. Use the Worksheet Column Column-Range command to change the width of a group of columns. A column width established for an individual column is shown in the top line of the control panel.

- You can insert and delete rows and columns. When you delete a row or column, you delete the contents of all the cells in the row or column.

- You can hide columns of data and redisplay them. Use this feature to remove confidential information from the worksheet area of the screen.

- You can erase a group of cells with Range Erase and the entire worksheet with Worksheet Erase. With Undo enabled, you can undo either of these actions with ALT-F4 (UNDO).

- Use Worksheet Global Label-Prefix to change the alignment for entries you are about to make. Use Range Label to alter the alignment of existing label entries.

- You can use Worksheet Status to review the current Global settings. With Release 2.3 you can also enter Worksheet Global to see the Global Settings dialog box.

Commands and Keys

Entry	Action
/	Invokes the menu
ESC	Backs you out of the menu by one step

Entry	Action
CTRL-BREAK	Backs you all the way out of the menu to READY mode no matter how many levels deep you are in the menu
DEL	Deletes the current cell's contents from READY mode
F2	(EDIT) Activates a dialog box
RE	Range Erase eliminates entries from a contiguous group of worksheet cells
RF	Range Format changes the appearance of numeric entries in a contiguous group of worksheet cells
RL	Range Label changes the alignment of a contiguous group of label entries on a worksheet
WCCS	Worksheet Column Column-Range Set-Width changes the width of a contiguous group of worksheet columns
WCS	Worksheet Column Set-Width changes the width of the current worksheet column
WD	Worksheet Delete deletes a contiguous group of worksheet rows or columns
WGC	Worksheet Global Column-Width changes the width of all columns that have not been set individually with the Worksheet Column or Worksheet Column Column-Range command
WGF	Worksheet Global Format changes the format of all worksheet cells whose formats have not been set with the Range Format command
WI	Worksheet Insert inserts blank rows and columns on a worksheet

4

Working with Files

New computer users always find the concept of files a little difficult to understand. This is partly because you cannot *see* a file, the way you can see entries that you place on the worksheet. But files are really quite simple to work with. They use concepts that are very similar to those you use every day for storing written documents in your office. The main difference is that computer files are stored on a disk instead of in a drawer. In this chapter, you will learn about basic file concepts and explore the basic file commands that 1-2-3 has to offer. You will then learn about new features in Release 2 and higher that allow you to temporarily exit 1-2-3 and access the file-handling features of your computer's operating system. If you are using Release 2.3, you can use the Viewer add-in to make it easier to retrieve and look at files. There are a few additional differences between Release 1A and Releases 2 and higher, most of them very subtle and relating to the use of directories or the display of files stored on the disk. If you are using Release 1A, check the special information in the examples that describe some of these differences.

File Concepts

Every day you undoubtedly work with a number of different pieces of paper. Periodically, you probably place some of these papers in file folders in a cabinet or desk drawer to make space for new information on your desktop. Then, when you want to review these papers again, you search for them in the cabinet or ask your secretary to bring you the file folder you wish to see. Assuming that you have an organized filing system, the papers you want will arrive back on your desk.

Your computer uses very similar procedures to maintain its information. Taking a look at the similarities and differences will help you understand the important role that files can play for you.

Storing Information on Disk

When you store information in your computer, you provide the machine with an organizational challenge similar to the one faced by you or your secretary. In the computer's case, the "desktop" is the RAM memory of the system; and, like your desktop, it has a limited amount of space. How much space it has available in memory will dictate how much information you can place in it at any one time. Part of this space can be used for a program such as 1-2-3; another part can be used to store a worksheet that you are building with the package. Only one worksheet can be on your computer's desktop at any one time; this keeps things organized for you. Just as you use file folders to store papers, so your computer uses disk files to store information. The computer's files are maintained on disk rather than in a cabinet. When you build a model, it will be stored in the computer's desktop—its temporary memory. You generally will want to store a copy of this model in a file on your disk before you exit 1-2-3 or start creating a second model. This storage makes it possible for the computer to recall the first model another time so that you can work on it again.

When working with a computer, you need to save your model before you complete it, as 1-2-3 does not automatically maintain a permanent record of your model. As soon as you turn your system off or exit 1-2-3 (whether deliberately or accidentally), the model is lost from memory. In order to use this model again, you must already have stored a copy of it in a file on your disk. The disk provides a more permanent memory since its contents are not lost when the power is off in your computer. As long as you store the file on disk, you can retrieve a copy of the file from disk and place it in the memory of your computer system again. With Release 2.3 of 1-2-3, there is a built-in safeguard to remind you to save a copy of your models to disk. The addition of a prompt message when you attempt to exit from 1-2-3 will remind you if you have not as yet saved changes to the current worksheet.

When you are working with data in the form of papers stored in your office files and you retrieve a file so that you can work with it again, the file no longer contains a copy. But storing data in computer disk files works differently. Once you store a copy of a model on disk, it remains there until you take some special action to remove it from the disk. Even when you retrieve a copy of the model to place it in memory again, the original copy is maintained on the disk. This feature offers a tremendous advantage over paper storage methods: If you accidentally destroy the copy in the computer's memory, you can always retrieve another copy of the model from the disk.

4

Organizing Disk Data

When you create file folders for your office, you probably have a system—even a rudimentary one—for labeling these files. One rule of your system is probably that no two folders have exactly the same label. If they did, you would have a lot of difficulty finding the papers you need once they were filed. Perhaps your system for labeling file folders is quite organized. It may include color coding or some other scheme that makes it easy to categorize your files.

Storing files on disk also uses a system. Part of this system involves rigid rules you must follow; there is also room for some flexibility, however, so that you can personalize the system to suit your needs. You need not be concerned with the specifics of how the data is stored on disk. Your only concern is the rules that you need to follow when working with these files, especially those rules that center around the names you use for your files and the location of these files when they are stored.

Filenames

Before you can store a file on your disk, you must determine what to name it. Since the naming process follows particular, although somewhat flexible, rules, first review the options before considering the mechanics for storing the file.

Each file on a disk must have a unique name. This *filename* will consist of from one to eight characters. You can create a name using the alphabetic characters, numeric digits, and some of the special symbols. Since it can be difficult to remember which symbols are permissible and which are not, it is best to limit your use of special symbols to the _ (underline symbol). This symbol is particularly useful as a separator in a filename. For example, the name Sales_89 might be used to store the sales data for 1989. Be aware that spaces are not allowed in 1-2-3 filenames; Sales 89 would not be a valid name. Although Release 2.3 will accept a numeric digit in the first position, you may want to avoid an initial numeric character for compatibility with other releases.

Although there is no flexibility in the rules already discussed, you can assign the eight allowable characters any way you like. It is best to develop some consistent rules for naming your data, as consistency can help you determine a file's contents when you see the filename later on. If you are storing sales data for a number of years, keeping one year's worth of data in each file, you could use the method already described and create names such as Sales_89 and Sales_90. You could also use names such as 89_Sales or Sls1989. It really does not matter what pattern you select for your names. What is important is that once you decide on a naming pattern, you apply it consistently for each file that you create. It is not a good strategy to name files 87_Sales, Sales_88, Sls_1989, and Sales90; this pattern is too inconsistent. You can enter filenames in either upper-case or lowercase letters, or even a combination of the two. Regardless of which type of entry you make, it will be translated into uppercase. All filenames are stored in uppercase on the disk.

You can also add *filename extensions*. These are one to three optional characters that you add to the end of a filename. They too can be entered in upper- or lowercase. They are separated from a filename by a period. For example, in Sales_89.WK1, the filename extension is .WK1. These extensions can be used to categorize files or to provide an extra three characters of description. Some programs automatically add extensions for you. 1-2-3 does this. Table 4-1 shows some of the most common filename extensions that you will encounter and the types of files they are used for.

If you are working with Release 1.0 or 1A, the extension .WKS is added to the filename every time you save a file. With Releases 2 and higher, the extension that is added is .WK1. You do not need to memorize this information; 1-2-3 handles it all for you. You only need to realize what these extensions are when you want to work directly with the data stored on your disk, using commands from your operating system. These filename extensions appear when you use operating system commands. They could cause confusion if you were not at least aware that 1-2-3 was creating them and using them to distinguish different types of files.

Storing Your Data

Files can be stored on either hard or floppy disks. The lower-cost hard disks, thanks to today's technology, are a popular storage medium for

Table 4-1. *Common Filename Extensions*

Filename Extension	Use
.WK1	Worksheet files in Release 2
.WK3	Worksheet in Release 3 format. Must be saved as .WK1 file to use in Release 2.3
.WKS	Worksheet files in Release 1A
.PIC	1-2-3 graph files
.PRN	Print files
.DRV	1-2-3 driver files
.COM or .EXE	Executable program files
.BAT	DOS batch files
.BAK	Backup files for Releases 2.2 and 2.3
.ENC	Encoded printer files
.ALL	Allways worksheet format file
.FMT	WYSIWYG worksheet format file

business computer systems. A floppy disk holds from 360,000 to over 1,440,000 characters, depending on whether you are using the standard double-sided, double-density disks or the new high-density disks. Today's typical hard disk installed in a computer system has a capacity of over 20,000,000 characters of information.

When new files are added to disks, their names are added to a directory on the disk that keeps track of every file on the disk. Although you could use a single directory to maintain a hard disk, such a directory could become so lengthy that it would be difficult to work with. This would be like having a single index to catalog a whole library of reference volumes; it would take a long time to read. More likely, each book in the collection has its own index. Some books may even have chapter outlines that can be referenced for contents.

To lessen the burden of the main disk index, you can set up *subdirectories* for your disk. Subdirectories function as a second-level index to group files that are related. You can create these groupings on any basis you like, including for each individual who uses the system, for each application category on the system, or by application program. In all cases, common files such as DOS utilities normally are maintained in the *root directory* (the main directory on the disk). When subdirectories are added, their names are placed in the root directory; however, the names of the files they contain are kept in the subdirectory, not in the root directory. Subdirectories are organized in a hierarchical structure, as shown in Figure 4-1. Here, the entries in the main directory include two references to subdirectories. These subdirectories must be created through commands in your operating system. Although 1-2-3 cannot create the directories, it will use whichever directory is current on the disk, and it gives you commands that let you activate another directory.

1-2-3 always assumes that you want to work with files on the current or default directory. This means that if you are content to use the current directory, you do not need to specify it when saving your data. However, if you want to use a different disk drive or a directory other than the current default, you must either change the default or enter the file location along with the filename (depending on which release of 1-2-3 you are using). You will look at both of these possibilities in the next section.

Figure 4-1. *Directory and subdirectories*

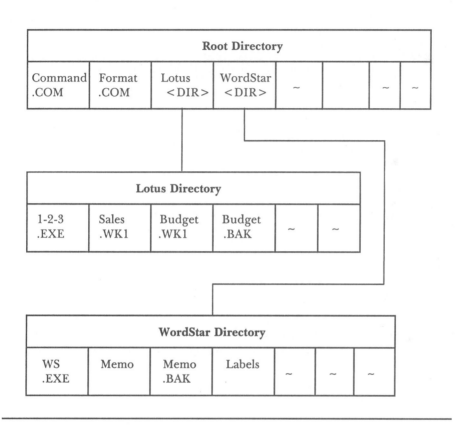

1-2-3 File Commands

You can use commands on 1-2-3's menu to handle your file-management tasks. There are menu selections for saving your data into disk files and retrieving copies of these files to place in memory. 1-2-3 has grouped each of the file-management commands under the File selection in the main menu. You bring this menu to your screen by selecting File. The following will appear:

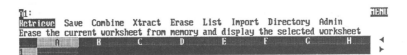

File Save

1-2-3 does not save your files automatically. It is your responsibility to save the data you enter in memory. It is best to do this periodically; do not wait until you are ending your 1-2-3 session before you save data for the first time. A good guideline is to save every 20 to 30 minutes. If you save with that frequency, you can never lose more than 20 to 30 minutes of your work, even if the power goes off unexpectedly.

Saving the First Time

You use a slightly different procedure to save your data the first time. Since you have never saved the data before, you need to enter a filename to identify your data on the disk. If you are saving onto floppy disks, you also need to ensure that a formatted disk is placed in the current drive. At this point, make a few entries on the current screen and then save the data.

1. Erase memory by selecting Worksheet Erase Yes.

2. Move the cell pointer to B2 and type **Qtr1**. Press the RIGHT ARROW key or click on C2. Type **Qtr2** through **Qtr4** in C2 through E2.

3. Select File Save to produce the following display:

The exact appearance of your screen will depend on which drive you are using as the default and the names of the files you have already stored on this drive. The top line allows you to use the mouse in place of keystrokes, as described later in the chapter, when you retrieve Files.

4. Type **QTRSALES** and press ENTER to supply a filename.

> After you have completed the last entry, the disk drive light will activate momentarily while your data is being written to disk. When the file has been placed on the disk, the indicator light will change from its WAIT status back to READY. At this point, you can continue to work on this model or start a new one, since you know that this one has been saved to the disk. For now, you will want to make some additions to this model to see how the process differs for subsequent saves.

Subsequent Saves

Each time you save a model that is already on the disk, you have the option of replacing the copy on the disk with the information that is currently stored in memory, of entering a new name, or in Releases 2.2 and above of creating a backup file. If you have saved the model previously, 1-2-3's default will be to save the model under this name. Make the following changes and save the model again with these steps:

1. Move the cell pointer to A3 and type **Sales**. Press DOWN ARROW or click on A4. Type **Expenses** in A4 and **Profit** in A5.

2. Select File Save. 1-2-3 will present this display:

Notice that 1-2-3 is suggesting that the file be saved under the same name you used previously. If you are working with Release 1A, your display will be slightly different, as Release 1A does not display the drive and directory.

3. Press ENTER. 1-2-3 will present this menu:

1-2-3 is asking if you wish to cancel the save request, replace the copy of the model stored on disk with the current contents of memory, or back up the original file using the same filename but a new filename extension for the original file and the same filename with a .WK1 extension for the current contents of memory.

4. Select Replace. 1-2-3 will save the updated model under the name you used previously.

If you want to save a model under a new name, 1-2-3 makes this possible. When 1-2-3 suggests that you use the original name, all you need to do is type a new name. Then, when you press ENTER, the file will be saved under the new name. This feature is especially useful when you need to create two similar copies of a model. You can create identical entries on both files, then save the model under two different names before entering the changes on the duplicate file.

If you are working with Release 2 or higher, you can save a file to a directory other than the current one. To do this, specify the directory you want when you use File Save. If 1-2-3 suggests that you use C:\LOTUS\QTRSALES but you wish to use A:SALES, when 1-2-3 presents its suggestion, do the following:

1. Press ESC.

2. Press ESC two more times to remove the entire suggestion. The first ESC removes the filename, the second the extension, and the third the drive and directory.

3. Type the complete *pathname,* which includes the drive, directory, and filename (A:SALES for this example).

Backing Up the Worksheet

Sometimes when you revise a document, you keep the previous version of the document in the file cabinet along with the current version. For example, if you revise a budget projection, you may keep the previous projection until after the budget meeting for comparison purposes. You can refer to the previous copy in the event that you want to revert to any of the old projections or as a backup in case you lose the later copy. Releases 2.2 and above offer the same feature for your worksheet files. The third choice in the File Save command that does not appear in other releases is Backup. When you select this option, 1-2-3 renames the worksheet file stored on disk with a .WK1 extension to a file with the same name but with a .BAK extension. Then 1-2-3 saves the current worksheet using the .WK1 extension. As an example, make the following changes to the model and save the model again with these steps.

1. Move the cell pointer to A1 and type **ABC Company.** Press ENTER.

2. Select File Save. 1-2-3 suggests that the file be saved under the same name you used previously.

3. Press ENTER. 1-2-3 displays the options Save, Backup, and Replace.

4. Select Backup. 1-2-3 saves the updated model under the name you used previously. The previous version of the file is saved with a .BAK extension.

4

To understand what the File Save Backup feature offers, imagine looking inside the QTRSALES.WK1 and the QTRSALES.BAK files. Their contents are shown in Figure 4-2. On the top, the QTRSALES.BAK file does not have ABC Company in the upper left corner of the worksheet, since this file contains the worksheet as it existed after the previous save operation. On the bottom, the QTRSALES.WK1 file has ABC Company in the upper left corner, since this file was created by the most recent save operation. If you ever need to use the backup version, you can use it just as you would use a normal worksheet file. Each time you back up the file, 1-2-3 replaces the .BAK file with the .WK1 file on disk; then it copies the worksheet in 1-2-3's memory to disk using the .WK1 extension. The use of the Backup option always allows you to save the current file on disk and its most recent previous version as a backup. This allows you to subsequently access either version of the model. You can also use Undo to toggle between the two files if you try it immediately after retrieving the .BAK version of the file.

File Retrieve

A *file-retrieve operation* reads a worksheet file from disk and places it in the memory of your computer. When it places the model in memory, it erases the memory's previous contents. This means that you must always save a copy of your worksheet in memory in order to retain a copy before

Figure 4-2. *Worksheet file and backup file*

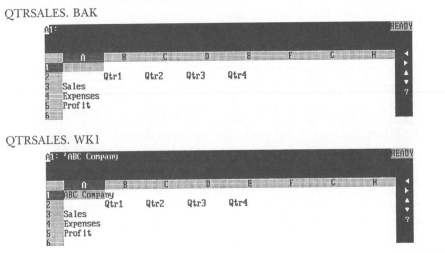

you bring another worksheet into memory. Of course, if Undo is enabled, you can use it to eliminate a big mistake like retrieving a file before saving the current file as long as you remember to use it immediately after retrieving the file.

Retrieving from the Default Drive

When you want to bring a worksheet file into memory, most of the time you will want to use the default drive since this is the same drive you have been using for data storage. If you don't take any special action, 1-2-3 assumes that this is where it should look for worksheet files and automatically displays a list of all the worksheet files on this drive. Release 2 or higher even displays the file list in alphabetic sequence to make it easy for you to find the file you want. You can press F3 (NAME) to see a full-screen listing of all the filenames. You can select a file by pointing to it with the highlighted bar 1-2-3 provides you. You can also type the name of the file from your keyboard either before or after 1-2-3 displays its list. However, one thing you cannot do is use a first-letter entry. This feature will work with all of 1-2-3's other menus, but not with a File Retrieve operation.

Follow these steps to retrieve the QTRSALES file from the disk in the current directory:

1. Select File Retrieve.
   A list of filenames similar to this display will appear.

2. Use the arrow keys to move the highlighted bar through the list until it is on QTRSALES or with a mouse, point to the file you want and click on it. Then press ENTER.

   If you need additional information about the files to make a selection and are using Release 2 or higher, you can press F3 (NAME) before you make a selection. 1-2-3 expands the list to provide information on the size of each file and the date and time it was last updated, as shown in Figure 4-3. If you are using a mouse, List, two periods (..), a question mark, and four arrows will be displayed in the control panel. Clicking on List is equivalent to pressing F3 (NAME). Clicking on the two periods is equivalent to pressing BACKSPACE. Clicking the question mark is equivalent to pressing F1 (HELP). The four arrows move the highlight in the direction you choose. The drive letters (A: through E: in these examples) let you switch between the disk drives on your system by clicking the drive specification.

Figure 4-3. *Expanding the list for files to retrieve*

```
List  ◄  ►  ▲  ▼  ?  ..  A:  B:  C:  D:  E:                    FILES
Name of file to retrieve: C:\123R23\*.wk?
            1ST_QTR.WK1    02/14/91        14:09           1798
1ST_QTR.WK1    2ND_QTR.WK1    H.WK1       CASE.WK1     FORMAT.WK1
JOU.WK1        M23X12XX.WK1   MENUS.WK1   MT4_5.WK1    MA.WK1
NUMBERS.WK1    PAYMENT.WK1    QTR1VALU.WK1 QTRSALES.WK1 QTRTOTAL.WK1
QTRTOTSL.WK1   VEHICLES.WK1   M23CHAP.2\
```

In Release 2.2, if you need to retrieve a backup file, you must type the filename and include the .BAK extension. For example, if you want to retrieve the backup of QTRSALES.WK1, you would enter QTRSALES.BAK for the filename to retrieve. Typing the filename is required since 1-2-3 displays only the list of files with WK as the first two letters in the filename extension.

Retrieving from Another Location

Release 2 or higher lets you retrieve a file that is not on the current disk or in the current directory, but the retrieve procedure changes slightly. Release 1A does not allow you to change directories without first using the File Directory command (discussed later in this chapter). After using this command to change the directory, you can use the standard command sequence for a file retrieve to achieve your goal.

To change the directory for a retrieve operation, you must override the default directory setting for this one activity. The difference in the process is subtle: You begin and end the same way as usual, but you change the directory in the middle.

Assuming that you have data disks that you can place in two of your drives and that the default drive is drive A, use these steps to try the procedure.

1. Select File Retrieve.

2. Press ESC twice to delete the reference to the default drive and directory. The following display appears:

3. Type the full name of your file, including its path and directory, and press ENTER.

You can also change from the current directory to its parent directory by pressing BACKSPACE or clicking on the two periods. You can change from the current directory to a subdirectory by selecting the subdirectory name from the list (subdirectory names appear after filenames).

Using the Viewer Add-In to Retrieve Files

Release 2.3 includes a viewer add-in that you can use to verify that you are retrieving the file you want. Follow these steps to use this feature:

1. Select Add-In Attach.

    Unlike other menus, you can display the Add-In menu by selecting Add-In from the 1-2-3 menu or by pressing ALT-F10. After you select Attach, 1-2-3 displays the files with .ADN extensions that represent the add-ins available in the current directory.

2. Select VIEWER.ADN.

    1-2-3 next prompts for how you want to activate this add-in. You may select No-Key, 7, 8, 9, or 10. No-Key means that the add-in is invoked by using the Add-In Invoke command, or another special key combination, or that it does not need to be invoked to be used. 7, 8, 9, and 10 represent the key combinations ALT-F7, ALT-F8, ALT-F9, and ALT-F10 that you can use to invoke the add-in. We will use 7 for this example.

3. Select 7 to invoke this add-in by pressing ALT-F7.

4. Select Invoke and select VIEWER from the list.

    The initial Viewer add-in menu contains Retrieve, Browse, and Link. (Link is used to build external file references.)

5. Select Retrieve.

    If the current worksheet had any unsaved changes, you would need to select Yes to confirm that you wanted to retrieve the new worksheet in place of the one in memory. The Viewer add-in displays the screen shown in Figure 4-4. The right side of the display shows the contents of the file highlighted on the left side. You can switch between the left and right side of the worksheet by pressing the LEFT and RIGHT ARROW keys.

6. Highlight the file you want to retrieve on the left side using the UP ARROW or DOWN ARROW.

7. Press ENTER or click on the filename to retrieve it.

When you are in the worksheet on the right side of the Viewer add-in, you can use all of the keys you would use in 1-2-3 to move to different cells.

Figure 4-4. *The Viewer add-in screen*

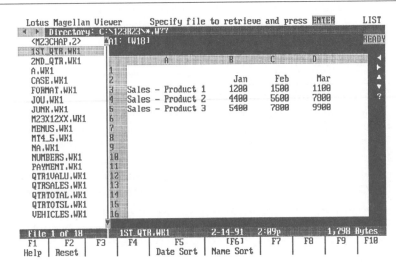

The control panel displays the cell's contents and formatting information. Cells containing formulas display (formula) instead of the formula itself, as well as formula results. You cannot change a worksheet in the Viewer. If a file is password protected, you cannot see its contents.

You can also change the highlighted file by using the UP and DOWN ARROW keys to move from one file to another. PGUP or PGDN will move a screen at a time, and HOME or END will move to the first or last file in the list. Initially, the current directory is displayed. You can change the drive and directory of the listed files by pressing the LEFT ARROW key. When the highlight is on a specific file or directory, F3 (NAME) changes the list to display the files in the parent drive. If you are in the root directory, pressing the LEFT ARROW key again lets you change the drive. When the highlight is on a drive or directory you want to display, press the RIGHT ARROW. To use the mouse, either point to what you want and click on it, or use the arrows and press ENTER (shown in a different color or intensity). You can also click on F2 at the bottom of the screen to return the displayed directory to the 1-2-3 default directory, F5 to list files in order by date, or F6 to list files in alphabetical order.

The results of retrieving a file with the Viewer are the same as if you used the File Retrieve command. The advantage of the Viewer is that you can visually check that you are retrieving the correct file.

Another option you may want to try on your own is selecting Browse from the initial Viewer menu. This option displays all files in a directory, not just the worksheet files. When you want to return to the current worksheet, press ENTER.

Determining What Files Are on Your Disk

Just as you might look at the names of the different file folders in an office file cabinet, sometimes you may wish to look through the names of the files on your disk. The File List command will handle this type of request for you. It lets you determine what types of files you want to view, by offering the menu selections of Worksheet, Print, Graph, Other, and Linked. Release 1A displays only the first three selections. Linked files, available in Releases 2.2 and above, are covered in Chapter 10.

1-2-3 checks the files whose filename extensions correspond to the type of file you choose. Enter the following sequence of commands to view all the worksheet files on your disk.

1. Select File List.

2. Select Worksheet.

3. If you have Release 2 or higher, move the highlighted bar around in the list to point to various filenames.

    As each filename is highlighted, an expanded description of the file entry appears at the top of the screen, as shown in Figure 4-5. This extra information allows you to determine the date and time for the last file update. It also lets you see the relative size of the file.

4. Press ENTER to return to READY mode.

To list files on another disk or in another directory, use the same approach described in the preceding discussion for retrieving from another disk. For Release 1A, as always, the only way to access a different directory is to activate it by using File Directory.

Figure 4-5.   *Exploring the list of files on your disk*

```
List  ◄  ►  ▲  ▼  ?  ..  A:  B:  C:  D:  E:                          FILES
Enter extension of files to list: C:\123R23\*.wk?
               1ST_QTR.WK1    02/14/91        14:09           1798
1ST_QTR.WK1    2ND_QTR.WK1    A.WK1          CASE.WK1         FORMAT.WK1
JOU.WK1        M23X12XX.WK1   MENUS.WK1      MT4_5.WK1        NA.WK1
NUMBERS.WK1    PAYMENT.WK1    QTR1VALU.WK1   QTRSALES.WK1     QTRTOTAL.WK1
QTRTOTSL.WK1   VEHICLES.WK1   M23CHAP.2\
```

Removing Files

The files that you save on your disk are retained indefinitely. In fact, 1-2-3 never eliminates any of them; it will remove a file only if you make a specific request for it to do so. The command used for eliminating files is File Erase. To remove a file from your disk, follow these steps. (Execute them only if you have a file you wish to eliminate—these steps work!)

1. Select File Erase.

    This produces the following display for you to select the type of file you want to erase:

```
G5: 'Profit                                                        MENU
Worksheet  Print  Graph  Other
Erase a worksheet file
     A         B         C         D         E         F         G         H     ◄
```

The display is slightly different for Release 1A since it does not support the Other option.

2. Select Worksheet to produce a list of your worksheet files like this:

```
List    ..  ◄  ►  ▲  ▼                                              FILES
Enter name of file to erase: C:\123NEW\*.wk?
1ST_QTR.WK1    2ND_QTR.WK1    CASE.WK1       FORMAT.WK1       INSERTS.WK1
     A         B         C         D         E         F         G         H
```

If you wish to expand this list to include file sizes and date and time stamps, press F3 (NAME).

3. Use the arrow keys to position the highlighted bar on the file that you want to permanently remove from the disk, and press ENTER. To select the file with a mouse, point to the file you want to delete and click it.

4. Select Yes to confirm that you want to delete the file.

Once you have deleted a file, there is no practical way to restore it. There are utility programs that can restore a file that has been deleted in this fashion, but they are not part of 1-2-3. Therefore, you must be extremely cautious when removing files from the disk.

Changing Directories

You have already seen how, if you have Release 2 or higher, you can access data on another disk or in another directory on a one-time basis with the File Retrieve and File Save commands. Each time you wish to use a directory other than the current one, you must enter the complete pathname for the file. The pathname includes the disk drive and an optional subdirectory along with the filename. This approach is cumbersome if you have to use information in these other locations repeatedly. A better solution is to make the other disk or directory the active one. You also use the File Directory command to change the active directory on your hard disk. First select File Directory. The current directory is displayed as follows:

In this example, the current directory is C:\123NEW\. Next, type the new directory. If the new directory were C:\ACCT\, you would type **C:\ACCT**. The directory must already exist since 1-2-3 will not create a directory that does not already exist.

1-2-3's dependence on a *default directory* — the drive and subdirectory you are using — saves you a considerable amount of time. If you are working with a hard disk system, your data will probably be stored in a subdirectory. To work in it for a period of time, you need to be able to change to another one. A default directory means that 1-2-3 assumes that the directory you are referencing is the current default, unless you specify otherwise. If you keep this default set to the drive containing your data, you will not need to enter the directory in order to make most of your file requests. The package does provide capabilities that let you alter the directory setting. This feature means that when you want to work with worksheet files that are on the floppy disk in drive A, it will be easy to have the directory set at drive C and alter it to a floppy drive.

Using Another Drive

You can change the drive that 1-2-3 File commands use. Before changing the drive, make sure both drives have readable disks in them since 1-2-3 will read both the current default drive and the new one. To change to drive B, for example, follow these steps:

1. Select File Directory.

2. Enter **B:** and then press ENTER.

    When you switch drives in Release 1A, you will get an erroneous Error Message, which reads "Directory does not exist." Ignore this message. Press ENTER a second time to change the directory.

The Operating System

The *operating system* that your computer uses is in some ways similar to a foreman in a production environment. A foreman manages the operation of the production line and coordinates the resources required to complete a job. The operating system in your computer is a program that manages the tasks that your computer performs and coordinates the resources required to complete a task. The operating system must always be in memory along with 1-2-3 or any other application program to ensure that these programs can access the resources of the computer system. The operating system you will be using on your computer is probably MS-DOS or PC-DOS or, in the latest computers, OS/2.

In Releases 2 and higher, 1-2-3's System command allows you to temporarily exit from 1-2-3 to perform file-management tasks directly with the operating system. Since 1-2-3 provides a number of file-management commands in its menu structure, it is easier to use 1-2-3's menu selection when these commands are available. The DOS commands are useful for performing tasks that 1-2-3's menu does not support. Before examining how the system feature works, let's cover a few basics about your computer's operating system.

Some of the basic tasks that the operating system performs are reading and writing data to and from the disk. The operating system also contains a variety of utility programs that copy files or disks, prepare disks for data storage, and check the directory of a disk. You can use these utility features before you enter a program like 1-2-3 to handle many tasks relating to file and disk information. After you place an application program like 1-2-3 into the memory of your machine, you usually can no longer access the operating system features. With Releases 2 and higher of 1-2-3, Lotus has provided a temporary exit from 1-2-3 that retains all your current worksheet data in memory while you work with DOS tasks.

The System Command

Normally, once you are in 1-2-3 you want to forget about the operating system and enjoy the ease with which you can use 1-2-3's menu to handle tasks. But there are exceptions. One of the most important exceptions is when you want to save data on a disk and don't have a formatted disk available to save on. Without the System command, if you do not have a formatted disk available, you will lose all the data that is in memory. With the System command, you can exit temporarily and format another disk. You can then use this newly formatted disk to save your data. You can also make a copy of a file on your disk to give to another business associate: You can remain in 1-2-3, temporarily switch to DOS to complete your task, and switch back again. The steps for each of these special uses are covered in the following sections.

Formatting Disks

The DOS command for preparing, or *formatting*, a disk is FORMAT. In the following exercise, you will use this command to format a blank disk that you will place in drive A. Follow these steps to complete the exercise and return to 1-2-3.

1. Select System.

2. If you are working with a floppy disk-based system, place the DOS disk in drive A.

3. Type **FORMAT A:** and press ENTER.

4. Place a blank disk in drive A in response to the following prompt on your screen:

    Insert a new diskette for drive A:
    and press ENTER when ready...

    With some releases of DOS, the message will be a little different.

5. Press ENTER to begin formatting.

6. Type **N** and press ENTER to indicate that you do not want to format additional disks.

7. Type **EXIT** and press ENTER to return to 1-2-3.

    A transcript of the entries for this process through step 6 is shown in Figure 4-6. Your display will look similar. However, if any bad sectors were encountered in your disk, FORMAT will skip them and notify you that it has done so with a message about the number of bad sectors excluded.

When DOS formats a disk it uses the program FORMAT.COM, which is supplied on your operating system disk. If you are working with a floppy disk system and follow the instructions in this exercise, everything will work fine. If you are working with a hard disk, the directory that contains FORMAT.COM must be the active directory or a directory DOS automatically checks when you type the format instructions. For a hard disk system where FORMAT.COM is not in the current directory, replace step 2 in the instructions with "Type **CD **". This changes the directory to the root directory on your hard disk where, presumably, you will have a copy of FORMAT.COM stored.

Figure 4-6. *Using the System feature to prepare a disk*

```
(Type EXIT and press ENTER to return to 1-2-3)


The IBM Personal Computer DOS
Version 3.30 (C)Copyright International Business Machines Corp 1981, 1987
                (C)Copyright Microsoft Corp 1981, 1986

C>format a:
Insert new diskette for drive A:
and strike ENTER when ready

Format complete

    1457664 bytes total disk space
    1457664 bytes available on disk

Format another (Y/N)?n
C>
```

4

Copying Files

You can use the DOS COPY command to copy a file on your disk to another disk without leaving 1-2-3. To copy the file SALES from the disk in drive A to a formatted disk in drive B and return to your task in 1-2-3, follow these steps:

1. Select System.

2. Place the disk containing SALES in drive A and the formatted disk in drive B.

3. Type **COPY A:SALES.WK1 B:** and press ENTER.
   The filename extension .WK1 was used in this example. If you are using Release 1A, the proper extension is .WKS.

4. Type **EXIT** and press ENTER.

Creating New Directories

You can create a new subdirectory for your hard disk without leaving 1-2-3. This option lets you create a logical section on the disk, which you can begin to use for specialized storage of worksheet data or other information. In the following example, the subdirectory will be added directly to the root directory of the disk, which is the main directory. In most cases, this is where directories should be added. Using too many levels causes confusion and makes it difficult to locate individual files. Follow these steps if you have a hard disk and wish to establish a subdirectory called BUDGET.

1. Save your current worksheet and clear memory with Worksheet Erase Yes, if data from a previous task remains on your screen.

2. Select System.

3. Type **cd ** to make the root directory active.

4. Type **md \ budget** to create a subdirectory named budget.

5. Type **cd \ budget** to make your new directory active.

6. Perform any DOS tasks you wish in this directory.

7. Type **Exit** and press ENTER to return to 1-2-3.
   Note that the current 1-2-3 directory would now be C:\123\, since 1-2-3 returned to the directory that was active before the temporary DOS exit was taken.

You may have noticed in the previous examples that when you finished entering DOS commands, you returned to 1-2-3 by typing **Exit** and pressing ENTER. When you exit to DOS and return, everything is the same as it was before you entered the System request. The same worksheet will be on the screen and 1-2-3 will be ready to continue where you left off.

Review

- Files provide permanent storage for your worksheets. You can save and retrieve worksheets to a floppy or hard disk.

- You can save a worksheet with the File Save command. When you save a file the first time, you must provide a filename. When you save it again, 1-2-3 displays the filename to select. If you press ENTER to select the displayed filename, you must select between

Cancel, Replace, and Backup (Releases 2.2 and above). You can also enter a new filename to save the worksheet in memory under the new filename.

- You can retrieve a worksheet with the File Retrieve command. When you execute the File Retrieve command in Release 2 or higher, 1-2-3 lists the files in alphabetical order that you can select.

- You can list files in a directory using the File List command. With Release 1, you can list worksheet, graph, or print files. With Releases 2 and higher, you can list worksheet, graph, print, linked, or all files.

- You can select where 1-2-3 looks for the files that you work with by using the File Directory command. When you use this command, you can provide a new directory before pressing ENTER. With Release 1A, you must change the directory before retrieving or saving a file to the new directory.

- With Releases 2 and higher, you can access the DOS operating system with the System command while keeping 1-2-3 and the worksheet in the computer's memory. You can use this feature to format disks, copy files, and create subdirectories.

Commands and Keys

Entry	Action
FD	File Directory allows you to change the default directory.
FE	File Erase eliminates a copy of a file on disk.
FL	File List displays a full screen list of all the files in the current directory or disk.
FR	File Retrieve retrieves a file from disk and places it in memory.
FSB	File Save Backup renames the .WK1 extension with a .BAK extension and saves the current version as .WK1.

Entry	Action
FSC	File Save Cancel cancels a save request without saving when 1-2-3 prompts that the file already exists.
FSR	File Save Replace replaces the current copy on disk with the current contents of memory.
S	System temporarily leaves 1-2-3 and activates the operating system. Type **EXIT** and press ENTER to return to 1-2-3.
F3 (NAME)	Switches a file list between using only the control panel and using the full screen to list files.

5

Making 1-2-3 Do Most
of Your Work

Until now, you have had to enter every worksheet entry that you needed for your models. While that is similar to using a columnar pad for your entries, it does not take advantage of the productivity features offered by a package like 1-2-3. This chapter introduces some of these features. Making only a few entries, you often can complete your model by putting 1-2-3 to work.

In this chapter, you will be introduced to commands that can move worksheet data to a new location. This means that if the requirements of your application change, it will be easy to restructure the worksheet. You will also learn how to restructure data stored in a column to a row orientation and vice versa. Again, this is quite an improvement over the eraser method that manual spreadsheets provide. Finally, this chapter introduces you to a command in Releases 2.2 and 2.3 that allows you to search for characters in labels or formulas. This new command also offers a Replace feature that you can use to modify labels and formulas quickly.

1-2-3's Copy command, also covered in this chapter, has more potential than any other command to increase your productivity with 1-2-3. You will learn the ins and outs of copying both label and formula data. You will also learn about other 1-2-3 features, such as repeating label entries and generating a series of numeric entries. Once you have mastered the Copy feature, you will want to master some of the tools that can help you monitor your expanded worksheet. For example, you will learn how to control the recalculation of formulas stored on the worksheet. In addition, you will be introduced to commands for splitting your screen display into two windows and freezing certain information on the screen.

Copying Data

Copying entries on a manual worksheet is a laborious task. To make an additional set of entries that duplicate existing ones, you must pick up your pencil and physically copy each entry that you wish to make. Naturally, duplicate entries take just as long to make as the original entries.

When you make duplicates with 1-2-3, however, this is not the case. For any entry that you wish to duplicate, you can have 1-2-3 complete most of the work for you. Just tell 1-2-3 what you want to copy and where you want it copied to. 1-2-3 does all the remaining work. It can take a column of label entries and copy it to ten new columns. It can even take a row of formulas that calculates all your sales projections for the month of January and copy it down the page to the next 11 rows, thus giving you all the calculations for February through December. Amazingly, 1-2-3 even adjusts the formulas as it copies them.

This section uses a building-block approach in covering all the Copy command features. First, it explains how to use Copy to duplicate a label entry. Then it looks a little more closely at the Copy command's inner workings, examining its ability to adjust formulas.

Copying Labels

Many situations call for the time-saving feature of copying labels. Perhaps you want to create a worksheet that uses account titles or months of the year in two different locations. Rather than typing them again, you can use the Copy command. Not only does it save you time, but it also guarantees that both sets of entries are identical. Copy is also useful when you have a number of similar entries to make. Often, you can copy your original entries and make minor editing changes in less time than it would take to type each of the complete entries.

Invoking Copy

Copy is somewhat different from the other menu commands you have used. It does not have a submenu like Range Format or Worksheet Insert. Instead of using a multilayered menu approach, the Copy command uses prompts. You must respond to these prompts in order to define the source location you wish to copy information from and the target location you wish to copy information to.

When you invoke Copy by selecting Copy, this is the first prompt message you see:

1-2-3 is asking what cells you wish to copy from. Different releases of 1-2-3 will display slightly different prompts in different locations, but the type of information they expect is the same. Think of this "from" range as the source of information to be copied. It suggests a range that encompasses only one cell. This suggested location is always the location of the cell pointer at the time you invoke Copy. If the location that 1-2-3 suggests is acceptable, you can press ENTER. If you like the beginning of the range but wish to enlarge it to include a row or column of cell entries, you can expand it with your pointer movement keys or the mouse. If you don't like the beginning of the range, you must unanchor the starting position by pressing ESC. You will then be free to move the beginning of the range. When you want to anchor it again, use the same strategy that worked with the Format commands and type a period. In Release 2.3, if you select a range before selecting the Copy command, 1-2-3 will use the selected range as the source range and only display the command's second prompt. Once you have finalized the source selection, 1-2-3's interest shifts to the target location (the location the data is copied to).

The prompt message displayed by 1-2-3 Release 2.3 for the target range looks like this:

1-2-3 again initially suggests the location of the cell pointer. The suggested location is not a range but a single cell, since you will almost always need to move the cell pointer to define the target range. And this is *all* you need to do, since it is displayed as a cell address rather than a range. You do not have to press ESC, as there is no range to unanchor. Once you select a location to start the copy, either you must press ENTER to finalize the location or modify it to represent a range. You can create a range with the standard method of typing a period and using the arrow keys to mark the end of the range. You can even press F3 (NAME) to select a named range to copy to.

Reviewing an example will help clarify how easy it is to copy a label entry. Follow these steps:

1. Move the cell pointer to A1, type **Sales — Product A**, and then press ENTER.

2. Select Copy to generate the prompt for the range to copy from.
   Notice that the suggestion for the source range is A1, the location of the cell pointer when you invoked the Copy command.

3. Press ENTER or click on the control panel.
   The prompt message generated next also suggests the original location of the cell pointer as the target range. However, you must change it.

4. Move the cell pointer to A2 and press ENTER to generate these results:

The new label generated is identical to the original entry, but it required far fewer keystrokes to create. Later, you will learn how to extend this productivity even further by copying to many locations with one command. For now, here are a few additional hints for the simplest copying task: copying an entry to one new location.

Modifying Copied Labels

The entry in A2 is currently identical to the original. Sometimes this situation is exactly what you need; other times, however, a slight modification might be required. If you wanted the label "Sales − Product B" in A2, the Copy approach is still best. However, fixing the label would require these extra steps:

1. Move the cell pointer to A2.

2. Press F2 (EDIT).

3. Press the BACKSPACE key, type **B**, and press ENTER to finalize. The results will look like this:

Keep this possibility in mind when you look for opportunities to copy. A Copy followed by a quick edit can still be much quicker than making new entries. Since you can use this feature with numbers as well, one potential application of Copy is to generate a list of numbers with only one digit different.

Copying Formulas

In one sense, copying formulas is no different from copying label or number entries. It is accomplished with the same Copy command. You respond to the prompts just as you do when you are copying label and number entries. With formulas, however, you need to be able to control how 1-2-3 copies the cell addresses a formula uses. If you have one constant interest rate and want all formulas to refer to it, you must be able to direct 1-2-3 to carry out that instruction. On the other hand, you need a different approach if you enter a formula for January profit that subtracts the cost of goods sold in January from the sales for January and want to copy this formula to generate formulas that calculate profit for the other 11 months. You cannot calculate February's profit by subtracting the January cost-of-goods-sold figure from January sales. You need to subtract February's cost of goods sold from February sales. Fortunately, 1-2-3 can handle this type of situation as well. These different options are handled by the type of references contained in the original formula and are not an option selected after the Copy operation begins. Let's examine an example of Copy for different reference types to help clarify this.

Address Types

All the cell addresses you have entered in formulas thus far have contained a column name immediately followed by a row number—for example, A1, E4, IV2000. This is the cell address specification that is used most frequently with 1-2-3. This type of address is called a *relative address*. There are two additional types of addresses: *absolute* and *mixed addresses*. They are distinguished by the way they are recorded in your formulas and the way in which 1-2-3 performs a Copy operation for each of the three types. Master the differences in the three types of addresses; the type of address references you use is critical in determining how your formulas are copied to new worksheet locations.

Relative Addresses   Relative addresses are the only type of cell address covered up to this chapter. They are easy to enter in formulas, whether you use the typing or the pointing method of formula creation. When 1-2-3 records your entry, it appears to store the formula exactly as you entered it. In fact, if you move your cell pointer to any cell that holds one of the formulas you have entered, you will see the exact formula you entered in the control panel.

However, 1-2-3 remembers your instructions in a slightly different way from what it displays. If you store the formula +A1+A2 in cell A3, 1-2-3 will interpret your instructions in this way: "Add the two cells above the location that will store the result." Everything is remembered as relative direction and distances from the cell that will contain the result when your formula contains relative references.

These relative references will mean that when you copy this type of formula to another location, 1-2-3 will adjust the formula in the new locations to reflect the same relative distances and directions. For example, if you were to copy the formula stored in A3 to B3, the formula you would see in the control panel for B3 would be +B1+B2. This formula uses different cell addresses from the original, but it still records the same relative directions: "Take the value that is two cells above the cell that will contain the result and add this value to the value that is one cell above the cell that will contain the result." This adjustment is handled automatically as long as you use relative references when you build your formulas.

You will build a model that allows you to practice the formula copy process. This model records profits for the current year and projects them for the next five years. The final result of your entries will look like Figure 5-1. Follow these steps to create the model:

1. Select Worksheet Erase Yes to start with a clean worksheet. In Releases 2.2 and above, you must select Yes a second time to confirm that you will lose unsaved changes.

2. Move the cell pointer to C1, type **Sales Projections 1992 − 1996**, and then press ENTER.

3. Move the cell pointer to A4 and then make these entries:

    A4:   Sales
    A5:   Cogs
    A6:   Profit

Figure 5-1.   *Completed sales projection model*

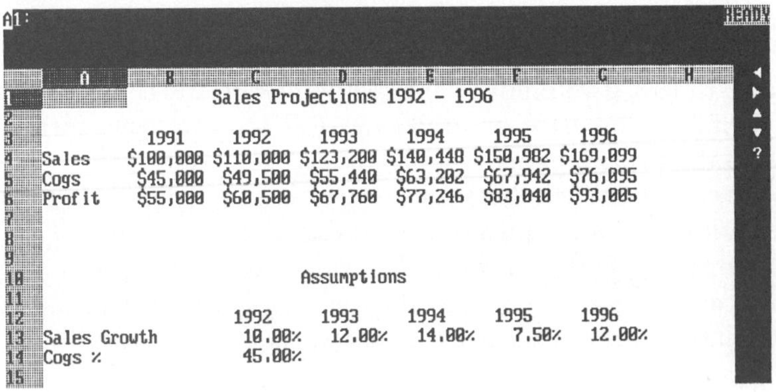

	B3:	^1991
	C3:	^1992
	D3:	^1993
	E3:	^1994
	F3:	^1995
	G3:	^1996

The caret (^) symbols in front of the year entries will cause the numeric digits to be treated as labels and will center them within the cell.

4. Move the cell pointer to B4 and make these entries for 1991:

	B4:	100000
	B5:	45000
	B6:	55000

These entries are not computed, as they are assumed to be the actual numbers at the end of 1991.

It is time to begin thinking about how you want to project sales for the remaining years. You can use a constant growth rate that would apply to all years, or you can assume that sales will grow at varying percentages each year. Several choices abound for computing the cost of the goods sold each year. One method is to use a percentage of sales. Even if you select this method without evaluating other options, you must again decide if one percentage will be used for all years or if the percentage will vary by year. The profit calculation does not require you to make a decision, since it is always equal to sales minus the cost of goods sold. This model assumes that sales will grow at varying rates but that cost of goods sold will be the same percentage of sales each year. You must enter these assumptions before projections can be made.

5. Move the cell pointer to D10, type **Assumptions,** and press ENTER.

6. Complete these entries:

A13:	Sales Growth	E17:	^1994
A14:	Cogs %	F17:	^1995
C12:	^1992	G17:	^1996
C13:	.1	E18:	.14
C14:	.45	F18:	.075
D12:	^1993	G18:	.12
D13:	.12		

7. Select Worksheet Global Format Currency. Type **0** and press ENTER. The percentages will display as zeros.

    This instruction will set the Global format to Currency, but you will also need to use a Range Format for the percentages that will be used in the model.

8. Move the cell pointer to C13; then select Range Format Percent and press ENTER to accept two decimal places. Use the RIGHT ARROW and DOWN ARROW keys to move the cell pointer to G13, and then press ENTER.

    The range of cells you just selected includes all the values you want formatted as percentages. The reformatted percentage entries are shown in Figure 5-2.

Figure 5-2.   *Model after initial entries*

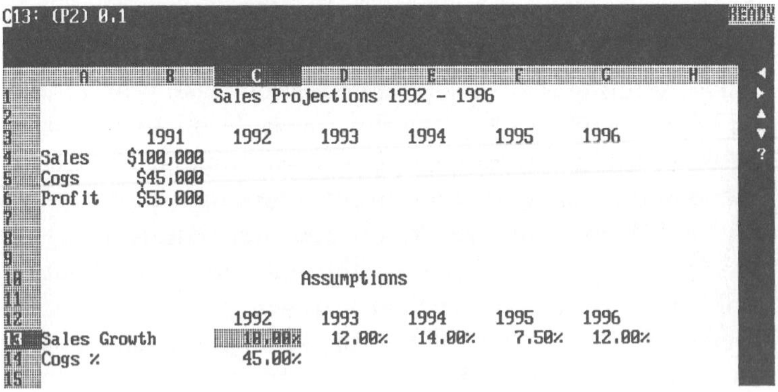

9. Move the cell pointer to C4, type **+B4*(1+C13)**, and press ENTER.
    This will compute the sales projection for 1992. Rather than
    typing this formula for each year, a better option is to copy it.

10. Select Copy. Press ENTER in response to 1-2-3's prompt message.

11. Move the cell pointer to D4 and press ENTER. The cell pointer will
    remain in C4, where the cell pointer was located before you used
    the Copy command.

12. Move the cell pointer to D4 to look at the new formula shown in
    Figure 5-3.
    Notice that 1-2-3 has adjusted each of the cell references to
    take the new location of the result into account. Each reference in
    the formula is the same distance and direction from the result in
    D4 as the original references were from C4, where the original
    result was computed. Before completing the copy process for
    sales, you will want to take a look at an absolute reference—a
    reference that will not be updated by a Copy operation.

Absolute Addresses   Absolute cell references are references that remain
the same regardless of where the formula is copied to. The formula
reference is effectively frozen in place and not allowed to change. Some

Figure 5-3. *The completed formula*

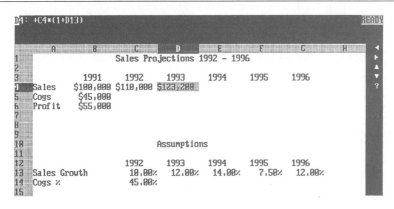

special action must be taken to create these references, since they have the $ character in front of both the row and column portion of the address. A3 or D8 are examples of absolute cell references.

You can create an absolute reference in one of two ways— by typing or pointing. Both parallel the creation method for relative references. If you choose to build the formula by typing, you will need to type the $ signs. If you choose to build the formula by pointing, you can press F4 (ABS); 1-2-3 will then add the $ signs in front of the row and column portion of the address.

Use this approach to build the cost-of-goods-sold data, to clarify how the feature works. Follow these steps to enhance the sales projection model you were working on earlier in the chapter:

1. Move the cell pointer to C5.

2. Type +.

3. Move the cell pointer to C4 with the UP ARROW key or move the mouse.

4. Type *.

5. Move the cell pointer to C14 with the DOWN ARROW key or the mouse.

6. Press F4 (ABS) once to add the $ signs.

   Your formula is now +C4*C19. Since you are in POINT mode, you could add the $ signs with F4 (ABS). If you were typing the address, you could also press F4 (ABS) to add the dollar signs to a cell or range address for absolute or mixed addresses in the POINT, VALUE, or EDIT mode. If you use F4 (ABS) on a range address, 1-2-3 will change both corners of the address. Mixed addresses are described below.

7. Press ENTER to complete the formula.

8. Select Copy and press ENTER to accept C5 as the source range.

9. Move the cell pointer to D5 and press ENTER.

   If you move the cell pointer to D5, you will see that the new formula also references C14 for its cost-of-goods-sold percent, as shown in Figure 5-4.

Mixed Addresses   Mixed addresses borrow something from each of the other two types of addresses. A mixed address is "mixed" in that one part is fixed and the other part is relative. This means that either the row or the

Figure 5-4.   *Copy operation completed for the Cogs formula*

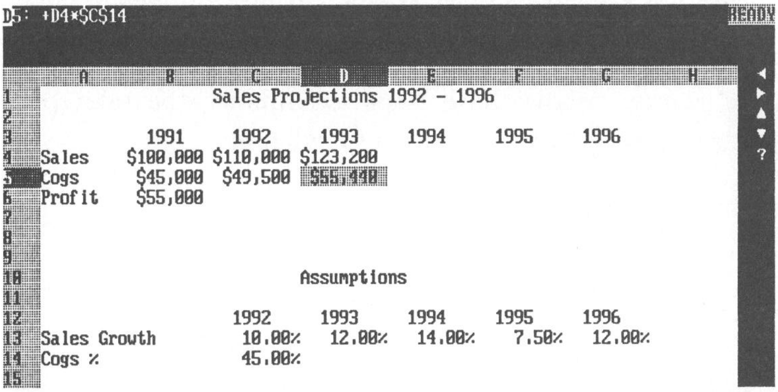

column portion of the address is fixed, but never both. During the copy process the fixed portion behaves like an absolute address, and the other portion functions like a relative address and is adjusted based on the location it is being copied to.

A fixed address can be written like A$5 or $D7. In the first example, the column portion of the address will be adjusted as the formula is copied to different columns, yet the row portion will remain fixed if the formula is copied to other rows. In the second example, the exact opposite takes place: The column portion of the address will always remain fixed, regardless of where the formula containing it is copied. The row portion of this address will be updated when the formula is copied to a different row.

The Mixed-Address feature is used only if you are building complex models. Still, it is important to know that it exists, in case you ever see a mixed address in a formula.

Scope of Copy

You have learned how to copy a formula to a new location on the worksheet, using the exercises you have completed thus far. This is just one of the ways you can use Copy. Other options are copying the contents of one cell to many additional locations and copying many locations to many additional locations.

One Entry to One Location You have already used this facet of the Copy operation. You used it to copy the sales and cost-of-goods-sold projections for 1992 to create the same projections for 1993. Now you will use it one more time to copy the profit calculation from 1992, but first you must enter the formula for 1992 profit and complete the assumption area. Follow these steps to add a formula for profit and then to copy the formula to one additional location.

1. Move the cell pointer to C6.

2. Type **+C4 − C5** and press ENTER.
   Since you wish both components of this calculation to be updated for the appropriate year when the formula is copied, both references are relative.

3. Select Copy.

4. Press ENTER to accept the source range generated by 1-2-3.

5. Move the cell pointer to D6 with the RIGHT ARROW key and press ENTER.

You have been making slow but steady progress in completing your model. Now it is time to step up the pace and copy to more than one location at a time.

One Entry to Many Locations   1-2-3's Copy command is not restricted to the single-copy approach we have been using. By expanding the size of the target range, you can copy the entry in one cell to a range that is as large as a row or column of the worksheet. You can put this expanded version of Copy to use in completing the sales projections for the remaining years of the model. Follow these steps.

1. Move the cell pointer to D4.

2. Select Copy and press ENTER to accept the source range.

3. Move the cell pointer to E4 in response to the prompt for the target range.

4. Type . (period).
   The period will anchor the beginning of the range and let you expand it.

5. Move the cell pointer to G4.

6. Press ENTER to produce the results shown in Figure 5-5.
   This one command will copy the sales projection formula into E4, F4, and G4. With a mouse, you would perform steps 3 through 5 by clicking on E4 and dragging the mouse to G4. After copying the formulas, E4 contains the formula +D4*(1+E13), F4 contains the formula +E4*(1+F13), and G4 contains the formula +F4*(1+G13).

Many Entries to Many Locations   You can step up the pace by copying a column or a row of formulas to many columns or many rows all in one step. To accomplish this, you must expand both the source and target ranges to include a range of cells. You can use this approach to complete the formulas for your model. Although the column of formulas you need to copy includes only two cells, it is still a column. You will be able to copy this column of formulas to columns E, F, and G. Follow these directions to complete the Copy operation:

Figure 5-5. *Copying the Sales formula to many cells*

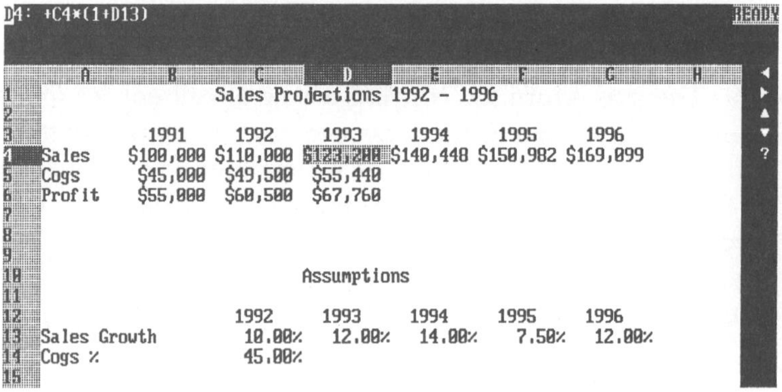

```
D4: +C4*(1+D13)                                                    READY

          A        B        C        D        E        F        G        H
1                         Sales Projections 1992 - 1996
2
3                    1991     1992     1993     1994     1995     1996
4    Sales        $100,000 $110,000 $123,200 $140,448 $150,982 $169,099
5    Cogs          $45,000  $49,500  $55,440
6    Profit        $55,000  $60,500  $67,760
7
8
9
10                                Assumptions
11
12                   1992     1993     1994     1995     1996
13   Sales Growth   10.00%   12.00%   14.00%    7.50%   12.00%
14   Cogs %         45.00%
15
```

1. Move the cell pointer to D5.

   This location is the upper leftmost cell in the range to be copied. As long as you remember to place the cell pointer in the upper leftmost cell in the range to be copied, the copy process will be easy to follow for either rows or columns.

2. Select Copy.

3. Expand the source range to D6 by moving the cell pointer with the DOWN ARROW key or by dragging the mouse.

   The cells you are copying from should be highlighted. The location where you should place the cell pointer when expanding the source range is always the lower rightmost cell in the range to be copied. Again, keeping the lower rightmost cell in mind will make these directions work even when you wish to copy a row of data.

4. Press ENTER, move the cell pointer to E5, and type . (period).

   This anchors the upper leftmost cell in the target range.

5. Move the cell pointer to G5.

   You are probably thinking that G6 would have been the correct location. Since 1-2-3 already knows from your definition of the target range that you are copying a column of formulas, it only needs to know how far across the worksheet you wish to copy this column. G5 answers that question.

6. Press ENTER to see the results shown in Figure 5-6.

   The procedure for copying a row of cell entries follows the same basic pattern as this example. First you must define which row of cells is in the source or from range. Next, you must tell 1-2-3 where to begin copying this row to and how far down the worksheet to copy it. Keep in mind that all these copy methods can be used just as easily for values and labels as for formula entries.

Rearranging the Worksheet

Planning is the best assurance that your completed model will both look good and meet your business needs. But even when you plan, there will be occasions when you want to rearrange the data contained in your model. 1-2-3 has commands that will reorganize the worksheet for you.

Figure 5-6.   *Result of the Copy operation for Cogs and Profit*

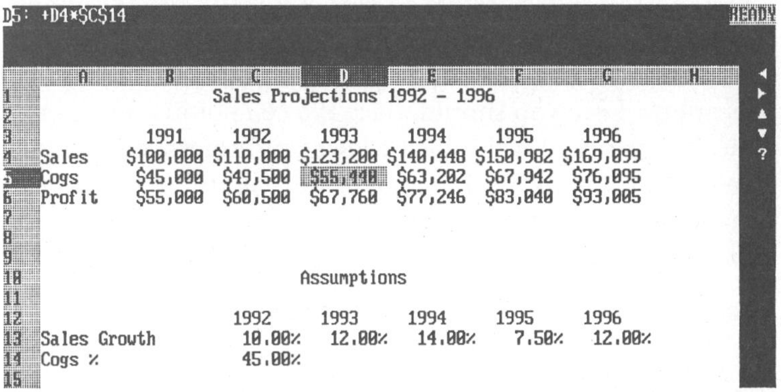

This means that you do not have to reenter and erase entries the way you would with a manual version of your model. These special commands include one that can move any range of data to another range that is the same size and shape. A second command allows you to take a row of data and place it in a column or to take a column of data and place it in a row.

Moving Worksheet Data

The Move command is used to move data in one range of the worksheet to another range. This range can be a single cell, a row of cells, a column of cells, or a rectangle with multiple rows and columns. The size and shape of the relocated data are determined by the original location of the data. This means that a row of data can only be moved to another row, not placed into a column of cells.

You can use the Move command to relocate labels, values, and formulas. When Move relocates formulas, it adjusts the cell references in the formulas being moved to account for the new location of these formulas on the worksheet. Move also adjusts absolute references to conform to the new worksheet location.

The Move command is very similar to the Copy command, except that here the original location of the data is not retained. To use this command, select Move. 1-2-3 prompts you for the source range. Just as with the Copy command, it is easiest to specify the range if you position your cell pointer in the upper leftmost cell in the range before requesting Move. Also like the Copy command, you can press ENTER to specify a single cell as the source or you can move the cell pointer to expand the size of the range.

After you finalize the source range with ENTER, 1-2-3 prompts you for the target range, the new location for your data. Unlike the Copy command, Move's source range determines the size and shape of the data being moved. Therefore, all you need is a beginning location for the relocated data, which you can define by specifying the upper leftmost cell of the new area. Once you have specified the target range and finalized it with ENTER, the Move operation is complete.

You can use Move to relocate your assumptions on the current model by following these steps:

5

1. Move the cell pointer to A10.

   This is the upper leftmost cell in a rectangle that will include all the entries in the assumption section, including the label in row 10.

2. Select Move.

3. Move the cell pointer to G14.

   Everything to be moved will be highlighted.

4. Press ENTER to finalize the source or from range.

5. Move the cell pointer to B22 and press ENTER.

6. Press PGDN to see where the range was moved.

   The entire range of cells containing assumption data will be relocated to B22..H26, as shown in Figure 5-7.

7. Select File Save, type **SALESPRJ**, and press ENTER to save this worksheet.

Transposing Data

1-2-3's *transpose* features are available in Releases 2 and higher. Not only does the Range Trans command (called Range Transpose in Release 2.01) copy a range, but it also alters its orientation. Transpose places data with a row orientation into a column. Likewise, it places data with a

Figure 5-7. *Move completed*

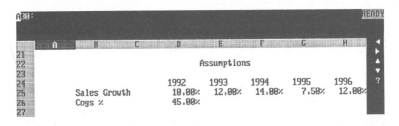

column orientation into a row. The power of this command will become apparent the first time you need to do major restructuring of a worksheet. You will have an opportunity to try both types of transposition.

Both versions of Range Trans can be used with labels and numbers. For Release 2.01, do not transpose formulas that contain relative references. Since the Range Trans command is actually a special form of Copy, the references in the formulas will be altered as they are written to the new cells if you are using Release 2.01. However, the data the formulas reference will still be in its original position and will cause disastrous results in the new formulas. In Releases 2.2 and above, Range Trans copies the formula's values to the new locations instead of the formulas themselves. This allows you to copy the formula's results without concern for whether or not the new orientation will damage the resulting entries. The resulting copy contains values but not formulas. In all versions, the original entries remain intact, allowing you to erase either these entries or the transposed entries.

5

Rows to Columns

Range Trans makes it easy to change data that was entered in a row to a column orientation. You do not even need to tell 1-2-3 whether the data you are transposing is in a row or column. 1-2-3 can figure it out from the range that you define. All you need to do is define the data to transpose, and then specify the upper leftmost cell where you wish to place the data. The following example illustrates how this command works:

1. Select Worksheet Erase Yes to clear the worksheet.

2. Select Worksheet Global Column-Width, type **14**, and press ENTER.

3. Make these entries in cells B2..F2:

B2:	Sales - Balls
C2:	Sales - Kites
D2:	Sales - Rafts
E2:	Sales - Jacks
F2:	Sales - Blocks

4. Press the HOME key.

A few of the entries appear as follows:

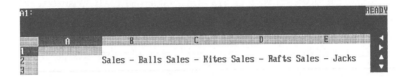

The entries are so wide that only a few are visible on the screen at once. You may decide to try a different orientation using the Range Trans command.

5. Move the cell pointer to B2 and select Range Trans.

6. Select B2..F2 as the source or from range and press ENTER. This selection can be accomplished quickly with the END key, followed by the RIGHT ARROW key.

7. Move the cell pointer to A4 and press ENTER.

    This will place the entries in column A, but the original entries are still in row 2. Your screen should match the display shown in Figure 5-8.

Columns to Rows

Transposing column data to a row is just as easy as the other way around. Try this example with the months of the year:

Figure 5-8.   *Transposed data*

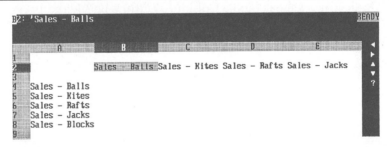

1. Start a new worksheet by selecting Worksheet Erase Yes. In Releases 2.2 and above, you must select Yes a second time to confirm that you want to erase the worksheet that you have not saved.

2. Using Figure 5-9 as your guide, enter the first six months in A3..A8.

3. Move the cell pointer to A3. Then select Range Trans.

4. Select the range A3..A8 and press ENTER.

5. Move the cell pointer to B2 and press ENTER.

   You can see the month names in Figure 5-10. The original entries will remain unless you use the Range Erase command to remove them.

Generating Cell Entries

This section covers the entries that you can have 1-2-3 generate for you. The generating features are so easy to use that it is like having someone perform data entry for you free of charge. 1-2-3's *repeating label* feature can generate dividing lines and other quick entries in worksheet cells. The other feature can generate a series of numbers that have the same increment between each value in the series—for example, 1, 2, 3, 4, or 25, 50, 75, 100.

Figure 5-9. *Data entered in a column*

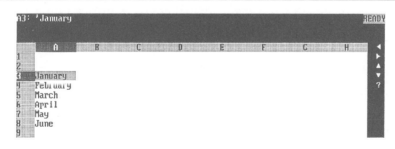

Figure 5-10.   *The result of transposing data to a row*

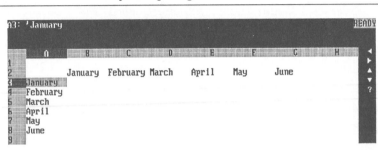

Creating Repeating Labels

You do not need a menu command to generate repeating labels. Instead, you accomplish it with the special label indicator backslash (\), followed by either a single character or a series of characters. Whichever you choose, 1-2-3 will duplicate your entry automatically to fill the complete display width of the cell and adjust the entry if you change the cell width.

You can use this feature to make a dividing line between sections of a worksheet or to create the top and bottom lines when you want to draw a box around your assumptions. Follow these steps to draw a box around the assumptions section of the worksheet:

1. Select File Retrieve, type **SALESPRJ,** and press ENTER.
    In Release 2.3, select Yes when 1-2-3 displays an additional prompt to confirm that you want to retrieve the file over the current worksheet, which has unsaved changes.

2. Move the cell pointer to A21.

3. Type ***** and press ENTER.
    Notice how the asterisks completely fill A21.

4. Select Copy and press ENTER.

5. Move the cell pointer to B21, type **.** (period), move the cell pointer to H21, and press ENTER.

6. Move the cell pointer to A22 and type *****, and then press ENTER.

7. Select Copy and press ENTER.

8. Move the cell pointer to A23, type **.** (period), and then move the cell pointer to A27 and press ENTER.

9. Move the cell pointer to A21 and select Copy.

10. Move the cell pointer to H21 and press ENTER.

11. Move the cell pointer to A28 and press ENTER.

12. Move the cell pointer to I21, type *****, and press ENTER.

13. Select Copy and press ENTER.

14. Move the cell pointer to I22 and type **.** (period); then move the cell pointer to I28 and press ENTER.

15. Select Worksheet Column Set-Width, type **2** and press ENTER.

16. Move the cell pointer to A21.

17. Select Worksheet Column Set-Width, type **7** and press ENTER.

    The final result of your entries is a line of asterisks on all four sides of the assumptions, as shown in Figure 5-11.

18. Select File Save, press ENTER, and then select Replace.

19. Select Worksheet Erase Yes.

Figure 5-11. *Box generated with repeating labels*

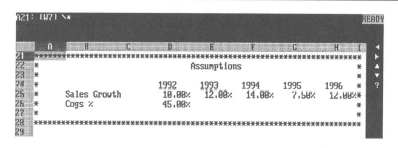

Generating a Series of Numbers

It can be tedious to enter a long list of numbers. In one special situation you can assign this task to 1-2-3: when the list of numbers is a series with equal intervals. The interval can be either positive or negative, but it must be the same between every number in the series. This means that lists such as 10, 20, 30, 40; 7, 9, 11, 13, 15; 52609, 52610, 52611; and 30, 29, 28, 27 can be generated by the package. A list such as 1, 3, 7, 15 could not be generated because the intervals between the numbers in the list are not the same.

Follow these instructions to generate a list of invoice numbers:

1. Type **Inv. No.** in A3.

2. Move the cell pointer to A4.

   This is the upper leftmost cell in the range where you will have 1-2-3 generate numbers.

3. Select Data Fill, type **.** and select the range A4..A20. Then press ENTER.

4. Type **57103** and press ENTER in response to the prompt for the start number.

   This is the first value that 1-2-3 will insert in the range to fill.

5. Press ENTER to accept 1 for the "step" increment number.

   This is the value that is added to each value in the list to create the next entry.

6. Type **59000**.

   The entries in the control panel should look like this:

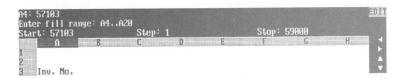

The stop value must always be as large as the last value in the list. This means that there are two factors that can end a list. The fill numbers stop being generated at the end of the range selected.

They can also stop sooner if the stop value is not large enough to accommodate the numbers you are generating.

7. Press ENTER.

The list of numbers generated is shown in Figure 5-12. Naturally, you can make your range larger to generate a larger list of numbers. You can also choose a horizontal range of cells and create an entry for each cell in the row.

8. Select Worksheet Erase Yes. In Releases 2.2 and above, select Yes a second time to confirm that you want to erase the worksheet that you have not saved.

Commands for Expanded Data

5

Now that you have learned the secrets of creating these models quickly, you can create many more models as well. Some of the models you

Figure 5-12. *Numbers generated by the Data Fill command*

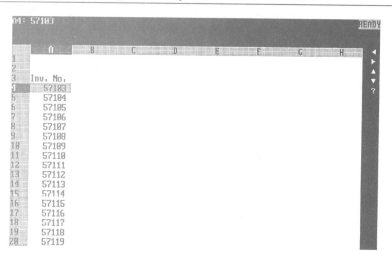

create will contain data for many months or years. You will also want to learn some of the tricks that make working with these models easier, such as controlling recalculation. This is a helpful trick, because as your models grow larger, 1-2-3 takes longer to recalculate after each of your entries. 1-2-3's speed seems quite good, compared to manual alternatives, when you do what-if analysis; but if you are entering a long list of account names or invoice numbers, it is annoying to have to wait for the program to finish recalculating. In this section you will learn how to put yourself in charge of the recalculation process.

You will also need additional tools to use for large models, since the entire model cannot be kept on the screen. And you will learn the techniques of creating a second window and freezing certain information on the screen. Both of these techniques are covered in this section.

Recalculation

1-2-3's recalculation options are accessed with the Worksheet Global Recalculation command. This is actually three commands in one, since it lets you change three different aspects of recalculation. You can select when the worksheet will recalculate, the order in which it will recalculate formulas, and how many times it recalculates the worksheet. The latter two options are advanced features of recalculation that are seldom required. If you are curious about these, check your 1-2-3 manual. The first option affects when the recalculation occurs. This is a real time-saver that can be used with any large worksheet. Releases 2.2 and above use minimal recalculation, allowing 1-2-3 to recalculate only those formulas affected by a change to the worksheet. This makes 1-2-3 faster and more efficient with all your calculations. If you are using Release 2.2 or above, you probably will not want to change recalculation to manual since it will result only in minimal time saving.

To alter the timing of recalculation for the sales projection worksheet, follow these steps:

1. Select File Retrieve, type **SALESPRJ**, and press ENTER.
2. Select Worksheet Global Recalculation.
   This command displays the following menu options: Natural, Columnwise, Rowwise, Automatic, Manual, and Iteration. The first

three options in this menu refer to the order of recalculation. The last option refers to the number of times the worksheet recalculates. The other two options, Automatic and Manual, let you determine whether the package will automatically update the model after a change or whether you wish to control recalculation.

3. Select Manual.

This option means that 1-2-3 will not recalculate formulas after a worksheet change. To recalculate them you will need to press the F9 (CALC) key.

4. Move your cell pointer to B4, type **200000**, and press ENTER.

Notice that this change does not affect the results in any category, although it does turn on the CALC indicator at the bottom of your screen. This indicator warns you that changes have been made and the worksheet has not been recalculated.

5. Press F9 (CALC).

Now you will see the results of the change.

6. Change the value in B4 back to 100000 by typing **100000**.

Again, the results are not affected.

7. Press F9 (CALC).

Your display should again show the results you started with.

8. Select Worksheet Global Recalculation Automatic.

From this point on, every worksheet entry will cause recalculation. You can also use the Global Settings dialog box in Release 2.3 to set when 1-2-3 recalculates the worksheet. You activate the dialog box by clicking on it or pressing F2 (EDIT). Select the Automatic check box under Recalculation to remove the mark and recalculate the worksheet manually. When you want to return to automatic recalculation, select the Automatic check box again to mark it and the worksheet will recalculate automatically. Keep this easy-to-make change in mind; it is a great option when you have a significant amount of data to enter.

5

Using Windows to Monitor Data

1-2-3 allows you to split the screen into two different sections and to view a different portion of the worksheet in each section. You have the option of splitting the screen vertically or horizontally. Which method to select will depend on how your worksheet is arranged and which sections you want to view. If you want to see columns in two different areas, you will split the screen vertically. If you want to view rows from two different locations, you will want to choose a horizontal split.

The command that you use to create the split is Worksheet Window. It is different from any other 1-2-3 command you have used: It requires you to position your cell pointer before invoking it. The location of the cell pointer determines the size of the two windows, and the window size cannot be changed while the menu is active.

After invoking the Worksheet Window command, you must select Horizontal if you want two horizontal windows. The split will be made above the cell pointer at the time the command is invoked. Selecting Vertical will draw two vertical windows, the first of which ends immediately to the left of the cell pointer's location when the command was invoked.

Once the screen is split into two windows, you can use the F6 (WINDOW) key to move to the other window. Regardless of which window you are in, F6 (WINDOW) always takes you to the opposite window.

The Worksheet Window menu has three additional options. The Clear option allows you to return to a display with one window. Cell pointer position is not important when you plan to choose Clear. The Sync and Unsync menu options let you control whether the two windows move in the same direction at the same time.

Try this exercise with your sales projection model to clarify how it works. Follow these steps:

1. Press the HOME key.

2. Move the cell pointer to A10.

3. Select Worksheet Window Horizontal.
   1-2-3 splits the worksheet into two windows at the cell pointer's location.

4. Press F6 (WINDOW) to move the cell pointer to the lower window.

5. Press PGDN to view the assumptions in the lower window as shown in Figure 5-13.

6. Select Worksheet Window Clear.
   The display will return to a single window.

Using Titles with Large Worksheets

One of the problems with large worksheets is that you cannot see all the data on the screen at one time. This problem is magnified when you move your cell pointer to the right or down and find that the labels at the left of the rows and the tops of the columns scroll off the screen. You can find yourself in a sea of numbers with no visible indication of what each of these numbers represents. The solution in 1-2-3 is to fix some of this label information on the screen.

Figure 5-13. *Two horizontal windows*

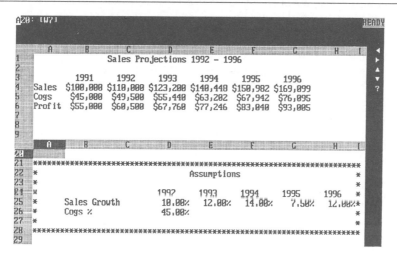

The command that freezes label information on the screen is the Worksheet Titles command. As with the Worksheet Window command, the position of the cell pointer at the time you invoke this command is critical. The cell pointer location defines what information will be frozen on the screen. The command has four options: to fix titles both vertically and horizontally; to fix them vertically; to fix them horizontally; and to clear all fixed titles from the screen. This last option does not eliminate the data in the titles. 1-2-3 will not let you select row titles if the cell pointer is in row 1 or column titles if the cell pointer is in column A since there would be no rows or columns selected.

If you choose to freeze vertical titles with either the Vertical or Both options, when you invoke Worksheet Titles any columns to the left of the cell pointer will become fixed on the screen. You will not be able to move your cell pointer into these columns with the arrow keys. If you move to the right of the point where columns would normally scroll off the screen, only columns to the right of the fixed titles will scroll off the screen. The columns defined as titles will always be visible.

The situation is similar for horizontal titles, whether you choose Horizontal or Both. All rows above the cell pointer at the time Worksheet Titles is invoked will remain frozen on the screen, even when the cell pointer moves far enough down on the worksheet to cause rows to scroll off the screen. The rows below the frozen titles can scroll off the screen, but the titles you have fixed on the screen cannot.

Looking at an example of this command with the sales projection worksheet will show you how it works. If you wanted to bring the right edge of the assumptions box into view, the left edge would scroll off the screen unless you first fixed the titles. Use these steps for fixing columns A through C:

1. Press the HOME key, and then press PGDN. Move the cell pointer to D25.

   You may think you could have just moved the cell pointer to D25, but the instructions given ensure that you have just the desired rows and columns above and to the left of the cell pointer.

2. Select Worksheet Titles Vertical.

3. Move the cell pointer to K25 to produce the display shown in Figure 5-14. Notice that columns A, B, and C are frozen on the screen, yet columns D and E are scrolled off the screen.

Figure 5-14.   *Vertical titles displaying columns A, B, and C*

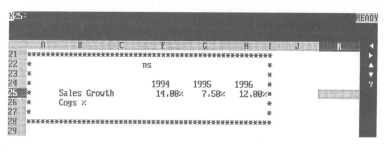

4. Select Worksheet Titles Clear.

This will unfix the titles, and columns A through C will scroll off the screen. These title-fixing features will be useful in situations where the total is at the bottom of a long column or to the right side of a long row. By fixing the titles you can check the total yet keep the corresponding labels on the screen for readability.

Searching and Replacing

Once you master 1-2-3's features, you will be creating large worksheets that model your business operations. Working with larger models can make it more difficult to find a particular entry as it is no longer practical to scan the model for a particular entry. If you are working with Release 2.2 or above, you can have 1-2-3 scrutinize entries for you. 1-2-3 can match a string of characters in either labels or formulas. In addition, you can use 1-2-3's Replace option to change one or more occurrences to another set of characters. These new search-and-replace features can save you time in reviewing entries and in the editing that would be required for entries you want to change.

The Range Search command is used for finding and replacing worksheet data. You can find text in cell formulas and labels. Since 1-2-3 can replace text as well as find it, you can use this command to correct a misspelling, change a cell address that formulas use, or find a name in a worksheet. The options for replacing text or cell addresses allow you to make all of the changes at once. If you would prefer to move a little more slowly, you can skip a matching entry, find the next matching entry to replace, or replace the current matching entry and move to the next one.

Searching Data

1-2-3 can find text stored in formulas and labels. This feature cannot be used to search a cell that contains only numbers. Using the feature with the sales projection worksheet will show you how it works. With the SALESPRJ file in memory from the previous example, use these steps to try the Range Search command to find the text "Sales":

1. Move the cell pointer to A1.

2. Select Range Search. 1-2-3 prompts for the range to search.

3. Type a period to anchor one corner of the search range and press the arrow keys to highlight A1..G6. With a mouse, click on A1 and drag the mouse to cell A1 to select the range A1..G6. Press ENTER. 1-2-3 prompts for the string to search for. You can use either upper- or lowercase letters when typing the search string since 1-2-3 treats them as equivalent entries.

4. Type **Sales** and press ENTER. 1-2-3 prompts for where you want to look for the string.

5. Select Labels. 1-2-3 will search all label cell entries for the string "Sales". 1-2-3 asks whether you want to find the string or replace the string with something else.

6. Select Find. 1-2-3 finds "Sales" in A4 (1-2-3 searches a column at a time, starting at the leftmost column) and creates the following display:

```
A4: [W7] 'Sales                                                    MENU
Next  Quit
Find next matching string
```

7. Select Next. 1-2-3 finds "Sales" in C1 and shows the same prompt. If you select Next, 1-2-3 will not find another "Sales" in

the worksheet. 1-2-3 will beep and display an Error Message. If you see this message, you can press ESC or ENTER to remove it and return to the READY mode.

8. Select Quit to return to the READY mode.

You can also use this command to find text in formulas. To find which cells use the 1994 sales growth in F25, you can search for a cell reference to F25 in formulas within the model by using the following steps:

1. Select Range Search. 1-2-3 prompts for the range to search and highlights the one you selected to find "Sales".

2. Press ENTER. 1-2-3 prompts for the string to search for and displays "Sales".

3. Press ESC to remove the previous entry, type **F25**, and press ENTER.
   1-2-3 prompts to see what type of entries it should check for the string.

4. Select Formulas.
   1-2-3 asks whether you want to find the string or replace the string with something else.

5. Select Find.
   1-2-3 will search all cells containing formulas for the cell reference F25. 1-2-3 finds F25 in E4 and prompts you to determine if you want it to find the next occurrence or to quit.

6. Select Next.
   1-2-3 cannot find another formula that uses F25, so it beeps and displays the "String not found" Error Message.

7. Press ESC. 1-2-3 returns to the READY mode.

Replacing Data

If you make a few mistakes when reentering labels and formulas, the Replace option in 1-2-3's Range Search command can handle the corrections for you. Replace not only locates your text but changes it to whatever character string you specify. You can use the SALESPRJ file and follow these steps to replace the text "Profit" with "Gross Profit":

1. Select Range Search. 1-2-3 prompts for the range to search. It displays the range you selected for searching the worksheet earlier.

2. Press ENTER to select A1..G6. 1-2-3 prompts for the string to search for and suggests F25 from the last Range Search command.

3. Press ESC, type **Profit**, and press ENTER.

   Since upper- and lowercase are equivalent in the search string, you can use either with identical results. 1-2-3 prompts for the type of entry within which you want to look for the string.

4. Select Labels.

   1-2-3 will search all label cell entries for the string "Profit". 1-2-3 asks whether you want to find the string or replace the string with something else.

5. Select Replace. 1-2-3 prompts for the replacement text you want to insert.

6. Type **Gross Profit** and press ENTER.

   1-2-3 finds "Profit" in A6 and creates the following display:

```
A6: [W7] 'Profit                                                    MENU
Replace All  Next  Quit
Replace string and proceed to next matching string in range
```

7. Select Replace.

   1-2-3 replaces "Profit" in A6 with "Gross Profit" and then searches for the next occurrence of "Profit". Since 1-2-3 cannot find another label that contains "Profit", 1-2-3 beeps and displays a message indicating that it cannot find more search strings.

8. Press ESC. 1-2-3 returns to the READY mode.

When you use the Range Search command to replace text in formulas or labels, you must be careful about what you supply as a search string. If the text that you search for is not clearly defined, you may wind up replacing text that you did not want replaced. As an example of an unintentional replacement, suppose you want to use the sales growth rate for 1994 in 1995. One method of doing this is to replace the G25 cell reference with F25. If you use a search string of "G" and a replacement text of "F", 1-2-3 returns unexpected results since it prompts you on many unexpected matches. To show how this happens, follow these steps:

1. Select Range Search.

   1-2-3 prompts for the range to search and highlights the one you selected in the last Range Search command.

2. Press ENTER to accept A1..G6.

   1-2-3 prompts for the string to search for and displays "Profit".

3. Press ESC to remove the previous entry, type **G**, and press ENTER.

   1-2-3 asks where it should look for the string.

4. Select Both to search both labels and formulas.

   1-2-3 asks whether you want to find the string or replace the string with something else.

5. Select Replace.

6. Type **F** and press ENTER.

   1-2-3 finds "G" in "Cogs" in A5 and asks whether to replace this one, replace all of them, find the next one, or quit.

7. Select All. 1-2-3 finds all occurrences of "G" in the worksheet and replaces them with "F".

   When 1-2-3 cannot find another "G", it beeps and displays an Error Message.

8. Press ESC. 1-2-3 returns to the READY mode. The screen looks like the one in Figure 5-15.

   Since the search string is not specific enough, the Range Search command replaced every "G" in the specified range. The entries in column G will highlight the error. A better solution is to enter G25 as the search string and F25 as the replacement string. Although you must type more characters, you exclude cells that you do not want to alter.

9. Select Worksheet Erase Yes to erase the worksheet. In Releases 2.2 and above, you must select Yes a second time to confirm that you want to erase the worksheet that you have not saved.

5

Figure 5-15. *Worksheet after supplying an inadequate search string*

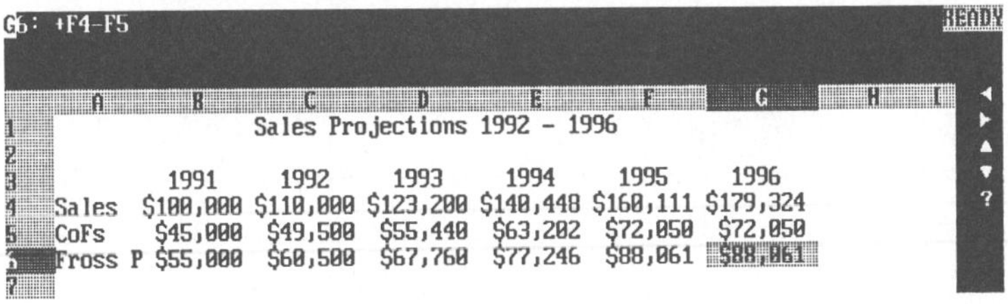

Review

- The Copy command can copy cells within a worksheet. You can copy one cell to one cell or one cell to many cells. You can also make one copy of an entire range of cells or make many copies of the same range. When you copy cells, 1-2-3 adjusts the formulas in the range depending upon whether the formulas use absolute, mixed, or relative cell addresses.

- The Move command can move cells within a worksheet. When you move cells, 1-2-3 adjusts the formulas so that all cell formulas reference the same cell contents they did before cells were moved.

- The Range Trans command in Release 2.2 (Range Transpose for Release 2.01) copies a range of cells and changes the cells' orientation from row to column or column to row. If you transpose formulas in Release 2.01, the relative references are distorted. If you transpose formulas in Releases 2.2 and above, the command copies and transposes the values of the formulas rather than the formulas themselves.

- You can create a repeating label using the backslash (\) label prefix. The characters that you enter after the backslash are repeated for the width of the cell. This repeating label adjusts the label's width for the column's width.

- The Data Fill command generates a series of numbers that are evenly spaced. To use this command you must provide the worksheet range that you want to fill with numbers, the number that you want to start the series with, the increment between values (positive for ascending and negative for descending), and the maximum value that can appear in the series.

- The Worksheet Global Default Recalculation command determines whether 1-2-3 recalculates the worksheet whenever a worksheet entry is made or only when you press the F9 (CALC) key. For releases before 2.2, setting the recalculation to manual can increase the speed of data entry significantly.

- The Worksheet Window command lets you create vertical and horizontal windows. These windows divide the screen so you can see two sections of your worksheet at once.

- The Worksheet Titles command locks rows and columns on the screen display so you can always see the column or row header. The command options let you select horizontal titles (rows that always appear on the screen), vertical titles (columns that always appear on the screen), both titles (columns and rows that always appear on the screen), or clear titles (removes the titles from the screen).

- The Range Search command, which is available in Releases 2.2 and above, can search for text in label or formula cell entries. The Replace option allows you to replace the text the command finds with different text.

Commands and Keys

Entry	Action
\	As a label prefix character, repeats the string that follows until the column width is filled
F4 (ABS)	Converts the address at the cursor's location to an absolute, mixed, or relative address
F6 (WINDOW)	Switches between the active windows
F9 (CALC)	Updates the calculations in the worksheet

5

Entry	Action
C	Copy copies one or more cells to new locations
DF	Data Fill generates a series of numbers that are specific intervals apart
M	Move moves one or more cells to another location
RS	Range Search finds or finds and replaces text in formulas and label cell entries
RT	Range Transpose copies one or more cells to a new location and changes the column and row orientation
WTB	Worksheet Titles Both freezes the rows above the cell pointer and the columns to the left of the cell pointer as worksheet titles
WTC	Worksheet Titles Clear clears worksheet titles created with other WW commands
WTH	Worksheet Titles Horizontal freezes the rows above the cell pointer as a horizontal title
WTV	Worksheet Titles Vertical freezes the columns to the left of the cell pointer as a vertical title
WWC	Worksheet Window Clear removes the second horizontal or vertical window
WWH	Worksheet Window Horizontal splits the screen display in half with a horizontal line, allowing you to view different sections
WWV	Worksheet Window Vertical splits the screen display in half with a vertical line, allowing you to view different sections of the worksheet
WGDRA	Worksheet Global Default Recalculation Automatic sets 1-2-3 to recalculate the worksheet whenever an entry is made
WGDRM	Worksheet Global Default Recalculation Manual sets 1-2-3 to recalculate the worksheet when F9 (CALC) is pressed

6

Printing Your Worksheet

In this chapter you will have an opportunity to explore 1-2-3's print features. You can use them to create a quick draft copy of your worksheet, using only a few instructions. When you are ready for a final copy, you can create a professional-looking report with a few new commands. These commands will allow you to control the print margins, access the special print options offered by your printer, and even add headers and footers to every page.

First, you will learn to use the basic print options. Then you will learn more complex print options, using the building-block approach, until you have a full set of print features that you can use. You will also have the opportunity to explore options for printing formulas and using worksheet commands to further customize your print output. Additional enhancements through the Allways and WYSIWYG add-ins are covered in Chapter 12, "WYSIWYG and Other Add-Ins." Since Release 2.2 includes the Allways add-in and Release 2.3 includes the WYSIWYG add-in, you will want to review Chapter 12 to learn about the significant printing enhancements these add-ins provide.

Print Basics

The basic print features are designed to give you quick access to a printed copy. This quick access is made possible by default values that 1-2-3 has set for options such as margins and page length. Later you will learn to override these default settings, but for now you might as well appreciate their presence; they make it easy for you to print your files.

Determining the Destination

What is the destination for 1-2-3's print features? At first the answer seems obvious. After all, if you are printing, you would expect to use the printer. But 1-2-3 offers you a choice: You can print to a printer or to a file on disk. The unexpected option of using a disk to capture print output adds considerable flexibility to the print features. In addition to these two destinations, Release 2.3 can print to an encoded file that includes special printer codes to print the worksheet correctly. Release 2.3 also includes a fourth option that allows you to print in the background while you continue to use the worksheet.

To select a destination, first access the print features by selecting Print. This will cause the submenu that includes Printer, File, and, in Release 2.3, Encoded and Background to display. 1-2-3 is asking whether to direct your output to the printer or to write it to a file. If you want to create printed hard copy immediately, choose Printer.

The Printer Option

When you select the Printer option, 1-2-3 assumes that the output device is the printer you selected when 1-2-3 was installed. As long as this printer is attached to your system and online when you tell 1-2-3 to begin printing, your print output will be sent to this device. Normally, the top or front of the printer has a series of small lights to indicate that the printer is online and ready to accept data. Verify that the printer is turned on and is online before you start to work with the Print commands. It is also a good idea to understand the defaults that will apply to your output before you learn about the instruction that actually starts the printing.

The File Option

The File option is designed to let you write your print output to a file. Unlike the files that contain worksheets, this file contains print data and is referred to as an *ASCII text file*. It will automatically be assigned the filename extension .PRN. Once you have stored the information in the file you can do various things with it: print it at a later time, modify it with many word processors, and use it as input to some application programs. Should you want to write your file to an ASCII text file, you can use any of the options presented in this chapter. Most of the examples in this chapter print to the printer using the Printer destination.

Encoded and Background Options

Release 2.3 adds the Encoded and Background options. Both of these print to an encoded file that has an .ENC extension. These files are only intended to be used to print the file to the printer that is selected when you create the file. With the Background option, this file is only temporary since 1-2-3 will delete this file as soon as 1-2-3 has finished printing it. All of the options for printing that are described in this chapter can be used with the new Release 2.3 printing destination options.

The Default Settings

One of the things that simplifies printing the first time you use a worksheet is the default settings that are provided for some of the Print options. These defaults affect the length of a page of output and the amount of white space, or the margin, on all four sides of a printed page. The defaults also apply to the printed pages you write out to disk.

The default page that is predefined for 1-2-3 has several areas affecting the amount of data that prints on a page. The layout of a printed page defining these areas is shown in Figure 6-1. 1-2-3 uses a default page length of 66 lines, yet not all these lines will contain print data. Some of them are reserved for top and bottom margins. Once two lines are deducted for a top margin and two more are deducted for a bottom margin, only 62 lines will print on a page. In addition to the top and bottom margins, 1-2-3 allows three lines at both the top and bottom for a header or footer, even if you choose not to use either one. This means that of the 66 possible lines, only 56 lines will be used for printing.

Similarly, standard print on an 8 1/2- by 11-inch sheet of paper allows 80 characters to print across the page, but the default settings will reduce

Figure 6-1. *Layout of a printed page*

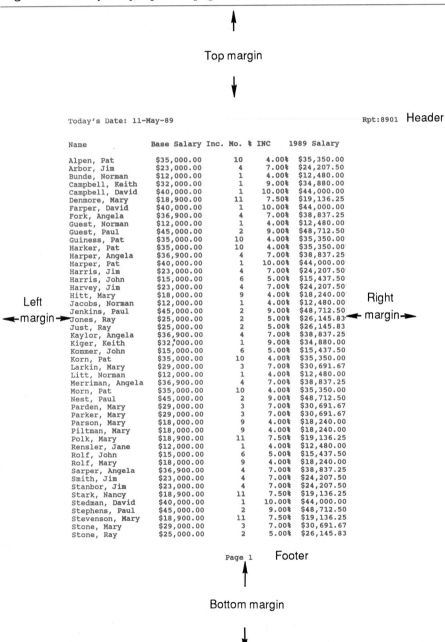

this number. 1-2-3 has a default left margin setting of 4 and a default right margin setting of 76. This means that a maximum of 72 characters can print across the page if you do not modify the defaults. Initially, try the Print operation without modifying any of these defaults.

The Basic Print Options

The second level of the Print menu is the same regardless of where you are printing. It is actually the main Print menu, since it is the root from which all the other Print options can be selected. Figure 6-2 shows the main Print menu and the Print Settings dialog box that tracks all the changes you make in the Print menu. The Print menu stays on your screen to allow additional selections. For this reason, it frequently is referred to as a "sticky menu." You will find it a real convenience, since most Print operations require more than one menu selection. When you select an option from 1-2-3's Print menu, the dialog box may disappear temporarily to allow you to select cells on the worksheet. As soon as you finalize your selection, the dialog box will reappear. Like all dialog boxes (or settings sheets in Release 2.2), you can hide them by pressing F6 (WINDOW). When you want the dialog box to return, press F6 again. Later in the chapter you will learn more about using the dialog box to make printing selections. Dialog boxes are discussed in Chapter 3, "Changing the Worksheet Appearance."

Another important distinction is that 1-2-3 can remember the results of any command that affects the print settings. To have 1-2-3 remember what you want to print or any changes that you make to the print settings in a later session, first complete the definition of your print specifications, and then save the worksheet.

Defining a Range to Print

At this point you want to tell 1-2-3 how much of the worksheet you wish to print. Therefore, select the Range option from the main Print menu. The next step depends on whether the worksheet already has a print range defined. If not, just move to the beginning of the print range, type a period, and move to the end of the print range. If the worksheet was printed previously, the range address used from that time will probably still be defined.

Before you can move the cell pointer to a new beginning location, you must press ESC to unlock the beginning of the range. Whether you have

Figure 6-2. *Main Print menu and Print Settings dialog box*

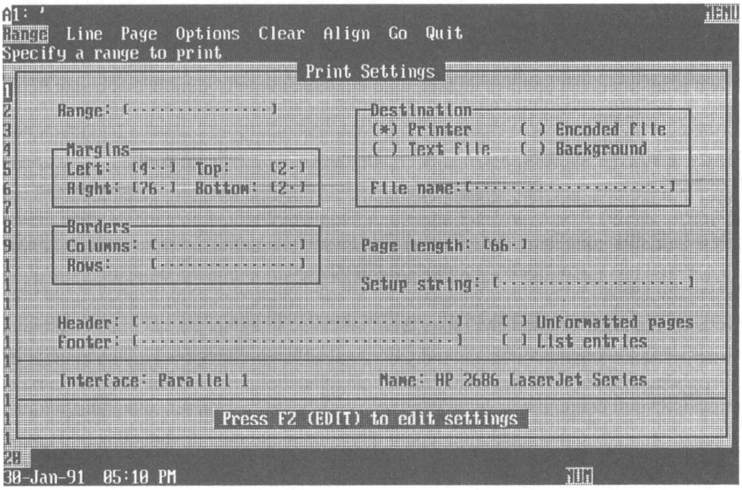

printed previously or not, you can type a range reference by entering the address of the beginning of the range followed by a period and the cell address of the end of the range—for example, B3.H15. If a current range exists, 1-2-3 will immediately replace it with the range you enter; you do not need to press ESC. The same is true for selecting a range to print with a mouse.

The size of the range you define will affect how 1-2-3 prints your data. If your defined range contains more data than will fit on one page, 1-2-3 will break the data into more than one page when you print. If the width of the range selected exceeds the number of characters that will print across one page, 1-2-3 will print as many columns across the first page as possible without exceeding the right margin setting. It will then break the output into more than one page. If the number of rows in the range selected exceeds the number of rows that can print on one page, 1-2-3 will generate a page break when the data prints.

To enter some data for printing and to try several options for specifying the print range, experiment with the following exercise. You could print worksheets you entered for other chapters, but you might not have one readily available. Therefore, this section offers instructions for creating employee data to be printed. You need to make quite a few entries to create this model, but it is designed to let you try each of the print options covered in this chapter without having to enter data again. You will use entries more than once to build a large file quickly. You will use the Copy command extensively to further reduce these entry requirements.

Follow these steps to enter the model and define the print range.

1. Enter the following labels across row 1:

   A1:   SS#
   B1:   Last Name
   C1:   First Name
   D1:   "Salary
   E1:   Location
   F1:   "Phone
   G1:   "Position
   H1:   Increase %
   I1:   '1992 Salary

2. Select Worksheet Global Column-Width, type **11**, and press ENTER.

3. Move the cell pointer to column A, select Worksheet Column Set-Width, type **13**, and press ENTER.

4. Make these entries in the cells shown:

   A2:   '516-75-8977   A3:   '541-78-6754
   B2:   Jones   B3:   Parker
   C2:   Paul   C3:   Mary
   D2:   45900   D3:   32100
   E2:   DAL   E3:   CHI
   F2:   980   F3:   541
   G2:   2301   G3:   1605
   H2:   .05   H3:   .04
   I2:   +D2*(1+H2)

6

A4:	'897-90-8769	A5:	'213-78-5412
B4:	Smith	B5:	Appel
C4:	Larry	C5:	Tom
D4:	61250	D5:	22300
E4:	ATL	E5:	BOS
F4:	342	F5:	219
G4:	1402	G5:	1750
H4:	.05	H5:	.06

5. Move the cell pointer to I2, select Copy, and press ENTER. Move the cell pointer to I3, type . (period), move the cell pointer to I5, and press ENTER.

   This completes the first four records. You need more rows of data to get the full effect of the Print features, but typing the entries would take too long. Instead, copy these entries until you have a sufficient number to print more than one page. You will, of course, have many duplicates.

6. Move the cell pointer to A2 and select Copy. Then press END and HOME or select the range A2..I5 with the mouse. Press ENTER to finalize the source range. Next move the cell pointer to A6 and press ENTER.

   This time you copied the first 4 rows of the worksheet to create another 4 rows. Next time you will copy the 8 existing data rows. After that you will copy the 16 entries and then the 32 entries (the number of records becomes larger each time you make a copy).

7. Proceed with the copy by selecting Copy. Then press END and HOME or use the mouse to select all the worksheet entries. Press ENTER, move the cell pointer to the next empty cell in column A, and press ENTER.

8. Repeat the previous step twice until you have entries in cells A1..I65.

9. Move the cell pointer to D2 and select Range Format Currency, type **0**, press ENTER, and then select D2..D65. Press ENTER.

10. Move the cell pointer to H2 and select Range Format Percent. Press ENTER, and then select H2..H65. Press ENTER again.

11. Move the cell pointer to I2. Select Range Format Currency. Type **0** and press ENTER. Select I2..I65. Press ENTER.

    The upper portion of your entries should match what is shown in Figures 6-3 and 6-4.

12. Select Print Printer Range and press the HOME key. Type . (period). Press END followed by HOME to highlight the range A1..I65. Press ENTER.

Figure 6-3. *A look at the left side of the entries*

```
A1: [W13] 'SS#                                                    READY

             A           B          C          D        E          F        ◄
  1   SS#          Last Name   First Name   Salary Location      Phone       ►
  2   516-75-8977  Jones       Paul         $45,900 DAL           900        ▲
  3   541-78-6754  Parker      Mary         $32,100 CHI           541        ▼
  4   897-90-8769  Smith       Larry        $61,250 ATL           342        ?
  5   213-78-5412  Appel       Tom          $22,300 BOS           219
  6   516-75-8977  Jones       Paul         $45,900 DAL           900
  7   541-78-6754  Parker      Mary         $32,100 CHI           541
  8   897-90-8769  Smith       Larry        $61,250 ATL           342
  9   213-78-5412  Appel       Tom          $22,300 BOS           219
 10   516-75-8977  Jones       Paul         $45,900 DAL           900
 11   541-78-6754  Parker      Mary         $32,100 CHI           541
 12   897-90-8769  Smith       Larry        $61,250 ATL           342
 13   213-78-5412  Appel       Tom          $22,300 BOS           219
 14   516-75-8977  Jones       Paul         $45,900 DAL           900
 15   541-78-6754  Parker      Mary         $32,100 CHI           541
 16   897-90-8769  Smith       Larry        $61,250 ATL           342
 17   213-78-5412  Appel       Tom          $22,300 BOS           219
 18   516-75-8977  Jonoo       Paul         $45,900 DAL           900
 19   541-78-6754  Parker      Mary         $32,100 CHI           541
 20   097-90-8769  Smith       Larry        $61,250 ATL           342
20-Feb-91  05:33 PM                                        NUM
```

Figure 6-4.   *A look at the right side of the entries*

```
G1: "Position                                                                  READY

            G         H          I         J          K          L            ◄
   1    Position  Increase %  1992 Salary                                      ►
   2      2301      5.00%      $48,195                                         ▲
   3      1605      4.00%      $33,304                                         ▼
   4      1402      5.00%      $64,313                                         ?
   5      1750      6.00%      $23,638
   6      2301      5.00%      $48,195
   7      1605      4.00%      $33,304
   8      1402      5.00%      $64,313
   9      1750      6.00%      $23,638
  10      2301      5.00%      $48,195
  11      1605      4.00%      $33,304
  12      1402      5.00%      $64,313
  13      1750      6.00%      $23,638
  14      2301      5.00%      $48,195
  15      1605      4.00%      $33,304
  16      1402      5.00%      $64,313
  17      1750      6.00%      $23,638
  18      2301      5.00%      $48,195
  19      1605      4.00%      $33,304
  20      1402      5.00%      $64,313
20-Feb-91  05:34 PM                                               NUM
```

Notice that the main Print menu is still in the control panel to let you make additional selections. Take advantage of its presence and enter the range specification a few different ways.

13. Select Range, press ESC to unlock the beginning of the range, and then move the cell pointer to B1; type . (period) and then press the END key followed by the DOWN ARROW key. Press the RIGHT ARROW key twice; then press ENTER to select the range B1..D65.

14. Select Range, type **A1.I65**, and press ENTER.

    When you type the address of a replacement range, you do not have to press the ESC key first.

Printing a Range

Once you have defined the range, simply select Go from the Print menu. Use the following step to immediately send the range you just defined to the printer:

1. Check to be sure that your printer is turned on and is online.

2. Select Go.

This will cause 1-2-3 to print the worksheet row by row and increment its internal line count with each line printed. When all the data in the defined range has been printed, 1-2-3 will return to the Print menu. The print output is shown in Figure 6-5. If you want a second copy you can select Go again, but 1-2-3 will not move to the top of a page before it starts printing again. You cannot solve this problem by paging with the formfeed or linefeed button on your printer, since 1-2-3 maintains its own line count to tell it how much more space it has on a page. If you were to physically advance the paper in your printer without setting 1-2-3's line count to zero, the new page would only contain data part of the way down the page; the line count would increment to 66 before reaching the bottom of the page. Look at the basic control options before printing a second time. To tell 1-2-3 to begin in the second copy at the top of the page, use the instructions for advancing a page, which follow.

Advancing a Line

Sometimes you want to print more than one print range. Depending on the size of each range of data, you may want to place all the ranges on a single page or place each one on a separate page. If you placed them on the same page, they would merge unless you added one or more blank lines after printing each range. 1-2-3 will do this for you when you give it the command Print Printer Line. (Normally you need only select Line, since the Print menu is likely to be on your screen.) Each time you select Line, 1-2-3 causes the printer to advance the paper one line and add one to the internal line count.

Advancing a Page

Advancing a line is fine for a small separation; but when you want data on separate pages you might have to select Line too many times to make this solution a practical one. Instead, use the command Print Printer Page. It will quickly advance the paper to the top of the next page. Try this now: Select Page. Only Page is needed since you are already in the main Print menu.

Setting the Line Count to Zero

When the paper in your printer is set at the top of a form, you will want 1-2-3's line count to be set to zero. The command for this is Align.

Figure 6-5.   *Output from the Print operation*

```
        1750       6.00%    $23,638
        2301       5.00%    $48,195
        1605       4.00%    $33,384
        1402       5.00%    $64,313
        1750       6.00%    $23,638
        2301       5.00%    $48,195
        1605       4.00%    $33,384
```

```
   Position Increase % 1992 Salary
        2301       5.00%    $48,195
        1605       4.00%    $33,384
        1402       5.00%    $64,313
        1750       6.00%    $23,638
        2301       5.00%    $48,195
        1605       4.00%    $33,384
```

```
  213-78-5412   Appel     Tom       $22,300 BOS        219
  516-75-8977   Jones     Paul      $45,900 DAL        980
  541-78-6754   Parker    Mary      $32,100 CHI        541
  897-90-8769   Smith     Larry     $61,250 ATL        342
  213-78-5412   Appel     Tom       $22,300 BOS        219
  516-75-8977   Jones     Paul      $45,900 DAL        980
  541-78-6754   Parker    Mary      $32,100 CHI        541
  897-90-8769   Smith     Larry     $61,250 ATL        342
```

```
  SS#           Last Name First Name    Salary Location   Phone
  516-75-8977   Jones     Paul       $45,900 DAL          980
  541-78-6754   Parker    Mary       $32,100 CHI          541
  897-90-8769   Smith     Larry      $61,250 ATL          342
  213-78-5412   Appel     Tom        $22,300 BOS          219
  516-75-8977   Jones     Paul       $45,900 DAL          980
  541-78-....   Parker    Mary       $32,100 CHI          541
                                     $61,250 ATL          342
```

Try it with this entry: select Align. It looks like nothing has happened, but 1-2-3 has completed its housekeeping chore of zeroing the line count.

Clearing the Print Settings

The Print menu has a special command for clearing print settings from a previous operation. If you select Clear from the Print menu, 1-2-3 displays a menu containing All, Range, Borders, and Format.

The first option clears everything connected with the previous print-ing, and is appropriately labeled All. It sets everything back to the defaults. This means that you must define the next Print operation, just as if you had never printed before.

The second option only eliminates the definition of the print range. After executing this command, you must define a print range before printing again. If you forget, nothing will happen when you tell 1-2-3 to begin printing since there will be no default settings for the print range.

The last two options, Borders and Format, will be discussed later in this chapter along with the more advanced features they relate to. Like the other options, they eliminate any special settings that have been made and leave the worksheet as if these special features had never been invoked.

Quitting the Print Menu

Since the Print menus do not disappear after you make your selec-tions, you need a way to let 1-2-3 know you are finished selecting print options. The Quit option in the Print menu is designed to do this. Once you select Quit you are returned to READY mode. If you are printing to a file, selecting Quit closes the file; pressing ESC also exits the Print menu and closes the file. Try it now with this command: select Quit.

Saving Your Specifications

When you update your worksheet data, you probably will want to produce updated copies of your report. It is easy to print a report on subsequent occasions if you have saved the worksheet file after printing. The File Save command saves any updates to worksheet data, as well as your print settings. This means that the print range and any special settings you have entered for margins or page length will still be available the next time you need to print. You will be able to select Print Printer Go to produce the output.

6

Adding Options

You have already mastered the basics of printing. You do not need any other commands to get a printed copy of your data. But you may not be content with the appearance of your printout. If you want to improve it, the print options can assist you. You can access them by selecting Options from the main Print menu to produce this menu:

This is another "sticky menu" like the main Print menu. It will stay around until you choose Quit or press ESC.

Margin Settings

To change margin settings, select Margins from the Options menu. You will be presented with a submenu that contains Left, Right, Top, Bottom, and None.

Each option on this menu represents one of the four areas where margins can be specified. The None option, which is new to Releases 2.2 and above, removes the margin settings from the worksheet, which causes 1-2-3 to use the widest area for printing your worksheet.

Whatever values you enter for margins will change the print defaults for this one worksheet. If you save the worksheet file after making changes to the margins, the changed values will be in effect for this worksheet the next time you retrieve it. If you want to make a temporary change, don't save the worksheet after changing the margins.

The limitations placed on potential margin settings for Release 1A differ from those for Releases 2 and higher. In Releases 2 and higher, the limits on top and bottom margins are 0 lines to 32 lines for each of these margin choices. In Release 1A, the settings for each margin can be between 0 and 10 lines. To enter a new margin setting, select the type of margin you wish to specify; then type a new value and press ENTER.

The range of acceptable values for the right and left margins is the same for all releases of the product. You can use settings of from 0 to 240 characters for both right and left margins.

Try the following exercise with the employee data to see how margins can affect the output:

1. Select Print Printer Options Margins.

2. Select Left, type **10**, and press ENTER.

3. Select Margins Right, type **70**, and press ENTER.

4. Select Quit.

    This Quit exits the Options menu and returns you to the main Print menu.

5. Select Go.

    You will see that one fewer columns print across the page because you have reserved more space for the right and left margins.

6. Select Page Align.

Headers and Footers

Headers and *footers* are lines that appear at the top or bottom of every page of print output. Information placed in the header (at the top of a page) typically includes the date or time, an identifying report number, a report title, the preparer's name, or a page number. The most frequent entry in a footer (at the bottom of the page) is the page number.

Headers and footers can be up to 240 characters each. However, do not make them any longer than the number of characters that will fit on one line, or 1-2-3 will truncate the extra characters. For example, if you use the default left and right margin settings of 4 and 76, do not enter a header longer than 72 characters. This limit applies whether you type the header or footer at 1-2-3's prompt or store the header or footer in a cell and reference the cell. The latter method is available in Releases 2.2 and 2.3.

Special Symbols

Two special symbols can be used anywhere in a header or footer to add special information. The @ makes 1-2-3 substitute the current system date at that location when it prints the header or footer line. The # makes 1-2-3 insert the current page number at that location in the header or footer. When a header or footer contains # for the page number, it is important to select Align. Besides resetting 1-2-3's line count on the current page, Align also resets the page numbering back to 1.

Either of these special symbols can be used alone or in combination with text characters. If you wanted the words "Page Number" to appear in front of the actual page number, you would place **Page Number #** in the header. Likewise, if you wanted to label the date you could enter **Today's Date: @**.

The Three Sections

1-2-3 allows you to define entries for the left, middle, and right sections of a header or footer. In other words, each header or footer has the potential to be divided into three sections. The sections are separated by the vertical bar symbol (|).

When you enter a header by selecting Print Printer Options Header, 1-2-3 prompts for the text you want to appear at the top of every page. Whatever you type will appear left-aligned in the header line. When you are finished entering information for the left section, type a vertical bar (|) to indicate that you would like to begin entering the center section. When you have completed the center section, type another vertical bar (|) to indicate the beginning of the entries for the right section. You can omit any section by entering the vertical bar to end the section without entering anything in it. For example, the header " | | Report Number: 3405" would not place anything in the left or middle sections of the header. It would right-align "Report Number: 3405" in the header line printed at the top of every page. You can enter everything on the left side of the page by using no vertical bar characters in your header.

Try this exercise to see how adding a header can affect your output:

1. Select Options Header, type **Report No: 2350 | | Page #**, and press ENTER.

2. Select Quit.

3. Select Go.

4. Select Page Align.

Figure 6-6 shows the header at the top of the first two printed pages. While this is an example of creating and printing a header, the steps for creating and printing a footer are identical.

Figure 6-6. *Header at the top of two pages*

```
Report No: 2350                                        Page 2

213-78-5412  Appel    Tom        $22,300 BOS        219
516-75-8977  Jones    Paul       $45,900 DAL        980
541-78-6754  Parker   Mary       $32,100 CHI        541
897-90-8769  Smith    Larry      $61,250 ATL        342
213-78-5412  Appel    Tom        $22,300 BOS        219

   Report No: 2350                                     Page 1

   SS#          Last Name  First Name    Salary Location   Phone
   516-75-8977  Jones      Paul       $45,900 DAL        980
   541-78-6754  Parker     Mary       $32,100 CHI        541
   897-90-8769  Smith      Larry      $61,250 ATL        342
   213-78-5413  Appel      Tom        $22,300 BOS        219
                                      $45,900 DAL        980
```

Using a Cell's Contents

If you are using Release 2.2 or above, you can use the contents in a worksheet cell for the header or footer. To refer to a cell's contents, enter a backslash and the cell address or range name that you want to use for the header or footer. If you enter a range name, 1-2-3 uses the cell in the upper left corner of the range. 1-2-3 uses the cell's contents just as if you entered the cell's contents at the header or footer prompt. This means you can include the vertical bars and the two special symbols in the cell. You may want to use this new feature to select from one of several headings when you print a report. To change a heading you would simply type the cell address that contains the header that you want.

As an example, you can create the same header shown in Figure 6-6 by entering **Report No: 2350 | |Page #** in K1. Then from the Print Options menu you would select Header, type **\K1**, and press ENTER. If you use a cell reference to select the header or footer, the header or footer cannot contain the other special header or footer characters.

Using Borders

The labels you enter at the top and/or left side of a worksheet provide descriptive information on the first page of a printed report, but the rows of labels at the top are not repeated automatically when the rows in the worksheet continue on subsequent pages. These pages will contain data that may be meaningless without labels. Similarly, when the rows in the worksheet exceed the width of one page, only the first page will contain the columns at the left. Data further to the right will be printed on subsequent pages but will probably be meaningless without labels.

The Borders option allows you to select rows or columns that will appear at the top or left side of every page. The columns or rows you select as borders should not be included in the print range. Otherwise, this data will print twice on the first page of the report—once as part of the border and once as part of the print range.

To use the Borders option, select Print Printer Options Borders. Then select Columns or Rows to select the columns or rows that you want to appear on every page. Next, select a cell or range address that contains one cell from every column or row you want to use in the column or row border.

You can put the Borders option to use for the employee file you started in an earlier chapter; the worksheet has more rows than will fit on one page, and the second page has no labels. Follow these steps to add the top row as a border:

1. Select Range from the main Print menu.

2. Type **A2.F65** and press ENTER.
   Notice that the row containing the labels is not included in the print range, since you will use it as a border row.

3. Select Options Borders Rows.

4. Move the cell pointer to A1 and press ENTER.

5. Select Quit.

6. Select Go followed by Page Align Clear All Quit when the printing stops.

The output contains labels at the top of both pages 1 and 2, as shown in Figure 6-7. The Clear All command eliminated all of the print settings, including the print range and borders. You can also remove column or row borders without affecting the other print settings with the Print Printer Clear Borders command.

Figure 6-7. *Borders option places labels on all pages*

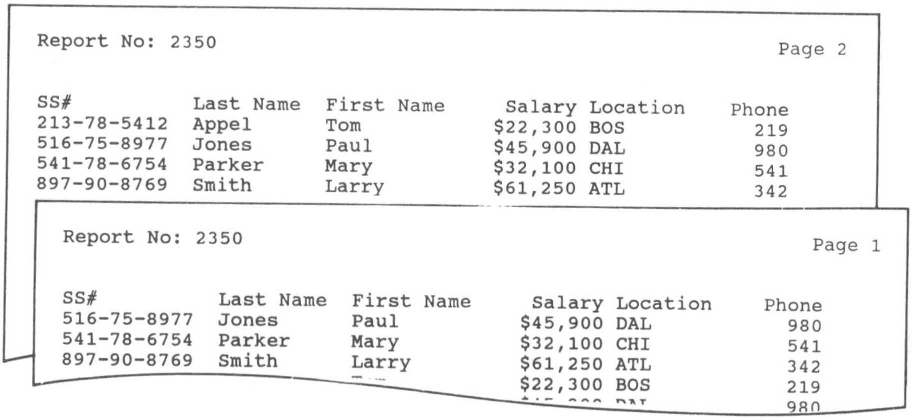

```
Report No: 2350                                               Page 2

SS#            Last Name   First Name    Salary Location    Phone
213-78-5412    Appel       Tom           $22,300 BOS           219
516-75-8977    Jones       Paul          $45,900 DAL           980
541-78-6754    Parker      Mary          $32,100 CHI           541
897-90-8769    Smith       Larry         $61,250 ATL           342

   Report No: 2350                                            Page 1

   SS#            Last Name   First Name    Salary Location    Phone
   516-75-8977    Jones       Paul          $45,900 DAL           980
   541-78-6754    Parker      Mary          $32,100 CHI           541
   897-90-8769    Smith       Larry         $61,250 ATL           342
                                            $22,300 BOS           219
                                                                  980
```

Changing the Page Length

The page length is set at a default of 66 lines for most printers. This is perfect for 8 1/2- by 11-inch paper on most printers when you are printing at 6 lines to the inch. But if you change to 8 lines to the inch or use a different size paper, you need to change the page length. Also, some printers, such as Hewlett-Packard laser printers, only print 60 lines per page.

Which length you can enter depends on which release of 1-2-3 you are using. Release 1A supports page lengths of any size between 20 and 100 lines. Release 2 has the same upper limit but supports a page size as small as 10 lines. Releases 2.2 and 2.3 also have the same upper limit but support a page size as small as 1 line.

To make a change, select Print Printer Options Pg-Length (Page-Length in Release 1A) and type the length you want before pressing ENTER. This change in length affects only the current worksheet. If you bring a new worksheet into memory and want to use a different page length, you need to invoke the command again.

Setup Strings

Setup strings are special character sequences that instruct your printer to activate special features. These special features allow you to override such standard settings as printing 6 lines per inch or using standard typeface. If you are using Release 2 or higher, you will want to use the Allways or WYSIWYG add-ins (discussed in Chapter 12) since they provide these customization features through menu selections. In essence, these add-ins have learned the setup strings for your printer; you do not need to remember them. This makes the printer's features easier to activate.

Special Print Options

The print features you have worked with up to now are the backbone of 1-2-3's print capabilities. You will want to master them because you will use them every day to produce printed copies of all your models. A few additional Print features are used less frequently but are still important. They can help you solve the occasional problems for which the regular Print features offer no solution. These additional Print features include special commands for printing data to a file and printing cell formulas, as well as Print options that are hidden in the Worksheet menu. Other Release 2.3 features such as background printing and using the Print Settings dialog box to print your data are also included.

Writing to a File

You can write all your print output to a file by selecting Print File rather than Print Printer. When this is the only change you make, the file that is created is identical to the data printed to a printer. You can also print to a file with Release 2.3's Print Encoded option to include printer setup strings that are appropriate for your printer. Since the file data is frequently used for a purpose other than printing, some of the information included in the file may not be appropriate. When writing data to a file, ask yourself whether page breaks, borders, and other formatting options should be applied. If you decide that you do not want the format options included—that you want your data written to the file without regard to page breaks or any other formatting such as margins, headers, or footers — select Print File, a filename, and Options Other Unformatted. Later, if you want to include the formatting when you print the worksheet data, you will first need to select Print Printer Options Other Formatted to restore formatting for the worksheet.

Printing Cell Formulas

1-2-3 provides a quick way to print a list of the contents of worksheet cells. This means that what is displayed is not the result of a formula but the formula you originally entered. Other attributes of the cell, such as width and format, will also be included in the list. Cells that are blank will be excluded from the list. Since 1-2-3 prints the contents of only one cell on a line, you can see how long this list might be for even a medium-sized worksheet.

You can try this technique for a section of the current worksheet. Follow these steps:

1. Select Print Printer Range.
2. Type **G2.I10** and press ENTER.
3. Select Options Other Cell-Formulas.
4. Select Quit to leave the Options menu, and select Go.
5. Select Options Other As-Displayed Quit.
   This command sequence will set the display back to the normal mode in which the printout of the worksheet matches the display you see on the screen.
6. Select Page Align Quit.
   The list produced should look like the one in Figure 6-8.

Enhancing Print Control

The Print options you have reviewed thus far have been located within the Print menu. This is exactly where you would expect to look for this type of feature. There are several additional options that can significantly affect print results, but they are activated in unexpected ways. Two of the commands are found in the Worksheet menus; the other is entered directly in worksheet cells.

Figure 6-8.   *Printing cell formulas*

```
G2:  2301
H2:  (P2)  0.05
I2:  (C0)  +D2*(1+H2)
G3:  1605
H3:  (P2)  0.04
I3:  (C0)  +D3*(1+H3)
G4:  1402
H4:  (P2)  0.05
I4:  (C0)  +D4*(1+H4)
G5:  1750
H5:  (P2)  0.06
I5:  (C0)  +D5*(1+H5)
G6:  2301
H6:  (P2)  0.05
I6:  (C0)  +D6*(1+H6)
G7:  1605
H7:  (P2)  0.04
I7:  (C0)  +D7*(1+H7)
G8:  1402
H8:  (P2)  0.05
I8:  (C0)  +D8*(1+H8)
G9:  1750
H9:  (P2)  0.06
I9:  (C0)  +D9*(1+H9)
G10:  2301
H10:  (P2)  0.05
I10:  (C0)  +D10*(1+H10)
```

Page Breaks

If you have Release 2 or higher, you can add a page break at any location within a worksheet to ensure that the information following the page break starts on a new page. This feature can prevent awkward breaks that can occur, for example, between the last number in a column and the total for a column. Once 1-2-3 has processed the manual page break that you insert, it will again begin processing the automatic page breaks from the location of the manual page break to the end of the document. If you do not want this, you must insert additional manual breaks to again interrupt the automatic page-processing feature.

To insert a page break in the worksheet, move your cell pointer to the leftmost cell in the print range in the row that you want to force to the top of a new page. Then select Worksheet Page. This causes 1-2-3 to insert a blank line above the cell pointer and to place |:: in the cell that contained the cell pointer. The cell pointer then moves down a line and stays on the line that contains the data it was originally with. If the page break symbol is anywhere but at the left edge of the print range, 1-2-3 will ignore the page break request. If this symbol is at the left edge of the range and you choose a range that is more than one page across, the break will occur across all pages in the range.

If you are using Release 2 or higher, follow these steps to insert a page break in the employee listing:

1. Move the cell pointer to A25.

2. Select Worksheet Page.

    The entries in row 25 and subsequent rows are moved down a row. The reason is that this command inserted a blank row and placed the page break symbol in the cell where the cell pointer was located when you requested the command, as shown here:

```
A26: [W13] '213-78-5412                                              READY
                  A              B           C          D          E        F
      23  541-78-6754  Parker     Mary       $32,100 CHI          541
      24  897-90-8769  Smith      Larry      $61,250 ATL          342
      25  ::
      26  213-78-5412  Appel      Tom        $22,300 BOS          219
      27  516-75-8977  Jones      Paul       $45,900 DAL          900
```

3. Select Print Printer Go.

    1-2-3 remembers your range from last time and automatically expands it by one row when you add the page break.

4. Select Page Align Quit.

    If you want to delete the page break later, use the Worksheet Delete Row command on the row containing the page break symbol, or erase the contents of the cell containing the page break symbol.

Hiding Columns

1-2-3's Worksheet Column Hide command introduced in Chapter 3 can enhance the features of the Print commands by letting you define a wide print range and hide those columns that you do not want printed. The Print Range command allows you to define only one contiguous print range. By hiding columns, you can effectively extend this to many separate columns of information by hiding the columns that lie between the areas you want to print.

This feature is especially advantageous when a worksheet contains confidential information. This allows you to create a list of employee names, locations, and phone numbers even when the confidential information is in the midst of the data columns you need. The hidden columns will not destroy the data; it merely removes the unwanted data from view temporarily. When you want to restore hidden data, use the Worksheet Column Display command and select one or more adjacent columns that are marked by asterisks to indicate their hidden status.

If you have Release 2 or higher, follow these steps to print a copy of the employee data without the salary or social security number columns:

1. Move the cell pointer to column A.

2. Select Worksheet Column Hide.

    The control panel asks that you specify the columns to be hidden.

3. Press ENTER to select column A.

4. Move the cell pointer to column D, where the salary information is stored.

5. Select Worksheet Column Hide and press ENTER.

6. Select Print Printer Clear All to remove any prior print settings.

7. Select Range, select the range A1..G10, and press ENTER.

8. Select Go.

    The printed report will appear like the one in Figure 6-9.

9. Select Page Align Quit.

    This command will position the paper at the top of a form, zero the line count, and exit from the Print menu, placing you back in READY mode.

10. Select Worksheet Column Display and select a range containing cells in column A through D before pressing ENTER.

    You can use a single command to display both hidden columns by selecting a range that includes cells from the hidden columns you want to display. 1-2-3 does not care that some of the cells in the range are not hidden.

The Print Settings Dialog Box

Most of the Print commands can be entered in Release 2.3's Print Settings dialog box. As described in Chapter 3, you can activate this dialog box by pressing F2 (EDIT) or using the mouse to click on the dialog box. In the Range text box, you can enter the range to print. If you want to change from SETTINGS mode to POINT mode to point to the range to print, press F4 (ABS). The same is true for selecting a cell or range address for the Columns or Rows text boxes under Borders.

In the Header, Footer, and Setup string text boxes, enter the text 1-2-3 should use just as if you selected Header, Footer, or Setup from the Print Printer Options menu. The Page length text box and the four text boxes under Margins use the same numeric ranges as if you used their equivalent commands available in the Print Printer Options menu.

With the Print Settings dialog box, you can change the print destination after you enter the main Print menu by selecting a different option

6

Figure 6-9. *Printed worksheet with hidden columns*

Last Name	First Name	Location	Phone	Position
Jones	Paul	DAL	980	2301
Parker	Mary	CHI	541	1605
Smith	Larry	ATL	342	1402
Appel	Tom	BOS	219	1750
Jones	Paul	DAL	980	2301
Parker	Mary	CHI	541	1605
Smith	Larry	ATL	342	1402

button under Destination. For all choices except Printer, you will also need to supply a filename; 1-2-3 will supply the appropriate extension.

The Unformatted pages and List entries represent the options available with the Print Printer Options Other command. When the Unformatted pages check box is marked, it is equivalent to selecting Options Other Unformatted from the main Print menu. When this check box is not marked, it is equivalent to selecting Options Other Formatted from the main Print menu. When the List entries check box is marked, it is equivalent to selecting Options Other Cell-Formulas from the main Print menu. When this check box is not marked, it is equivalent to selecting Options Other As-Displayed from the main Print menu.

The dialog box also includes the currently selected interface (how the computer is connected to the printer), and the printer name. These options are changed with the Worksheet Global Default Printer command, which is beyond the scope of this book.

Printing in the Background

If you are printing a large worksheet, you may not want to wait until 1-2-3 finishes printing it before you continue using other 1-2-3 features. In Release 2.3, you can print in the background, which means 1-2-3 stores the information to be printed in a temporary file. While you are working with other 1-2-3 features, 1-2-3 sends the contents of the file to the printer. You must wait when you print a large file because your printer may not be able to print as quickly as 1-2-3 can send information to the printer.

To print in the background, you must execute the BPRINT program before you load 1-2-3. To print in the background with Release 2.3, follow these steps:

1. Select File Save, type **EMP_LIST**, and press ENTER to save the file.

2. Select Quit Yes to leave 1-2-3.

3. Type **BPRINT** and press ENTER to execute the BPRINT program from the 1-2-3 directory.

4. Type **123** and press ENTER to start 1-2-3 again.

5. Select File Retrieve, select EMP_LIST, and press ENTER to retrieve this file.

6. Select Print Background, type **TEMP** and press ENTER.

    The prompt for the filename is the file that 1-2-3 will use to temporarily store the information to be sent to the printer as 1-2-3 prints in the background. This file has an .ENC extension and is erased when 1-2-3 is finished printing it.

7. Select Clear All to erase all previous print settings.

8. Select Range, press HOME, type . (period), and press END and HOME before pressing ENTER to select the entire worksheet as the range to print.

9. Select Align, Go, Page, and Quit.

1-2-3 will print the information to a file called TEMP.ENC. When 1-2-3 returns to the READY mode, you can continue using other 1-2-3 features, including erasing the current worksheet or retrieving another one. As you continue to work with 1-2-3, 1-2-3 is sending information to the printer. When it is finished, TEMP.ENC will no longer exist.

You will not want to use Release 2.3's background printing if you are using another printer spooler, working in Windows, or printing on a network.

6

Review

- The Print menus provide the commands and options that you use to print your worksheets. Your initial selection from the Print menu is the destination. You can print directly to the printer or to a file. Once you select a destination, 1-2-3 displays the main Print menu. Release 2.3 features a Print Settings dialog box below the Print menu to change and display all of your print settings.

- To print a worksheet, you must use Range from the main Print menu to select the area of the worksheet, and then select Go. Select additional enhancements before selecting Go.

- Print settings are saved with the worksheet data.

- You can control the printer with options in the Print menus. These options include Line to advance the printer one line, Page to advance the printer to the next page, and Align to reset the line count for the printer to zero.

- 1-2-3 makes several assumptions about how it should print a worksheet. These are the default settings. They include the margins and the page length, although options under Print Printer Options allow you to change these assumptions.

- The Print Printer Clear command selects which of 1-2-3's print settings are removed or returned to the default setting.

- A report can contain headers and footers that appear on every page. Headers and footers can contain the "at" symbol (@) for the current date and the number sign (#) for the current page number. Vertical lines (¦) can divide the header or footer sections to left align, center, and right align header and footer text. With Releases 2.2 and above, you can enter a cell address or range name to use the contents of the cell referenced.

- The Print Printer Options Borders command selects the rows and columns that appear at the top and to the left of every page. Borders allow lengthy reports to retain their identification labels.

- You can activate specific Print features by using Allways or WYSIWYG rather than entering strings of setup codes.

- You can prevent columns from printing by hiding them with the Worksheet Column Hide command.

- You can document a worksheet by printing the cell formulas. Normally, 1-2-3 prints the worksheet data as it appears.

- The Worksheet Page command inserts a page break into a worksheet. When 1-2-3 prints a worksheet with a page break, it advances to the next page when it reaches the page break.

- You can suppress the headers, footers, and page breaks when you print by using the Print Printer Options Other Unformatted command. This option is often used to print to a file that you want to use in another computer package.

- You can print in the background and continue using 1-2-3 while your data is printing if you execute the BPRINT program from DOS, and select Background for the printing destination.

Commands and Keys

Entry	Action
F6 (WINDOW)	Removes and displays a dialog box
PB	Prints a worksheet in the background
PE	Prints an encoded file
PF	Print File sends print output to a file with a .PRN extension
PP	Print Printer sends print output to the printer
PPA	Print Printer Align resets 1-2-3's line count to zero
PPC	Print Printer Clear removes all print settings, the range setting, the borders print settings, or the settings for margins, page length, and setup string
PPG	Print Printer Go starts printing the current selected print area
PPL	Print Printer Line advances the printer one line
PPP	Print Printer Page advances the printer one page
PPQ	Print Printer Quit exits the sticky Print menu
PPR	Print Printer Range selects worksheet area to print
PPOB	Print Printer Options Border selects the border columns and rows
PPOF	Print Printer Options Footer sets the footer that appears at the bottom of each page
PPOH	Print Printer Options Header sets the header that appears at the top of each page

6

Entry	Action
PPOM	Print Printer Options Margins sets the top, bottom, left, and right margins, or removes all margins (Releases 2.2 and 2.3)
PPOO	Print Printer Options Other sets additional print formatting, such as printing the worksheet as it appears or the cell formulas, and including the headers, footers, and page breaks or suppressing them
PPOP	Print Printer Options Pg-Length sets the page length
PPOQ	Print Printer Options Quit exits the sticky Print Options menu
PPOS	Print Printer Options Setup sets the setup string for Release 2 or earlier
WCH	Worksheet Column Hide hides worksheet columns and does not print them
WP	Worksheet Page inserts a page break into a worksheet

7

Worksheet Functions

Your 1-2-3 models have already shown you the importance of formulas. Formulas are actually the power behind a spreadsheet package like 1-2-3. They record your calculations and use them over and over again. But there is a problem with formulas: It takes a long time to record them, and when you are recording a long series of calculations, it is easy to make a mistake. Fortunately, 1-2-3 has built-in functions to reduce these drawbacks. These functions are prerecorded formulas that have already been verified for accuracy. All you need to do is specify which data they should operate on, each time you use them. The built-in functions also provide features that go beyond the capabilities of formulas and let you access the system date as well as calculations such as the square root and tangent.

In this chapter you will examine how 1-2-3's built-in functions are recorded on the worksheet. You will learn the syntax and the rules that provide a powerhouse of almost 90 prerecorded calculations that you can access easily. You will learn about seven of the eight function categories into which all 1-2-3 functions are grouped. The eighth category includes the data-management functions. These functions will be covered in

Chapter 9, "Data-Management Basics." In this chapter, however, you will examine a variety of functions from the different categories and learn how to use them in application models. This chapter is longer than previous ones because it explains the many diverse functions and exposes you to some of the variety offered by these functions.

Built-in Function Basics

A few general rules apply to all functions, regardless of their type. Yet individual functions may differ from one another in terms of how they expect you to convey the data with which you want them to work. You need to know the general rules and the individual exceptions, as well as which category of function is likely to handle the task you wish to address. This section provides such information. Read it before addressing the individual function categories; it is an important first step.

General Rules

Since built-in functions are formulas, they are value entries in worksheet cells. There are several new rules that do not apply to formulas, all pertaining to the syntax of recording the different components of a function. A diagram of these components is shown in Figure 7-1. The first rule for function entry is that all functions must start with the symbol @. After entering the symbol @, you must include the special keyword that 1-2-3 uses to represent the function. This keyword is the function's name. You can enter it in either upper- or lowercase letters, but it must follow 1-2-3's spelling exactly.

Function Arguments

The next component within a function is the *arguments*. Arguments specify the data with which the function will work. Arguments are required by most functions, since most functions must be defined exactly in the order to be used. However, there are a few exceptions to this rule. Arguments must be enclosed within parentheses; but if the function you are using does not require arguments, you do not need to use parentheses.

Figure 7-1.   *Function format*

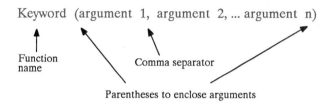

When using a function that requires multiple arguments, use a comma (,) to separate the arguments. With Release 2 and higher, a semicolon (;) is an acceptable alternative. Spaces cannot be used within a function; therefore, they are not valid as separator characters. The Worksheet Global Default Other International Punctuation command sets the argument separator, which may also include a period.

Function arguments can be provided as cell addresses, a range name that you assign to one or more cells, constants, formulas, and even other built-in functions. The examples you enter in this chapter may include some constants in functions to expedite data entry. However, it is preferable to store the data needed by the function in worksheet cells and to reference those cells within the function, since a change in an argument's value will not require that you edit the function. Much variety is possible; look at these examples of the @SUM functions, which total the values you provide as arguments:

    @SUM(9,4,8,7)
    @SUM(A1;D3;Y6;Z10)
    @SUM(Salaries,Rent_Exp,Equipment)
    @SUM(A1..H4)
    @SUM(A1,@SUM(B2..B3),Z2)

All five would be valid function entries, although you would need Release 2 or higher for the semicolons in the second example. As you progress through the exercises in this chapter, you will have an opportunity to use different types of arguments.

Most of the built-in functions expect value entries for arguments. Release 2 and higher have some built-in functions that require string or character data for arguments. You cannot substitute a type of data for an argument that is different from what 1-2-3 is expecting. For example, if you use 1-2-3's @SUM function, you will need to provide value entries as arguments. @SUM will add these together to produce a total. If you substitute label entries for the arguments, @SUM will return an error.

Types of Function Arguments

Different functions require different arguments and you use them in different ways. The three basic types of functions are those that require no arguments, those that expect a list of arguments in any sequence, and those that require a specific number of arguments in a specific order.

Examples of functions that require no arguments are @RAND, @NA, and @PI. *@RAND* is used to generate a random number and does not require any input. *@NA* is used when data is missing and you want to mark its position as not available at the current time. *@PI* is used to represent the special mathematical constant 3.14159265, which is used in geometric problem solving.

There are also a number of functions that expect a list of values for arguments. The entries in the list can be single cells or ranges of cells, and can be provided in any order you like. All the statistical functions fall within this category of argument types. For example, these two functions are equivalent:

@SUM(A1,B4,C5,D2..D10,F1,H2..M4)
@SUM(F1,H2..M4,A1,C5,D2..D10,B4)

In both cases all the individual values, as well as each of the values in the ranges, will be totaled to produce a single sum. Functions that allow this interchangeability of argument order specify "list" as their argument. For example, since @SUM accepts this type of argument, you can expect to see @SUM(list) when we discuss the syntax of this function in detail.

The last type of function argument is position dependent. Functions that require arguments in a specific order cannot have their arguments reordered without erroneous results occurring. For example, the @PMT function is designed to calculate the amount of a loan payment. The function requires three arguments: the principal, the interest, and the term of the loan. Later in the chapter you will see the functions specified like this:

@PMT(principal,interest,term of loan)

When using the function, you must provide the three arguments in this exact order.

Function Categories

There are seven categories of functions in 1-2-3, excluding the data management functions. The built-in functions are grouped into categories such that the functions within a category have some similarity of purpose. This logical grouping of functions allows you to focus easily on the special requirements of a category. It can also help you increase your knowledge of new functions whose purpose might be similar to some functions you are already using.

As you work through this section you will find that Releases 2 and higher have functions that do not occur in Release 1A. Release 2 uses a whole new category of functions for working with string data. Within individual categories, these new functions for users of Releases 2 and higher are appropriately marked.

Chapter Organization

The various function categories form the organizational structure of the rest of this chapter. You can use the remainder of the chapter in two ways. The preferred approach is to work through the exercises in each function category to become familiar with their use. There may be function categories that apply to your models, but unless you take an in-depth look at what they can do, you might not realize their potential. Another approach, if your time is limited, is to focus on function categories for which you have immediate use, then to come back and take a look at the other categories as you need them.

Statistical Functions

"Statistics" is a word that causes many people to be apprehensive. They recall statistics as complicated mathematical procedures from a required college math course. But 1-2-3's statistical functions need not invoke this sense of alarm. They are simple to use, and they compute the most basic statistical measures. These are computations that you perform every day without even thinking of them as "statistical." They include computations such as the average, sum, count, minimum value, and maximum value. Table 7-1 provides a list of the statistical functions.

1-2-3's statistical functions perform their magic on lists of values. Frequently these lists are a contiguous range of cells on the worksheet. Since the statistical functions all use a list for an argument, mastering one of these functions will allow you to use any of them.

Statistical functions can also be a series of individual values or a combination of a range and individual values. Blank cells can be included in the list, but all the values in the blank range will count as zeros. When a range contains multiple blank cells, 1-2-3 will ignore the cells that contain blanks.

The *@COUNT* function is an exception to the others in the statistical category. It counts the number of non-blank entries in the list. It can accept string values in its argument list in addition to numeric values. Entries that contain zero are not equivalent to blanks and will be counted. You must carefully choose which range of a worksheet to count since you want to select data for each record.

Table 7-1. *Statistical Functions*

Function Entry	Description
@AVG(list)	Computes an average for the values in list.
@COUNT(list)	Counts the non-blank entries in the list.
@MAX(list)	Locates the maximum value in the list.
@MIN(list)	Locates the minimum value in the list.
@STD(list)	Calculates the standard deviation of the values in the list.
@SUM(list)	Sums the values in the list.
@VAR(list)	Computes the variance for the values in the list.

You will use one model to test the @SUM function. It will contain information on the monthly sales for all the High Profits Company salespeople in region 4 as an example of the statistical functions. Follow these steps to create the basic model before continuing:

1. Select Worksheet Global Format Currency. Type **0** and press ENTER.

   This command establishes a Global format for the model before you enter data. Next you will format a section of the model that requires whole numbers to be displayed without the dollar sign.

2. Select Range Format Fixed. Type **0** and press ENTER. Type **B6.C9** or select the range with your mouse and press ENTER.

3. Move the cell pointer to column A and select Worksheet Column Set-Width. Press the RIGHT ARROW key four times and press ENTER.

   This action widens this column to 13 positions in preparation for the data to be entered. There is one more column to be widened. You could have entered these commands, like the formatting command, after you entered the data in the worksheet. However, if you know what your final report will look like, it is often best to perform the housekeeping tasks first.

4. Move the cell pointer to column G and select Worksheet Column Set-Width. Press the RIGHT ARROW key twice for a width of 11 and press ENTER.

   Once you have completed the housekeeping tasks, you are ready to begin entering the data for the model. You can use the model in Figure 7-2 as a guide to obtaining the entries, or you can use the detailed entries in step 5.

5. Place the following entries in the worksheet cells listed:

   C1: High Profits Quarterly Sales Figures
   D2: Region 4
   A5: Salesperson
   A6: Jason Rye
   A7: Paul Jones
   A8: Mary Hart
   A9: Tom Bush
   B5: District

B6:   1

B7:   3
B8:   1
B9:   2
B11:   TOTAL SALES
C5:   Branch
C6:   1705
C7:   3201
C8:   1705
C9:   4250
D4:   Jan
D5:   Sales
D6:   95800
D7:   56780
D8:   89675
D9:   91555
E4:   Feb
E5:   Sales
E6:   105650
E7:   52300
E8:   108755
E9:   87600
F4:   Mar
F5:   Sales
F6:   114785
F7:   48750
F8:   135400
F9:   92300
G4:   Qtr.
G5:   Total

6. Move the cell pointer to D4 and select Range Label Right. Move the cell pointer to G5 and press ENTER.

   Your model should match the one in Figure 7-2. You are now ready to use it in testing the @SUM function.

@SUM

The *@SUM* function totals a list of values. The syntax for the function is @SUM(list). The list can be a range of values, a list of individual values

Figure 7-2. *Right-aligning the labels*

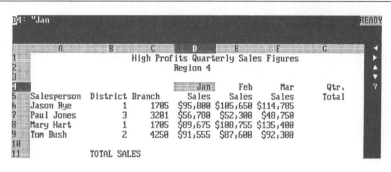

separated by commas (the argument separator), or a combination of the two.

@SUM is one of the most frequently used functions. It easily performs the laborious task of adding all of the numbers in a range without having to enter a long formula to add each value separately. It can be used just as easily to total a row of values. As with any other formula, once you have entered it for one row or column, you can easily copy it to other locations where you have similar needs.

Using @SUM to Total Sales   You will use the @SUM function to compute the total sales in each month and the total sales for each salesperson during the quarter. Follow these steps to add the sum computations:

1. Move the cell pointer to D11 and type **@SUM(**

2. Move the cell pointer to D6 and type a period (.) to lock the beginning of the range in place. Then move the cell pointer to D9 to highlight all the entries, as shown in Figure 7-3.

3. Type) and press ENTER to display the results shown in Figure 7-4.
    You have just entered your first @SUM function using the pointing method for specifying the range. If you prefer, you can always type the range address rather than pointing to it, but the pointing method helps prevent errors. As you point to the beginning of the range you want to sum, you get visual verification that this is the correct beginning location for the calculation. The same is true when you point to the end of the range, since

Figure 7-3.   *Highlighting the range*

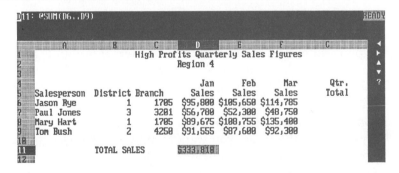

1-2-3 highlights everything in the range. Either way you choose
to enter the @SUM function, this function is a lot quicker than
typing +D6+D7+D8+D9 (the alternate method for computing
the desired result).

4. With the cell pointer in D11, select Copy. Press ENTER. Then move
   the cell pointer to E11 and type a period (.) before moving the cell
   pointer to G11 and pressing ENTER.

   This Copy command totaled all the columns for you, giving
   you maximum use from the one function you entered.

Figure 7-4.   *@SUM completed*

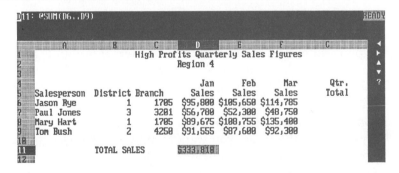

5. Move the cell pointer to G6. Type **@SUM(**. Move the cell pointer
    to D6. Type a period (.), then move the cell pointer to F6. Type
) and press ENTER.
          This formula produced a quarterly sales figure for Jason Rye.

6. Select Copy and press ENTER. Move the cell pointer to G7 and type
    a period (.). Then move the cell pointer to G9 and press ENTER.

This last instruction copies the totals down the column so that you now
have a total sales figure for each salesperson for the quarter.

Allowing for Expansion   The example you just completed computes the
monthly sales totals correctly. But if you want to add another salesperson
to the bottom of the list, you need to revise the @SUM formulas at the
bottoms of the columns so they include a reference to the cell containing
the figure for the new employee. You don't need to do this, however, if
you insert a blank row in the middle of the sum range and enter the new
data there. In that case, the new row will be included automatically since
1-2-3 will expand the range. The problem is that most of your additions
are at the very top or bottom of the range and 1-2-3 does not stretch the
range to include these new rows. However, you can overcome this revision
requirement by entering your initial sum formula a little differently.
    Leaving a blank row at the top and the bottom of the column you are
summing will give you the expansion capability you need. If your original
@SUM range includes a blank row at the top and bottom of the range, you
can insert blank rows at the top or bottom and 1-2-3 will adjust the range
for you. The blank rows do not affect the @SUM results since 1-2-3 treats
them as zero. To alter the original @SUM formula and then copy it across
again in preparation for adding a new salesperson, follow these steps:

1. Move the cell pointer to A6 and select Worksheet Insert Row.
    Then press ENTER to produce a display like the one shown in
    Figure 7-5.

2. Move the cell pointer to D12 and type **@SUM(D6..D11)**. Then
    press ENTER.

7

3. Select Copy and press ENTER. Move the cell pointer to E12 and type a period (.). Then move the cell pointer to G12 and press ENTER.

These new @SUM entries will allow you to expand your entries at either the top or the bottom of the database by placing the cell pointer in either row 6 or row 11 and using Worksheet Insert Row to add a new blank row for the new employee information.

4. Move the cell pointer to A7 and select Worksheet Insert Row and press ENTER.

5. Make these entries to add the new salesperson:

A7:   Jane Hunt
B7:   2
C7:   4590
D7:   87650
E7:   92300
F7:   93415
G7:   @SUM(D7..F7)

Figure 7-5.   *Inserting a blank row to facilitate expansion*

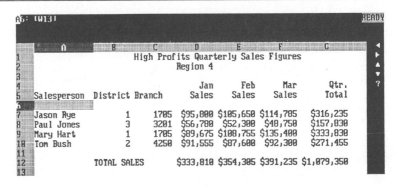

Notice in Figure 7-6 that the totals for each month have been adjusted to show the new results. This means that you will be able to add new entries in any location within the data and have the formula updated for you automatically. The district and branch values in this new line are formatted as fixed with 0 decimal place using the Range Format command. The original ranges that were formatted did not include these cells.

6. Move the cell pointer to B7 and select Range Format Fixed, type **0**, and press ENTER. Move the cell pointer to C7 and press ENTER. The results are shown in Figure 7-6.

Date and Time Functions

Date and time information is an important part of many business decisions. Date information is needed to tell if a loan is overdue or if there is still time remaining in the discount period for an invoice. Time information can be used to calculate the service time for various tasks or to log the delivery time for various carriers. Release 1A contains functions

Figure 7-6. *Total for the quarter*

```
G7: (W11) @SUM(D7..F7)                                          READY

         A         B        C         D        E        F          G         ◄
                            High Profits Quarterly Sales Figures             ►
 1                                   Region 4                                 ▲
 2                                                                            ▼
 3
 4                                   Jan      Feb      Mar       Qtr,         ?
 5  Salesperson  District Branch     Sales    Sales    Sales     Total
 6
 7  Jane Hunt       2       4590    $87,650  $92,300  $93,415   $273,365
 8  Jason Rye       1       1705    $55,800 $105,050 $111,786   $316,235
 9  Paul Jones      3       3201    $56,700  $52,300  $48,750   $157,830
10  Mary Hart       1       1705    $09,675 $100,755 $135,400   $333,830
11  Tom Bush        2       4250    $91,555  $87,600  $92,300   $271,455
12
13            TOTAL SALES          $421,460 $446,605 $484,650 $1,352,715
14
```

that support the date-stamping of worksheets and the use of dates in various calculations. Release 2 and higher have time functions that allow you to time-stamp a worksheet and perform calculations that involve time differences. The date and time functions are shown in Tables 7-2 and 7-3.

Working with Dates

1-2-3 can work with dates between January 1, 1900, and December 31, 2099. A unique serial number is assigned to each date: The number for January 1, 1900, is 1 and the number for December 31, 2099, is 73050. This serial date number represents the number of days since December 31, 1899. Although representing every date in terms of its distance from December 31, 1899, may seem strange, this is what provides the date arithmetic features of the package. Since all dates have the same comparison point, you can subtract one date from another to determine how many days apart they are. If a loan is due on a date whose serial date number is 32980 and today's serial date number is 32990, then it is obvious that the loan is overdue since the serial number for the due date is lower than today's serial date number.

All of this may seem a little confusing, but 1-2-3 can reduce some of the difficulty. You will not need to calculate or enter serial date numbers. 1-2-3 does that for you with its date functions. These functions also allow you to only extract part of a date, such as the month, for example.

1-2-3 also provides a format command that formats serial date numbers so they look presentable. You can choose from a variety of date formats that are familiar to you in the Range Format menu.

Table 7-2.   *Date Functions*

Function Entry	Description
@DATE(year,month,day)	Creates a date serial number.
@DATEVALUE(string)	Converts a text string in a valid date format to a date serial number.
@DAY(date serial number)	Extracts a day number from a date.
@MONTH(date serial number)	Extracts a month from a date.
@NOW	Enters the current date/time serial number in a cell.

Table 7-3.   *Time Functions*

Function Entry	Description
@HOUR(time serial number)	Extracts an hour from a time.
@MINUTE(time serial number)	Extracts the minute number from a time.
@NOW	Enters the current date/time serial number in a cell.
@SECOND(time serial number)	Extracts a second from a time.
@TIME(hour,minute,second)	Creates a time serial number.
@TIMEVALUE(string)	Converts a text string in a valid time format to a time serial number.

Date-Stamping the Worksheet

All releases of 1-2-3 provide a way for you to put a *date stamp* on the worksheet. With Release 1A, the function you will use is *@TODAY*. This function does not require arguments; when you enter it in a worksheet cell, it always accesses the system date and displays the serial date number for the system date in the worksheet cell where you entered the function. You can use Range Format to change the appearance of this serial date number to something more familiar.

Releases 2 and higher provide the identical feature, except that the function you enter is *@NOW*. You will learn some additional features of @NOW later, but for the moment the only important information about @NOW is that it enters a serial number in the worksheet cell.

The serial number contains two parts with @NOW. It consists of a whole number and a decimal fraction. The whole number represents the serial date number and the decimal fraction represents the current time. Both the date and time will be updated every time the current model is recalculated. If you save your worksheet file after entering the @NOW function, it will be available the next time you use the worksheet. Every time you boot your system, you will want to ensure that the correct date is being used so that your models can be time-stamped accurately.

You can try out this date-stamping feature with these instructions, but remember to adjust them for Release 1A by substituting @TODAY for @NOW:

1. Select Worksheet Erase Yes.

2. Type **@NOW** and press ENTER.

   If you are using Release 2 or higher, you should see a date number display that looks something like this:

   Your display will be slightly different, since it will be based on the date when you are using the worksheet. There will be an even greater difference if you are using Release 1A because the options are not the same. Once entered, this function will be updated every time the worksheet is recalculated; so if you work with the spreadsheet past midnight, you will see the date change. If you save the worksheet to disk, the next time you retrieve the worksheet an updated date will appear in the cell that contains @NOW.

3. Select Worksheet Column Set-Width and press the RIGHT ARROW key. Then press ENTER.

   This instruction widens the display so that you can view the date and time display in this column.

4. Select Range Format Date to produce this display:

   This display shows the various date-formatting options.

5. Use the RIGHT ARROW key and move to each of the menu options to view the date pattern that would be produced by selecting that option. Then select option 1 by typing **1** and pressing ENTER.

The serial date number should now be formatted with a pattern like this:

Remember that your display will look a little different, since your date is probably different from the one used for this example.

If you include @NOW in an area of your worksheet that you normally print, you will have an automatic date stamp on every printed report you create. Since you must retrieve the worksheet in order to print it, the date will automatically be updated every time the worksheet is printed.

Time-Stamping the Worksheet The *time-stamp* feature is accessed with the @NOW function and is only available for Release 2 and higher. The difference between using @NOW to date-stamp the worksheet and to time-stamp it is the format that you place on the result of the function. @NOW returns both a whole number and a fractional decimal. The whole number represents the number of days; the fractional decimal represents the portion of the current day that has already elapsed. If the decimal is 0.25, it represents a quarter of the day as having elapsed, or 6 A.M. A decimal fraction of 0.5 represents noon and 0.75 represents 6 P.M. Naturally, all the fractions between the ones listed also represent specific times within the day.

To see these time displays as other than decimal fractions, you will need to format the entries as Time. Do this by using Range Format Date Time, producing the following display for your selection:

```
A1: (D1) [W10] @NOW                                            MENU
(HH:MM:SS AM/PM)  2 (HH:MM AM/PM)  3 (Long Intn'l)  4 (Short Intn'l)
Lotus standard long form
      A          B          C          D          E          F          G        ◄
1  13-Feb-91                                                                      ►
2                                                                                 ▲
```

The variety of time displays will allow you to create a report that closely matches the organizational standards you are currently using.

You can time-stamp your worksheet by following these steps:

1. Move the cell pointer to A2, type **@NOW**, and press ENTER.
2. Select Range Format Date Time 2 and press ENTER.

Your display will be formatted like the following one, although the hour and minutes in the display will depend on the time of day when you make your entry.

Entering Dates   Many times when you work with dates, you do not want the current date. You want to record the date of hire, loan due date, or an upcoming anniversary date. 1-2-3 provides a way for you to record this date information in the worksheet. You use the *@DATE* function and supply arguments that represent the year, month, and day.

This function is the first one you have worked with where the arguments must be supplied in a specific order, as shown in this syntax:

@DATE(YR,MO,DA)

The first argument, *YR*, can be any number from 0 to 199, with 1900 represented by 0, 1989 by 89, and 2099 by 199. The month argument, *MO*, can be any number from 1 through 12. The day argument, *DA*, can be a number from 1 to 31, but it must be a valid day number for the month you select. For example, September cannot have 31 because 30 is the largest number of days in September. Since you will want the function to generate the correct serial date number for you, you must adhere exactly to the order shown for the three arguments.

You can put the @DATE function to work in a model that calculates the charges for video rentals. In this example, the charges will depend on the number of days that a patron has had the video. You will enter the customer number in column A, the video number in column B, the date the video was checked out in column C, and the date it was returned in column D. These last two entries will be used to compute the charges. The formula you use will subtract the date when the video was checked out from the date when it was returned and multiply the number of days by $2.25. Follow these steps to make the entries and apply the formats shown in Figure 7-7.

1. Select Worksheet Erase Yes and make these entries in the worksheet cells listed:

A4: Customer-id
A5: '21-876
A6: '23-765
A7: '34-651
B4: Video
B5: 350
B6: 610
B7: 212
C1: Every Rental Videos
C3: Checked
C4: Out
D3: Checked
D4: In
E3: Amount
E4: Due

Figure 7-7. *Result of subtracting two dates*

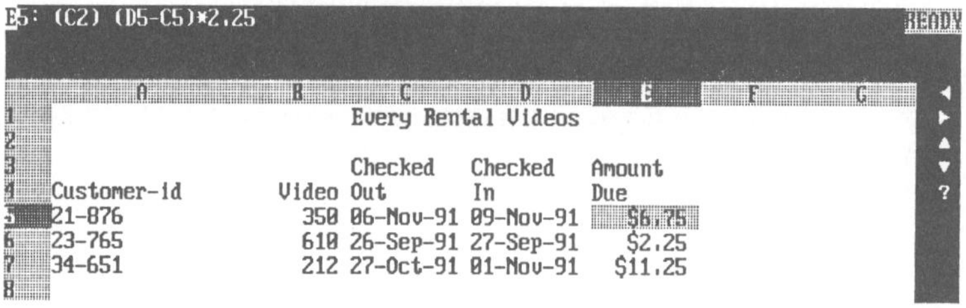

2. Now enter these dates using the @DATE function:

   C5:   @DATE(91,11,6)
   C6:   @DATE(91,9,26)
   C7:   @DATE(91,10,27)
   D5:   @DATE(91,11,9)
   D6:   @DATE(91,9,27)
   D7:   @DATE(91,11,1)

3. Move the cell pointer to E5 and type **(D5-C5)*2.25**.

   This entry is the computation for the cost of the rental. This computation is the number of days times the daily charge of $2.25. But first you must calculate the number of days by subtracting the two dates.

4. Select Copy and press ENTER. Move the cell pointer to E6 and type a period. Then move the cell pointer to E7 and press ENTER.

5. Press HOME, and select Worksheet Column Set-Width. Then type **16** and press ENTER.

6. Move the cell pointer to C5. Select Range Format Date 1. Type **C5.D7** and press ENTER.

7. Select Worksheet Column Column-Range Set-Width. Then press the RIGHT ARROW key and press ENTER to select columns C and D. Press the RIGHT ARROW key so that the dates display properly. Then press ENTER. If you are using Release 2, 2.01, or 1A, you must increase the width of each column separately.

8. Move the cell pointer to E5. Select Range Format Currency. Press ENTER. Then type **E5.E7** and press ENTER to produce the completed model shown in Figure 7-7.

Your model is now complete. However, you may be thinking that it would be just as easy to type the date in the way you want to see it by using a label entry such as "Apr-14-91." While this solution seems reasonable, the problem is that your entry would be a label and labels cannot be used in arithmetic operations. You would not be able to subtract two dates or compare the date against the current date without converting these label entries to dates.

Entering Times   Just as you must use a function to enter dates, you must also use one for making time entries on the worksheet. If you enter a time representation without using the special function, you will not be able to use it in time computations. The function available in Release 2 and higher that is used to make a time entry on the worksheet is *@TIME*. It uses this syntax:

@TIME(hour,minute,second)

In this function, *hour* is a number between 0 and 23, with 0 representing midnight and 23 representing 11 P.M. *Minute* is a number between 0 and 59, and *second* has the same acceptable value range as *minute*.

Follow these instructions to create a worksheet that measures the time elapsed from when a vehicle is logged in for repair to when it leaves the repair shop.

1. Make these entries:

A3:	Job
A4:	Number
A5:	1
A6:	2
A7:	3
A8:	4
B1:	QUICK CAR REPAIR November 12, 1991
B3:	Time
B4:	In
C4:	Repair
C5:	Tire
C6:	Brakes
C7:	Steering
C8.	Lube
D3:	Time
D4:	Out
E3:	Elapsed
E4:	Time

Your model should now look like this:

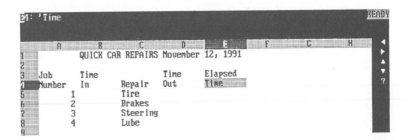

2. Move the cell pointer to B5 and select Range Format Date Time 2. Move the cell pointer to B8 and press ENTER.

3. Move the cell pointer to D5 and select Range Format Date Time 2. Move the cell pointer to D8 and press ENTER.

4. Move the cell pointer to E5 and select Range Format Date Time 4. Move the cell pointer to E8 and press ENTER.

5. Move the cell pointer to B5, then type **@TIME(8,5,0)**, and press the DOWN ARROW key.

   Notice the zero entry for seconds. It is used as a place marker even when you do not have a special value to enter.

6. Type **@TIME(8,10,0)**, and press the DOWN ARROW key.

7. Type **@TIME(8,30,0)**, and press DOWN ARROW.

8. Type **@TIME(8,32,0)**, and press ENTER to produce this display:

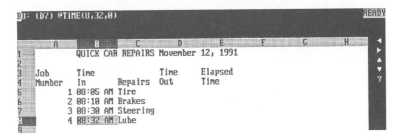

9. Complete the remaining time entries for the times the vehicles were completed by making these entries in column D:

        D5: @TIME(9,17,0)
        D6: @TIME(10,34,0)
        D7: @TIME(13,18,0)
        D8: @TIME(9,44,0)

       Notice the use of a 24-hour clock representation, with the number 13 used to represent 1 P.M.

10. Move the cell pointer to E5, type **+D5−B5,** and press ENTER.

       This computes the elapsed time for the repair of the first vehicle. When you copy this formula for the remaining entries, your job will be finished.

11. Select Copy and press ENTER. Move the cell pointer to E6 and type a period (.). Then move the cell pointer to E8 and press ENTER to produce these results:

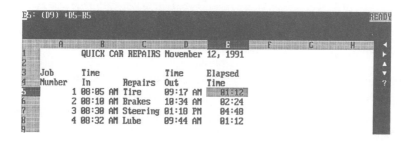

12. Select File Save, type **TIME**, and press ENTER.

13. Select Worksheet Erase Yes.

String Functions

       String functions are a feature that was added in Release 2. They provide a variety of character-manipulation formulas that give you flexibility in rearranging text entries. You can work with the entire label entry for a cell with the string functions, or with just a part of it. The functions in this category can be real lifesavers when you have to correct data-entry errors. Table 7-4 provides a list of all the string functions. You will work with abbreviated examples that correct errors in one or two entries, but the same formula you create for one entry could be copied down a column

Table 7-4.   *String Functions*

Function Entry	Description
@CHAR(x)	Returns an LICS character corresponding to x.
@CLEAN(string)	Removes control characters from the string.
@CODE(string)	Returns the LICS code of the first character in the string.
@EXACT(string1,string2)	Returns 1 if string1 and string2 are identical and 0 if they are not identical.
@FIND(search string, string,start-number)	Returns the position of the search string in the string.
@LEFT(string,n)	Extracts n number of characters from the left side of string.
@LENGTH(string)	Returns the number of characters in the string.
@LOWER(string)	Returns the string in lowercase.
@MID(string,start-number,n)	Returns n characters from the middle of string beginning with position start-number.
@N(range)	Returns the entry in the first cell of range as a value.
@PROPER(string)	Returns string in propercase.
@REPEAT(string,n)	Repeats the string n times.
@REPLACE(original, start,n,new)	Replaces n characters in original with new beginning at position start.
@RIGHT(string,n)	Extracts n characters from the right side of string.
@S(range)	Returns the entry from the first cell in range as a label.
@STRING(x,n)	Converts the value x to a label with n decimal places.
@TRIM((string)	Removes beginning trailing, and extra spaces from string.
@UPPER(string)	Returns string in uppercase.
@VALUE(string)	Converts a string that looks like a value to a value.

to correct a large portion of a worksheet. You will have the opportunity to work with functions that change an entry from uppercase to lowercase or even proper noun format. You will also learn how to repeat a character string.

When the string values you are working with are used as arguments for the string functions, they must be enclosed in quotation marks ("). However, when these same entries are referenced by a cell address, no quotation marks are required. For example, the function @UPPER converts text entries to uppercase. If you want to include the string jim smith as an argument in this function, you need to record it as @UPPER("jim smith"). However, if you store jim smith in A5, you can write @UPPER(A5), without quotation marks.

Some string functions produce another string as a result of the function. Other string functions produce numeric results that are equivalent to a position number within the string.

@UPPER

The *@UPPER* function will change selected characters to uppercase. This feature allows you to convert worksheet text data to all capital letters, if that is your preference. The syntax of the function is @UPPER(string).

Make these entries to try the function:

1. Move the cell pointer to A1, type **jim smith**, and move the cell pointer to A2.

2. Type **Bill Brown** and move the cell pointer to A3.

3. Type **JANE JONES** and move the cell pointer to B1.

4. Select Worksheet Global Column-Width, type **12**, and press ENTER.

5. Type **@UPPER(A1)** and press ENTER.

6. Select Copy and press ENTER. Move the cell pointer to B2, type a period (.), move the cell pointer to B3, and press ENTER.

7

The converted data appears like this:

@LOWER

The *@LOWER* function converts text entries to all lowercase. Regardless of whether the text is uppercase, lowercase, or in proper noun format (with the first letter capitalized), the @LOWER function produces a string that is guaranteed to be lowercase.

You can use the example you created to test the @UPPER function to test the @LOWER function. Follow these steps to add a new column to the model:

1. Move the cell pointer to C1, type **@LOWER(A1)**, and press ENTER.

2. Select Copy and press ENTER. Move the cell pointer to C2, type a period (.), move the cell pointer to C3, and press ENTER to produce this display:

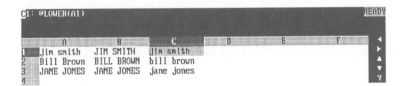

@PROPER

The *@PROPER* function converts text into the format you expect to see for proper nouns. The first letter in each word is capitalized and the remaining letters of the word are displayed in lowercase. This is another function you can use to establish consistency in the data on your work-sheet. The model that was used to test the @UPPER and @LOWER functions can be used with @PROPER. Add another column to this model by following these instructions:

1. Move the cell pointer to D1, type **@PROPER(A1)**, and press ENTER.

2. Select Copy and press ENTER. Move the cell pointer to D2, type a period (.), move the cell pointer to D3, and press ENTER to produce this display:

```
D1: @PROPER(A1)                                                      READY

         A            B            C            D         E        F      ◄
1  Jim smith    JIM SMITH    Jim smith    Jim Smith                       ►
2  Bill Brown   BILL BROWN   bill brown   Bill Brown                      ▲
3  JANE JONES   JANE JONES   jane jones   Jane Jones                      ▼
4                                                                         ?
```

3. Select File Save, type **CASE**, and press ENTER.

4. Select Worksheet Erase Yes to clear the worksheet.

@REPEAT

The *@REPEAT* function is used to duplicate a character string a specified number of times. The primary purpose of this function is to improve the appearance of the worksheet. @REPEAT can create dividing lines between the assumptions of a report and the display of the final results. In one sense, @REPEAT is similar to the backslash character (\) because it repeats labels. It differs in the sense that \ is restricted to filling a single cell, whereas @REPEAT can extend across many worksheet cells. In addition, @REPEAT can complete the dividing line with the entry of one function, whereas the \ character normally requires repeated entries or copying to complete its task.

If you wish, you can go back to the sales projections you entered in an earlier chapter and replace the asterisks with the backslash, using a new character sequence. For now, enter @REPEAT in a worksheet cell to see how it works. Follow these steps:

1. Move the cell pointer to A7.

2. Type **@REPEAT("+ −",36)** and press ENTER.

7

Your display should match this:

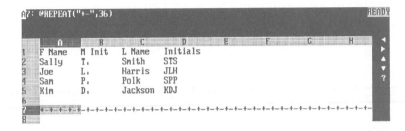

Notice that quotation marks were required in the function because a string value was placed in the function as an argument.

Math Functions

1-2-3's math functions perform both simple calculations and more complex operations suited to an engineering or manufacturing application. Rather than look at the trigonometric functions and more complex operations, you will benefit most from the general-purpose examples emphasized by the exercises in this section. You will look at the value of a number, and learn how to overcome rounding problems. Table 7-5 is a complete list of math functions.

@ABS

The *@ABS* function returns the positive or absolute value of a number, without regard to whether the number is positive or negative. The function is useful when you are concerned with the relative size of numbers and do not care if the number is positive or negative.

An example of this function is illustrated by the need of retail establishments to monitor cash overages and shortages in their registers. Consistent cash overages and shortages indicate a cash-control problem that should be corrected. Simply adding the overages and shortages doesn't always work: They might cancel each other out. However, examining the absolute value of the overages and shortages reveals the totalamount of the differences.

Table 7-5. *Math Functions*

Function Entry	Description
@ABS(x)	Returns the absolute value of x.
@ACOS(x)	Returns the arc cosine of the cosine of x.
@ASIN(x)	Returns of arc sine of the sine of x.
@ATAN(x)	Returns the arc tangent of the tangent of x.
@ATAN2(x,y)	Returns the arc tangent of the tangent of y/x.
@COS(x)	Returns the cosine of x.
@EXP(x)	Calculates the value of 2.718282 raised to the x power.
@INT(x)	Returns the integer portion of x.
@LN(x)	Calculates the natural log of x.
@LOG(x)	Calculates the base 10 log of x.
@MOD(x,y)	Returns the remainder when x is divided by y.
@PI	Returns the value 3.1415926536.
@RAND	Returns a random number between 0 and 1.
@ROUND(x,n)	Rounds the value x to the n place.
@SIN(x)	Calculates the sine of the angle x.
@SQRT(x)	Returns the square root of x.
@TAN(x)	Returns the tangent of the angle x.

Follow these instructions to set up a model for the Hot Dog House Register:

1. Select Worksheet Erase Yes and then Worksheet Global Format Currency. Press ENTER to accept the default of two decimal places.

2. Place these entries in worksheet cells:

   A5:   Monday
   A6:   Tuesday
   A7:   Wednesday
   A8:   Thursday
   A9:   Friday
   A10: Saturday
   A11: Sunday
   A13: TOTAL DIFFERENCE FOR THE WEEK:
   C1:   Hot Dog House Register
   C2:   Week of November 10, 1991

7

> C4: Over/Under
> C5: 42
> C6: −35
> C7: 22.78
> C8: −57
> C9: 12.58
> C10: .58
> C11: −2.10
> E4: Absolute Value

3. Move the cell pointer to E5, type **@ABS(C5)**, and press ENTER.
   This step computes the absolute value of the entry in C5.

4. Select Copy and press ENTER. Move the cell pointer to E6, type a
   period (.), move the cell pointer to E11, and press ENTER.
   Once you have completed this step, all the daily cash differences have been converted to their absolute values and stored in
   column E.

5. Move the cell pointer to E13, type **@SUM(E5.E11)**, and press
   ENTER to produce the results shown in Figure 7-8.

This step computes a total of the cash differences, without regard to
whether they were positive or negative, by using the absolute value of each

Figure 7-8.   *Using @ABS*

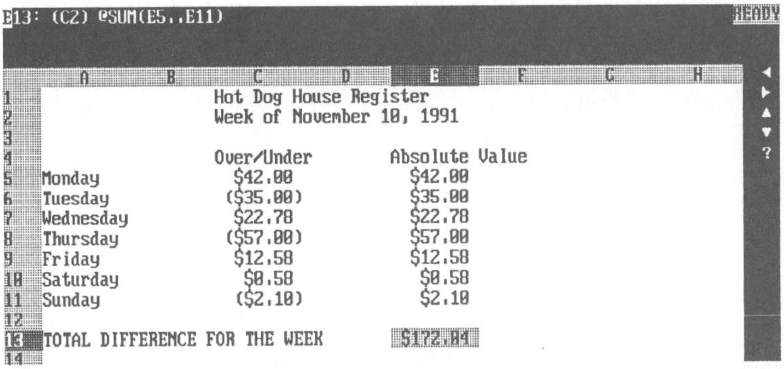

day's total in the sum calculation. This method prevents the cash differences from partially canceling each other out and seeming like less of a problem than they actually are.

@ROUND

The *@ROUND* function actually alters the way a number is stored internally by letting you specify the number of decimal places you want. This function can solve some of the problems caused by the discrepancy between how numbers are stored and the format you use to display them. In Chapter 3, "Changing the Worksheet Appearance," you learned that you could use the format commands (Worksheet Global Format and Range Format) to display numbers with a varying number of decimal places. But the problem with these changes is that the full internal accuracy is still maintained despite the change in the display appearance. The greater internal storage accuracy of the numbers being added can cause totals at the bottom of a column to appear as though they do not add properly.

Use the following steps to create a model that shows this discrepancy, and then apply the @ROUND function to the formulas in the model so that the internal accuracy is equal to the numbers that are displayed.

1. Make these entries:

    A2:   Product 1 Sales
    A3:   Product 2 Sales
    A4:   Product 3 Sales
    C1:   Price
    C2:   33.3333
    C3:   67.5068
    C4:   3.3335
    D1:   Quantity
    D2:   100
    D3:   50
    D4:   100
    E1:   Total $

2. Move the cell pointer to C2 and select Range Format Currency, type **4**, and press ENTER. Press the END key, followed by the DOWN ARROW key, and press ENTER.

7

3. Move the cell pointer to E2 and select Range Format Currency, type **0**, and press ENTER. Type **E2.E5** and press ENTER.

   The END and DOWN ARROW sequence will not work for this Format operation, since all the cells in the column are empty at this time and 1-2-3 would format to the bottom of the column.

4. Type **+C2*D2** and press ENTER.

   This formula computes the total cost of the purchase. A whole number is displayed; however, a decimal fraction exists in the number stored internally because of the decimals in the price.

5. Select Copy and press ENTER. Move the cell pointer to E3, type a period (.), move the cell pointer to E4, and press ENTER.

6. Move the cell pointer to E5 and type **@SUM(E2.E4)**. Press ENTER to produce these results:

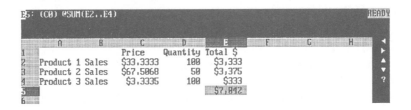

The column E figures suggest that the total should be $7041, not the $7042 shown. The difference of 1 is caused by the rounding discrepancy that occurs when the total $ numbers are displayed. The @SUM function is computed from the numbers that are stored, not those that are displayed. The @ROUND function can solve this problem. But first you need to learn a little more about its syntax.

The format of the @ROUND function is

@ROUND(number to be rounded, place of rounding)

The number to be rounded can be a number, a reference to a cell that contains a number, or a formula that evaluates as a number. The place of rounding is a positive or negative number that specifies the place of rounding. Rounding to the nearest whole number uses 0 as the place of rounding. Rounding to decimal places to the right of a whole number uses positive integers for each place farther to the right. Rounding to the left of the whole-number position is represented by negative integers. Table 7-6 shows the effect of some of the rounding options on a number.

Table 7-6.   *Effects of Various Rounding Options*

Number	Rounded Number	Formula for Rounding
12345.678123	12345.6781	@ROUND(A3,4)
	12345.68	@ROUND(A3,2)
	12345.7	@ROUND(A3,1)
	12346	@ROUND(A3,0)
	12300	@ROUND(A3,−2)
	10000	@ROUND(A3,−4)

You can apply this @ROUND function to the total $ computations with these steps:

1. Move the cell pointer to E2 and press F2 (EDIT).

2. Press the HOME key to move to the front of the entry. Press DEL to delete the +.

3. Type **@ROUND(**

4. Press the END key, type **,0)**, and press ENTER.

5. Select Copy and press ENTER. Move the cell pointer to E3, type a period (.), move the cell pointer to E4, and press ENTER to produce these results:

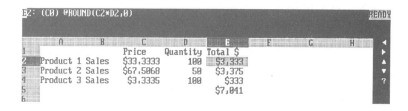

The addition of @ROUND to each formula makes the column total agree with the numbers displayed. This is because you altered the internal accuracy of each of the numbers to force it to match the display.

6. Select File Save, type **ROUND**, and press ENTER.

7. Select Worksheet Erase Yes.

Many worksheets will have @ROUND added to most of the formulas. To use it, follow the same procedure used in this example, making each formula an argument to the @ROUND function.

Special Functions

1-2-3's special functions are grouped together because they do not fit neatly into any of the other function categories. Some of them are used to trap error conditions. Others count the number of rows in a range or allow you to choose a value from a list of options. Still others let you examine the contents of worksheet cells closely, thus providing information about a cell's value or other attributes. For the most part, this group can be thought of as a smorgasbord of sophisticated features. Table 7-7 provides a complete list of the special functions.

@NA

This function causes *NA* ("not available") to appear in the cell where @NA is entered. Its impact does not stop there: All worksheet cells that reference this cell will also have the value NA. There are no arguments for this function: Its syntax is @NA.

@NA is used as a flag to remind you to complete missing entries before finalizing a report. Since cells that reference this cell take on the value NA, there is no way for you to erroneously assume that a total reflects all data entries.

Create a model that uses the @NA feature to flag missing grades for an instructor. All students who miss an exam have their grade entered as @NA rather than as a test score. This means that their final grade point average will show as NA since it will reference each of the exam grades, including the one recorded as @NA. An instructor could use this model at the end of a semester to identify those students who have not yet made up missing exams. The instructor would have the option to change the

Table 7-7. *Special Functions*

Function Entry	Description
@@(location)	Returns the address of location.
@?	Indicates an unknown add-in @function.
@CELL(attribute,range)	Returns specific information about the first cell in range as indicated by attribute.
@CELLPOINTER(attribute)	Returns information about the current cell as specified by attribute.
@CHOOSE(x,list)	Returns the x entry from list.
@COLS(range)	Returns the number of columns in the range.
@ERR	Returns the value ERR.
@HLOOKUP(x,range,row-offset)	Returns a value from range from the row indicated by row-offset.
@INDEX(range,column-offset,row-offset)	Returns an entry from the table range as indicated by the two offsets provided.
@NA	Returns the value NA.
@ROWS(range)	Returns the number of rows in range.
@VLOOKUP(x,range,column-offset)	Returns a value from range from the column indicated by column-offset.

missing exam grade to a 0, or to record an Incomplete for the student's final grade. Follow these steps to complete the model:

1. Make these entries to add a heading for each category and to place the students' names in the model after entering Worksheet Column Set-Width to End pressing ENTER:

C1:	Fall Semester 1991
A3:	Student
A4:	B. Black
A5:	S. Conners
A6:	F. Dalton
B3:	Exam 1
C3:	Exam 2
D3:	Exam 3
E3:	Final
F3:	Average

7

2. Record these grades for the first exam:

    B4:   75
    B5:   67
    B6:   78

3. Record these entries for the second exam:

    C4:   @NA
    C5:   78
    C6:   90

Since B. Black did not take exam 2, @NA was recorded for that student's score. Recording NA will not give you the same effect. @NA is a value entry that will affect calculations referencing the cell. NA is a label entry and cannot be used in arithmetic calculations.

4. Record these grades for the third exam and the final exam:

    D4:   82
    D5:   72
    D6:   89
    E4:   88
    E5:   81
    E6:   92

5. Move the cell pointer to F4, type **@AVG(B4.E4)**, and press ENTER.

6. Enter Range Format Fixed 1 and press ENTER twice.

7. Select Copy and press ENTER. Move the cell pointer to F5, type a period (.), move the cell pointer to F6, and press ENTER.

    The results are shown in Figure 7-9. Notice that the average for B. Black displays as NA. This average is not available because one of the values needed to compute it is missing.

8. Select File Save, type **NA**, and press ENTER.

9. Select Worksheet Erase Yes.

Figure 7-9. *Using @NA*

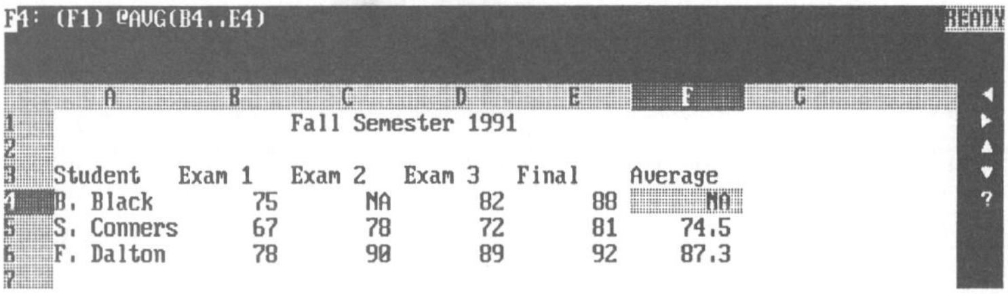

Financial Functions

1-2-3 provides an entire category of functions to use in investment calculations and other calculations concerned with the time value of money. You can use these financial functions to monitor loans, annuities, and cash flows over periods of time. With Release 2 and higher, some depreciation calculations are also included in these financial functions. You can quickly compare various financial alternatives since you can rely on the function to supply the correct formulas. As with the other functions, all you need to supply are arguments to tailor the calculations to your exact needs.

When you use financial functions, it is very important that all the arguments and the result use the same unit of time. For example, a function to compute the amount of a loan payment will require you to decide whether you want to calculate the payment amount on a yearly, quarterly, or monthly basis. Once you decide on one of these or on some other unit of time, you must apply it consistently across all arguments. If you choose to compute a monthly payment amount, the interest rate must be expressed as a monthly rate. Likewise, the term should be expressed as a number of months. Table 7-8 is a complete list of the financial functions.

@PMT

The *@PMT* function calculates the appropriate payment amount for a loan. The syntax for this function is

@PMT(principal,interest,term of loan)

Table 7-8.   *Financial Functions*

Function Entry	Description
@CTERM(int,fut-value,pres-value)	Number of compounding periods required to attain a future value.
@DDB(cost,salvage,life,period)	Calculates depreciation with the double-declining balance method.
@FV(payments,interest,term)	Calculates a future value for an investment.
@IRR(guess,range)	Calculates an internal rate of return.
@NPV(interest,range)	Calculates the net present value of a series of cash flows.
@PMT(principal,interest,term)	Calculates a loan payment amount.
@PV(payments,interest,term)	Determines the present value.
@RATE(fut-value,pres-value,term)	Calculates the interest rate needed to reach a future value.
@SLN(cost,salvage,life)	Calculates the straight-line depreciation.
@SYD(cost,salvage,life,period)	Calculates the sum-of-the-years-digits depreciation.
@TERM(payments,interest,fut-value)	Calculates the number of periods needed to reach a future value.

The *principal* is a numeric value that represents the amount of money borrowed. *Interest* is a numeric value that represents the interest rate. To specify a 9% interest rate, you can use 9% or .09. *Term* is the number of payments for the loan. It is a numeric value and should be expressed in the same time period as the interest.

You can test this function in building a model that determines whether you can afford the monthly payments on your dream home. This model will also use range name references for the function arguments. You learned how to apply these names to cells in Chapter 2, "Defining Your Calculations," but the process will be reviewed in this example as you apply range names to the principal, interest, and term for the loan before entering the function. Complete these steps:

1. Make the following entries:

    A1:   Principal:
    A2:   Interest:

> A3: Term:
> A5: Monthly Payments:
> C1: 150000
> C2: .09
> C3: 20
> D3: years

2. Move the cell pointer to C1, select Range Name Create, type **PRINCIPAL**, and press ENTER twice.

 This step applies the range name PRINCIPAL to C1.

3. With the cell pointer still in C1, select Range Format Currency and press ENTER twice.

4. Move the cell pointer to C2, select Range Name Create, type **INTEREST**, and press ENTER twice.

 This step applies the range name INTEREST to C2.

5. With the cell pointer in C2, select Range Format Percent and press ENTER twice.

6. Move the cell pointer to C3, select Range Name Create, type **TERM**, and press ENTER twice.

 This step applies the range name TERM to C3.

7. With the cell pointer in C5, select Range Format Currency and press ENTER twice.

8. Select Worksheet Column Set-Width, type **12**, and press ENTER.

9. Type **@PMT(**

10. Press F3 (NAME), highlight PRINCIPAL, and press ENTER. Type a comma (,).

11. Press F3 (NAME), highlight INTEREST, and press ENTER. Type /**12** to convert the annual interest rate to a monthly rate. Type a comma (,).

12. Press F3 (NAME), highlight TERM, and press ENTER. Type *****12)** to convert the number of years to number of months. Press ENTER.

 This function shows the use of formulas for function arguments since the interest rate must be divided by 12 to convert the annual percentage to a monthly figure, and the term must be multiplied by 12 to express it as months. 1-2-3 does not object to the use of these formulas since they return the value entries needed for each of the function arguments. The result is shown here:

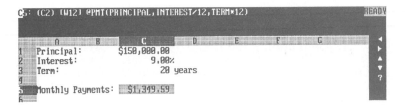

13. Select File Save, type **PAYMENT,** and press ENTER.
14. Select Worksheet Erase Yes.

Logical Functions

1-2-3's logical functions allow you to build conditional features into your models. The functions in this category return logical (true or false) values as the result of the condition tests they perform. They are a powerful addition to 1-2-3 because they allow you to alter calculations based on conditions in other locations of the worksheet. This flexibility lets you construct models patterned after "real world" business conditions, where exceptions are prevalent.

These functions let you have more than one calculation for commission payments, purchase discounts, FICA tax, or any other computation requiring multiple calculations that depend on other values in the worksheet. Table 7-9 is a complete list of the logical functions.

@IF

The example you will explore creates a salary model. With this model, you can estimate the various components of salary expense. After projecting a salary increase with a percentage growth factor, you can also estimate other salary expenses, such as your FICA contribution as an employer or

Table 7-9.   *Logical Functions*

Function Entry	Description
@FALSE	Returns a logical 0.
@IF(condition,x,y)	Tests a condition and returns x if it is true and y if it is false.
@ISAFF(name)	Tests to see if name is a defined add-in @function. Returns 1 if it is and 0 if it is not.
@ISAPP(name)	Tests name to see if it is an attached add-in. Returns 1 if it is and 0 if it is not.
@ISERR(x)	Tests x for the value ERR and returns a 0 for false and a 1 for true.
@ISNA(x)	Tests x for the value NA and returns a 0 for false and a 1 for true.
@ISNUMBER(x)	Tests x to see if it is a value and returns 0 for false and 1 for true.
@ISSTRING(x)	Tests x to see if it is a string and returns 0 for false and 1 for true.
@TRUE	Returns the logical value 1.

the cost of the benefits you are supplying for different personnel classifications. You can easily adapt the model to meet other conditions and situations—either by adding new expense categories (patterning calculations after the examples provided) or by altering the formulas for the existing calculations. Since this model is dependent on the @IF function, it is a good idea to review how the @IF function works before starting the model.

The @IF function lets you test a condition to determine the appropriate value for a cell. @IF is one of the most powerful built-in functions because it frees you from the limitation of deciding on one formula for a cell. Now you can set up two different values for a cell and determine which one to use, based on other conditions in the worksheet. You can create two or more discount levels, payroll deductions, commission structures, or other calculations involving more than one alternative.

The @IF function uses three arguments, in this sequence:

@IF(condition to test,value if true,value if false)

The first argument, *condition to test,* can be any logical expression that can be evaluated as true or false. Examples are A1 > 9, C2 = G10, and A2 + B6 > C3*H12. The expression returns a value of true only if the condition specified is met. For example, in the first expression, true will be returned only if A1 is greater than 9. If this expression evaluates as true, the cell will take on the value specified in the second argument of the function.

The second argument for the @IF function, *value if true,* is the value the cell will use if the condition is true and can take several forms. It can be an actual numeric value, a formula that needs to be calculated, or another @IF statement to be checked if multiple levels of conditions must be met before an action is determined. In Release 2 and higher, this argument can be a string value as long as it is enclosed in double quotation marks.

The third argument, *value if false,* is the value the cell containing the @IF statement will assume if the condition in the function is false. All the conditions mentioned for *value if true* also apply here.

Release 2 and higher also allow strings to be used with the logical @IF condition. For example, you could have an entry such as @IF(A10 = "Chicago",F2,G2). If A10 contains Chicago, the cell containing this entry will take on the value of F2. If A10 contains anything else, the cell containing the function will be equal to G2.

Salary Model Entries

To minimize your entries, enter data for only a few employees. Then a simple Copy operation and additional data entry allow you to expand this model to include as many employees as you want. You will be making entries for the model shown in Figure 7-10. Follow these explicit instructions for your entries:

1. Select Worksheet Erase Yes to clear the worksheet.

2. Select Worksheet Column Set-Width, type **13**, and press ENTER. This will widen column A to accept the name entries.

Figure 7-10. *Completed salary model*

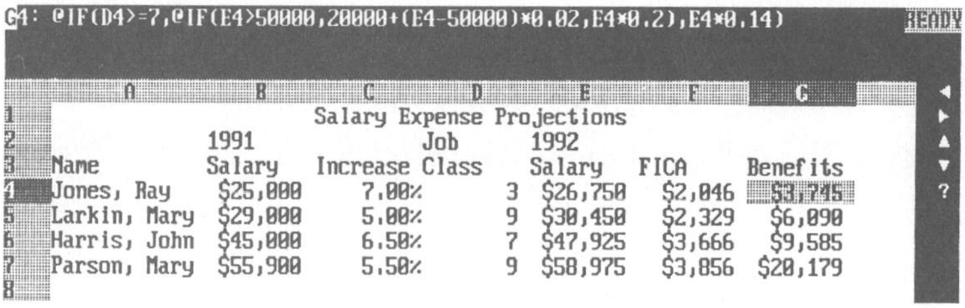

G4: @IF(D4>=7,@IF(E4>50000,20000+(E4-50000)*0.02,E4*0.2),E4*0.14) READY

	A	B	C	D	E	F	G
1			Salary Expense Projections				
2		1991		Job	1992		
3	Name	Salary	Increase	Class	Salary	FICA	Benefits
4	Jones, Ray	$25,000	7.00%	3	$26,750	$2,046	$3,745
5	Larkin, Mary	$29,000	5.00%	9	$30,450	$2,329	$6,090
6	Harris, John	$45,000	6.50%	7	$47,925	$3,666	$9,585
7	Parson, Mary	$55,900	5.50%	9	$58,975	$3,856	$20,179
8							

3. Make these entries on the worksheet:

A3: Name
A4: Jones, Ray
A5: Larkin, Mary
A6: Harris, John
A7: Parson, Mary
B2: '1991
B3: Salary
B4: 25000
B5: 29000
B6: 45000
B7: 55900
C1: Salary Expense Projections
C3: Increase
C4: .07
C5: .05
C6: .065
C7: .055
D2: Job
D3: Class
D4: 3
D5. 9
D6: 7
D7: 9

E2:   '1992
E3:   Salary
F3:   FICA
G3:   Benefits

4. Move the cell pointer to C4, select Range Format Percent, and press ENTER. Move the cell pointer to C7 and press ENTER again.

5. Move the cell pointer to D4, select Range Format Fixed, type **0**, and press ENTER. Move the cell pointer to D7 and press ENTER again.

6. Select Worksheet Global Format Currency, type **0**, and press ENTER to produce the display in Figure 7-11.

   All the remaining entries in this model must be calculated. Standard formulas will not work; various factors affect the computed results, and a regular formula cannot deal with these exceptions. After analyzing each of the required conditions, enter an @IF statement that captures the essence of how you would perform these calculations manually under all circumstances.

   FICA is not computed by the same method for all wage levels. It is calculated at 7.65% unless the individual earns more than the established cap amount for FICA. If earnings exceed the cap amount, you will only pay an employer's FICA contribution on the cap amount. You can record this with the @IF function if the

Figure 7-11. *Salary model before adding formulas*

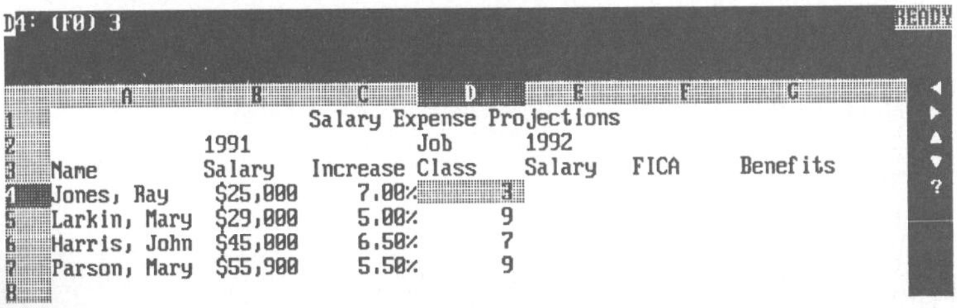

condition to be tested is recorded in the function and the two different methods for performing the FICA computation are recorded as the values for true and false conditions.

Follow these directions for making your entries:

7. Move the cell pointer to E4, type **+B4∗(1+C4)**, and press ENTER.

   This formula calculates the projected salary for 1992, based on the increase percentage.

8. Select Copy, press ENTER, move the cell pointer to E5, type a period, move to E7, and press ENTER.

9. Move the cell pointer to F4 and type **@IF(E4<50400,E4∗ .0765,50400∗.0765)**. Then press ENTER.

   The essence of this function is to check whether the salary is less than $50,400 and, if it is, to multiply the salary by 7.65%. If it is not less than $50,400, the rate will be applied to $50,400, the amount chosen for this example as the arbitrary limit for FICA payments. You now have the rules for two different ways to perform the FICA calculation, depending on the amount of the salary.

10. Select Copy, press ENTER, move the cell pointer to F5, and type a period (.). Then move the cell pointer to F7 and press ENTER.

    The results will look like the worksheet in Figure 7-12. Naturally, if you had more records on your worksheet, you could copy this formula farther down the worksheet than cell F7 before finalizing the copy. If you wish, you can also complete a calculation for benefits by using the formula you see in the control panel of Figure 7-10.

Figure 7-12. *Salary model with @IF formulas for FICA calculation*

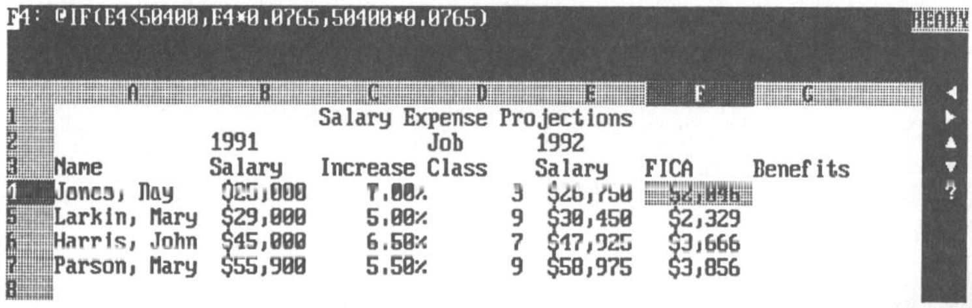

Review

- Functions are prerecorded formulas. They are accessed by using the symbol @ followed by a keyword. Most functions also have arguments that define your specific needs to 1-2-3. These arguments are enclosed in parentheses and separated by commas.

- There are eight categories of 1-2-3 functions. Statistical functions perform basic statistical computations. Date and time functions allow you to record dates and times in worksheet cells and work with these special entries in other ways. String functions are designed to provide a way to work with character strings. Math functions perform simple mathematical operations and provide access to trigonometric calculations. Financial functions compute depreciation and computations involving the time value of money. Special functions are a group of miscellaneous functions that do not fall into any of the other categories. Logical functions allow you to test conditions. Data-management functions allow you to perform computations on entries in a 1-2-3 database.

8

Creating Graphs

The worksheet provides an excellent way to *perform* all your financial projections, but it is not always the best way to *present* the results from these calculations. Important numbers that you want to highlight often get lost in a sea of other figures. How can you make sure that you and others who read your report, which contains hundreds of numbers, will focus on those conditions and trends that you think are important?

One answer is to use 1-2-3's graphics features, which let you present your data in an easy-to-interpret format. Graphs do not present all the specific numbers; instead, they summarize the essence of your data so that you can focus on general patterns and trends. And when you find something in a graph that warrants more detailed analysis, you can still return to the supporting worksheet figures for a closer look.

You do not have to reenter your 1-2-3 data to use the graphics features. You can use the data already entered for your spreadsheet application without making any changes. Nor do you need to learn a new system to create your graphs; 1-2-3's graphics features are accessed through menus that are just like 1-2-3's other menus. You only need to learn a few new commands. Once you have entered your worksheet data, you need make only a few menu selections to present this data in graphic format. (Incidentally, any changes you make to your data will be reflected in your graph.)

To view your graphs on the screen, you need a color monitor or a monochrome (one-color) monitor with a graphics card. But even if you do not have a monitor that will support graphics, you can still make the menu selections that define the graph and save it to disk for printing later on.

Release 2.3 significantly improves the quality of the graphs. This release is designed to take advantage of the new high resolution monitors and support much more detailed graphics. With 1-2-3 graphs, you can create professional-looking slides and transparencies for important business meetings.

Releases lower than 2.2 cannot print a graph directly. Graphs must be saved to disk and printed with the separate *PrintGraph program* or, in Release 2.2, with the Allways add-in that is part of your 1-2-3 package. A separate program is required because 1-2-3's graphics features are so extensive. There are different fonts, different sizes, and color, as well as support for a variety of printers and plotters. If all these options had been placed within 1-2-3's main program, so much memory would have been required that there would have been no room for your own data. The Allways add-in is covered in Chapter 12, "WYSIWYG and Other Add-Ins." This add-in provides additional features that are unavailable in 1-2-3, such as printing a graph and a worksheet on the same page.

This chapter will introduce you to the basic commands for defining a graph. You will learn about some of the special options that produce a more professional product. You will find out how to create and save multiple graphs in a single worksheet file. You will also learn how to obtain a printed copy of a graph using PrintGraph.

Creating a Graph

Creating a basic graph is really quite simple. There are three basic steps. First, decide what type of graph you wish to see. Second, tell 1-2-3 what data to place in this graph. And third, tell 1-2-3 to display the graph for you. Once you have completed these basics, you may want to add further enhancements.

Before you can begin to create your first graph, there are a few basic terms to understand. A sample graph, with the key terms and components marked, is shown in Figure 8-1. A discussion of each of the basic terms follows. More specialized terms are covered along with the implementation of specific features later in the chapter.

Data Series

1-2-3's graphs are designed to show from one to six sets of data values, depending on the type of graph that you select. A set of data values is referred to as a *series* and must consist of a range of contiguous cells on the worksheet. A series can represent, for example, sales of a product for a period of six months, the number of employees in the company each year for the last ten years, or the number of rejects on a production line for each of the last 16 weeks.

Figure 8-1. *A bar graph with titles and legend*

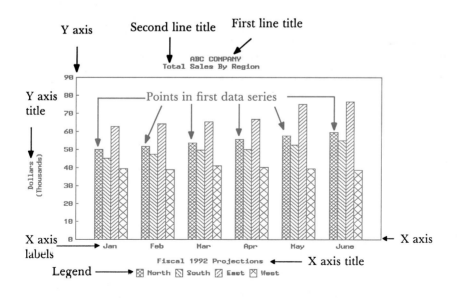

X Axis

The individual values in the series are represented as data points along the *X axis,* which is the horizontal axis at the bottom of the graph. Each point along this axis might represent a year, a month, or a quarter. It could also represent a division, a product, or a project. The points along this X axis can be labeled to make it clear what they represent. In addition, a title can be placed along the X axis to describe the general category of data shown along that axis. For example, if each of the points on the X axis represents a month between January and December, an appropriate title for the axis might be Fiscal 92 Projections, which describes the category to which each of these months belongs.

Y Axis

The *Y axis* is the vertical axis found on most of the graphs that 1-2-3 produces. It is used to measure the relative size of each value within a series. Once you tell 1-2-3 which data to display on the graph, this axis is labeled automatically. 1-2-3 will sometimes represent graph data in thousands or millions and label the Y axis appropriately. You can also make a title for this axis; you might describe the units of measure as dollars, number of employees, or some other appropriate unit of measure for the quantities shown on this axis.

Legend

If you choose to show more than one data series on a graph, you can describe each of the series with a *legend* at the bottom of the graph. The legend will show the symbol or pattern used to represent each series in the graph and will describe the data represented by that symbol or pattern.

Entering Graph Data

If you have worked through the examples in this book from Chapter 1, "Worksheet Basics," you already have a number of worksheets that 1-2-3's graphics features could represent nicely. Even though you have some data for a graph, you will enter a short new worksheet designed to let you work with a small amount of data, yet still experience the maximum number of graphics features. Follow these steps to enter the required data for the examples in this chapter:

1. Make the following entries in the worksheet cells shown:

D1:	′ ABC COMPANY
D2:	SALES BY REGION
A5:	North
A6:	South
A7:	East
A8:	West
B4:	Jan
B5:	50000
B6:	45000
B7:	62800
B8:	39550
C4:	Feb
C5:	+B5*1.035
C6:	+B6*1.05
C7:	+B7*1.02
C8:	+B8*.98
D4:	Mar
E4:	Apr
F4:	May
G4:	June

2. Select Worksheet Global Format Currency, type **0**, and press ENTER.

3. Move the cell pointer to B4, select Range Label Right, move the cell pointer to G4, and press ENTER.

   This aligns the labels on the right side of the cell as the numbers are aligned.

4. Move the cell pointer to C5, select Copy, and move the cell pointer to C8. Press ENTER, move the cell pointer to D5, type a period (.), move the cell pointer to G5, and press ENTER again.

5. Move the cell pointer to the following cells and type these numbers:

E6:	50000
F7:	75000
D8:	41000

Adding these numbers overlays the formulas in those cells and provides more variety in the graph than a growth at a constant rate.

6. Move the cell pointer to C5.

Your entries should look like those in Figure 8-2. Notice that the original formula is not altered by the addition of several numeric constants to the model. You have finished entering the data you will use with the graphics examples. Now it is time to define your requirements for the graph.

Graph Types

1-2-3 offers seven different graph types plus a variety of features that provide variations on a graph type. Your options are line, bar, stack-bar, XY, pie, HLCO, and mixed. A *bar graph* looks like the one shown in Figure 8-1. It uses bars of different heights to represent the data ranges you wish to graph. Bar graphs are especially appropriate when you wish to contrast the numbers in several series.

A *line graph* shows the points in the data range you specify, plotted against the Y axis. The points may be connected with a line, shown as symbols, or both. This type of graph is an excellent choice for plotting trend data over time, such as sales or expenses.

Figure 8-2.   *Worksheet for using graph features*

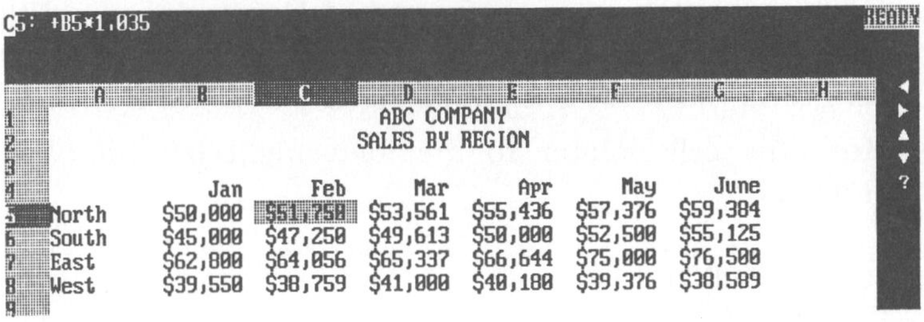

A *stack-bar graph* places the values in each of the series you select on top of each other for any one point on the X axis. A stack-bar is a good choice when you wish to see the level of the total as well as each of its components. You might use this type of graph to show the contribution to profit from each of the company's subsidiaries. Figure 8-3 shows a stack-bar graph that has been rotated 90 degrees by selecting Features Horizontal.

An *XY graph* plots the values in one series against the values from a second series. You might use this type of graph to plot age against salary, time against temperature, or machine repairs against the age of the machinery. Figure 8-4 shows an example of an XY graph.

A *pie chart* shows only one range of values. It represents the percent that each value is of the total by the size of the pie wedge assigned to that value. A pie chart is an effective way to show the relative size of different components of a budget or the contribution to profit from different product lines. An example of a pie chart is shown in Figure 8-5 where the pieces contain hatchmarks and one piece has been exploded (separated from the rest of the pie).

HLCO (High-Low-Close-Open) graphs are new to 1-2-3 Release 2.3. They are ideal for presenting stock and bond prices. Four different data

Figure 8-3. *A horizontal stack-bar graph*

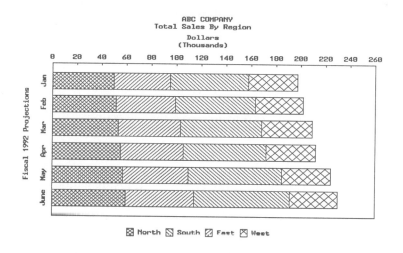

Figure 8-4. *An XY graph*

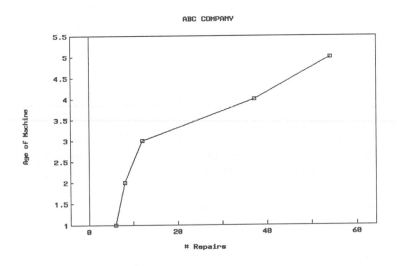

ranges are assigned to an HLCO graph with one data series representing each set of prices. Figure 8-6 shows an HLCO graph for XYZ Company's stock during May 1991.

A *mixed graph* allows you to combine a bar graph with a line graph. The first three data ranges are displayed as bars and the last three are shown as lines. Figure 8-7 shows a mixed graph where the Features option 3D-Effect was used to add a three-dimensional effect to the bars.

If you do not choose one of the graph types for your graph, 1-2-3 will use the default type, a line graph. Your first example will be of a bar graph, so use the following steps to make that selection:

1. Select Graph.

This will display the main Graph menu as shown in Figure 8-8. Below the menu is the Graph Settings dialog box. From this menu, you can access additional Graph menus that provide additional settings. As you make selections with the Graph menus, 1-2-3 displays the settings in the box. You can use this box to constantly monitor the status of your graph settings or, in Release 2.3, press F2 (EDIT) to change them. 1-2-3 Release 2.3

Figure 8-5. *A pie chart*

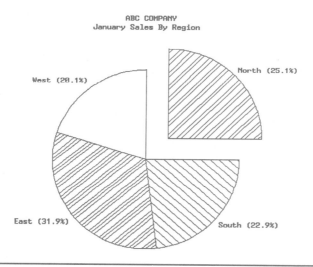

ABC COMPANY
January Sales By Region

North (25.1%)

West (28.1%)

East (31.9%)

South (22.9%)

provides a second settings sheet for legends, titles, data labels, and format. If you want to view the worksheet instead of the settings sheet, press F6 (WINDOW). Pressing F6 (WINDOW) again returns the settings sheet to the screen.

2. Select Type to see the following submenu:

C5: +B5*1.035   MENU
Line Bar XY Stack-Bar Pie HLCO Mixed Features
Line graph

3. Select Bar.

4. Select Type Features 3D-Effect to add a three-dimensional effect to the bars.

    If you are using a mouse, you can select 3-D bars in the dialog box to achieve the same effect.

Notice that once you have made the type selection, you are returned to the main Graph menu, not to the READY mode. The main Graph menu is another "sticky" menu, like Print. It will stay around so you can make additional selections for defining your graph, disappearing only when you select Quit.

8

Figure 8-6.   *An HLCO graph for XYZ Company's stock*

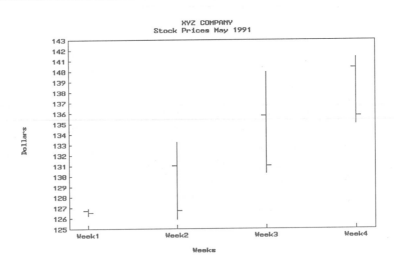

Specifying Graph Data

There are no defaults for the data to be shown in a graph. If you forget
to tell 1-2-3 which data to display on the graph, your graph will be blank.
Line, bar, stacked bar, and XY graphs can each show up to six data series
or ranges. These graph types can have data assigned to graph ranges A, B,
C, D, E, and F in the Graph menu. Pie charts are special; a pie chart
can only show one data range. In a pie chart, data is assigned to graph
range A.

Follow these steps to assign data to graph ranges A through D in the
current graph to see how data is assigned to the various graph ranges:

1. Select A to produce this display:

There is no need to select Graph because the Graph menu is
already on the screen.

Figure 8-7. *A mixed graph*

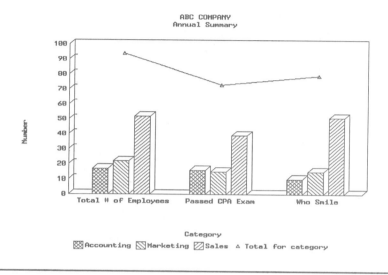

2. Move the cell pointer to B5 and type a period (.), move the cell pointer to G5, and press ENTER.

   This step assigns the range B5..G5 to the A range of the graph so that it will now represent the sales for the North region in the months of January through June.

3. Select B and move the cell pointer to B6. Type a period (.), move the cell pointer to G6, and press ENTER.

   This assigns the data for the South region to the B range of the graph.

4. Select C and move the cell pointer to B7. Type a period (.), move the cell pointer to G7, and press ENTER.

   This assigns the data for the East region to the C range of the graph.

5. Select D and move the cell pointer to B8. Type a period (.), move the cell pointer to G8, and press ENTER.

8

Figure 8-8. *Main Graph menu and Graph Settings box*

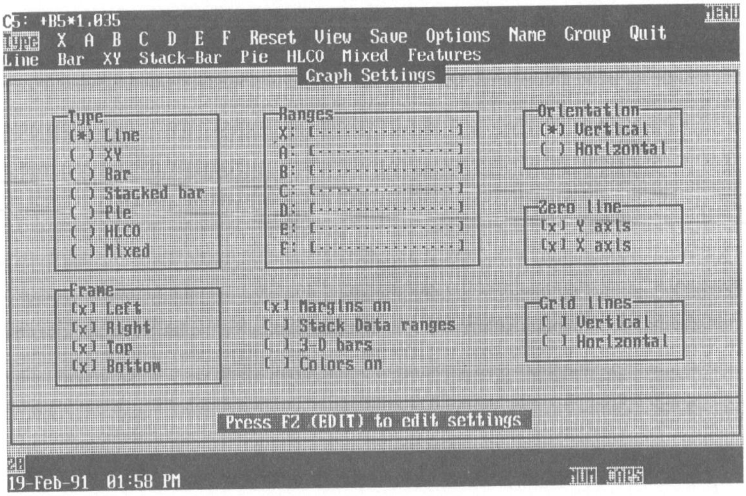

This assigns the data for the West region to the D range of the graph. Notice that this is the last region for ABC Company so that the E and F ranges are currently unassigned. Also notice that all the ranges assigned have the same unit of measure—dollars. If some ranges were measured in units of products sold and others in dollars, both could not be shown on the same graph. The unit of measure must be the same for all of the data shown on a graph.

Viewing the Graph

Although the graph is not quite finished, you can still view it to see how the various data ranges stack up against each other. Sometimes if one range is either extremely large or extremely small in comparison to the others, it is not practical to graph the data together; the values in the smaller range will seem to blend with the X axis. To view your graph and return again to the menu, follow these steps:

1. Select View.

   If your monitor can display graphics, this command will produce an image of the graph. All four data ranges are shown on the graph; the A range values are represented by the leftmost bar in each grouping. There are six different points on the X axis, each representing one month in the range. If your monitor can display colors, each range may appear in a different color instead of a different hatch pattern.

2. Press any key to return to the menu display.

   1-2-3 offers another method for viewing the current graph. The F10 (GRAPH) key displays the current graph when you are in the READY mode. To try this feature, follow these steps.

1. Select Quit.

   1-2-3 leaves the Graph menu and returns to the READY mode.

2. Press the F10 (GRAPH) key.

   1-2-3 displays the same graph again. To return to the READY mode, press any key. You can use this function key when you change the worksheet data a graph uses and you want to see the effect on the graph.

Viewing in Color or Black and White

If you have a monitor that shows a single color, your only option is to view the graph with the B&W (black and white) option. If you have a color monitor you can select Options Color, and different colors will be used for the various data ranges. Whether you use three colors or a more extensive palette when coloring the graph depends on the graphics support supplied by your system. If you are able to view the system in color, you will want to use the B&W option to switch back to black and white before saving the graph. This option distinguishes the various data series by placing hatch patterns within bars and adding symbols to line graphs. Although the Color option uses color to distinguish the various data ranges, these color differences are lost when the graph is printed on a standard black and white printer.

8

Enhancing the Display

The current graph is not useful. The bars are hatch-marked to distinguish them, but the only way to tell which set of bars represents which set of data is by remembering the sequence in which the different regions were assigned to the graph ranges. Nor can you tell whether the points on the X axis represent years, months, or days and whether the numbers graphed are sales, expenses, or number of employees. Some additional information must be added to the graph in order for it to be useful. In this section you will learn how to add titles to the graph, label the X axis points, and add legends and grid lines.

Labeling the X Axis

Without labels along the X axis it is impossible to tell what each group of values represents. You can solve this problem easily by assigning a range of labels to be displayed along the axis. This range of labels should correspond to the values in the data ranges that have been assigned and should have the same number of entries. Normally you will already have values like this in a column or row of the worksheet. For the current example, the labels that you need for the X axis are in B4..G4.

You can assign these labels to the X axis with the X range option from the Graph menu. Follow these steps to make the assignment:

1. Select Graph X.

    This will produce a display similar to the one used for the graph data ranges:

    You must enter the range address you want to use either by typing it or by using the pointing method.

2. Move the cell pointer to B4, type a period (.), and move the cell pointer to G4 before pressing ENTER.

3. Select View to see the graph with the addition of labels along the X axis.

4. Press any key to return to the Graph menu.

Using Shortcuts

If you are using Release 2.2 or above, you can sometimes consolidate range assignments into one easy step. Your data must be in tabular form for this to work with the data used to label the X axis at the top or left side of the detailed entries. Follow these steps to assign all of the data ranges with one command:

1. Select Group. 1-2-3 displays this prompt:

(Note that 1-2-3 prompts you with the current location of the cell pointer.)

2. Move to B4, type a period (.), press END, press HOME, and press ENTER to select B4..G8 as the worksheet data range for the data ranges, or use your mouse to select the range. 1-2-3 displays this prompt:

This selection determines whether 1-2-3 divides the worksheet data into graph data ranges according to rows or columns.

3. Select Rowwise.

1-2-3 automatically assigns the first row in the worksheet range to the X data range, the second row to the A data range, and so forth. By using the Graph Group command, you can assign all of the graph data ranges at once instead of one at a time.

4. Select View to create a display with the month names under each set of bars.

8

5. Press any key to return to the Graph menu.

Adding Titles

Titles can be added to your graph in four different locations to improve its appearance. You can add a title along either of the axes or at the top of the graph in one or two lines. The menu and dialog box you will see when you select Graph Options Titles looks like Figure 8-9. You will have 39 characters in which to enter any one of these four titles, once you select the option you want. The title can be even longer if you make it by using data that is already stored in a worksheet cell. Follow these steps to enhance your current graph with titles in all four locations:

1. Select Options to produce the following menu:

2. Select Titles First to add a title at the top of the graph.

Figure 8-9. *The menu and dialog box displayed after selecting Graph Options Titles*

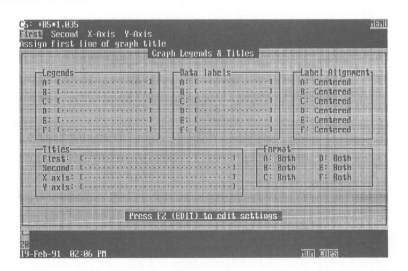

3. Type **\D1** and press ENTER.

This will use the current entry in D1 as the title at the top of the graph. Notice how the Options menu returns to the screen. It too is a "sticky" menu: You must choose Quit in order to leave.

4. Select Titles Second, type **Total Sales by Region**, and press ENTER.

This time the title was added by typing because there was no entry on the worksheet that exactly matched the desired title.

5. Select Titles X-Axis, type **Fiscal 1992 Projections**, and press ENTER.

6. Select Titles Y-Axis, type **Dollars**, and press ENTER.

7. Select Quit.

This will exit the Graph Options menu and place you in the main Graph menu.

8. Select View to produce a display with all four titles as in Figure 8-10.

9. Press any key to return to the Graph menu.

Figure 8-10. *A three-dimensional bar graph with titles*

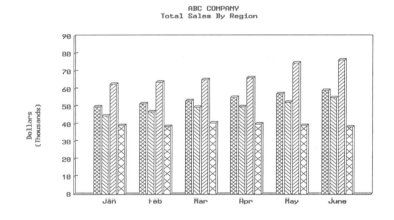

Adding Legends

Legends add clarity to a graph that presents more than one data series by identifying how each data series is represented on the graph. If symbols are used to distinguish the different data series, the legend will consist of the series indicator and the text describing the data shown by that series. If color or hatch patterns are used, a small square of the color or pattern is placed at the bottom of the screen along with the text description of the series. In Releases 2.2 and above, you can add all of the legends at once with a new menu option. Also, 1-2-3 will automatically adjust the legend display to use more than one line if the legend text needs it.

Selecting Legend from the Options menu presents the Legend sub-menu, as shown here:

When you select Legend you will be presented with a choice of the same six letters that you used to assign worksheet ranges to the different data series for the graph. Releases 2.2 and above include a Range option to select a worksheet range for all of the data range legends. To select a legend for a single range, select each of the data series that you assigned and enter a legend for each. You will need to select Legend and the appropriate letter each time until you have assigned a legend entry to each of the data series you used in the graph. Follow these steps to assign the legends for the current graph:

1. Select Options Legend A, type **\A5**, and press ENTER.

   The label stored in the cell A5 will be used for the legend. Your other option is to type **North** and press ENTER. The advantage of using the label entry in the cell is that if you decide to update it later, the graph title will automatically be updated for you the next time the graph is created.

2. Select Legend B, type **\A6**, and press ENTER.

3. Select Legend C, type **\A7**, and press ENTER.

4. Select Legend D, type **\A8**, and press ENTER.

5. Select Quit.

6. Select View to create the display shown in Figure 8-11.

7. Press any key to return to the Graph menu.

If you are using Release 2.2 or above, you can follow these simpler steps to assign worksheet data as the legend text for the data ranges:

1. Select Options Legend Range. 1-2-3 displays this prompt:

(Note that 1-2-3 prompts you with the current location of the cell pointer as the starting point for the legend range.)

2. Move to A5, type a period (.), press the DOWN ARROW key three times, and press ENTER to select A5..A8 as the worksheet data range for the data range legends.

Figure 8-11. *Adding a legend to the bar graph*

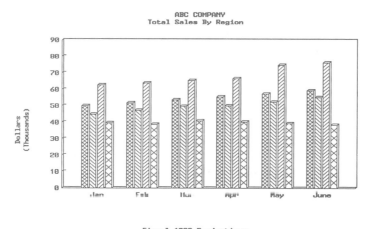

1-2-3 automatically assigns the first worksheet cell as the A data range legend, the second worksheet cell as the B data range legend, and so forth.

3. Select Quit.

4. Select View to create the display shown in Figure 8-11.

5. Press any key to return to the Graph menu.

Adding Grid Lines

Grid lines are a series of lines that are parallel to either the X axis or the Y axis and that originate from the markers on the axis. They are designed to help you interpret the exact value of data points by extending either up or to the right from these markers. These lines are called grid lines because choosing to use them in both directions at once will create a grid pattern on your graph.

To get the menu for Grid, select Graph Options Grid. The grid options can be used with all graph types except the pie chart; grid lines across a pie chart would detract from your ability to interpret the graph. The Grid menu contains these four options:

With a bar graph, only the first option, Horizontal, is appropriate. This choice will let you interpret the top of each of the bars more accurately. Try it now for the current graph with these entries:

1. Select Options Grid Horizontal.

2. Select Quit to leave the Options menu.

3. Select View to produce the graph shown in Figure 8-12.

4. Press any key to return to the Graph menu.

5. Select Options Grid Clear Quit.

This will remove the horizontal grid lines and return you to the main Graph menu. If you wish to verify that the lines have been removed, you can use the View command.

Figure 8-12. *Adding horizontal grid lines to the bar graph*

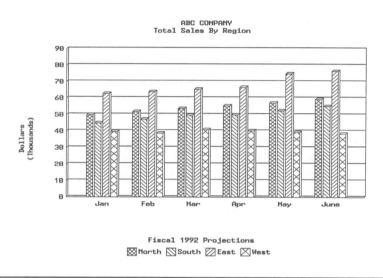

Naming the Current Graph

1-2-3 can only maintain one set of graph definitions at a time unless you assign a name to these definitions. Now that you have completely defined a graph, assign a name to these specifications before you create a second graph. The command to use is Graph Name Create. Once you have used this command to assign a name, you are free to reset the current graph settings. This lets you start fresh to define a new graph or make a few changes to create a second graph that has many of the same options as the first graph. Follow these steps to assign a name to the current graph settings so you can create additional graphs.

1. Select Name Create.

    You do not need to select Graph since you are already in the Graph menu.

2. Type **Sls_bar** and press ENTER.

More Graph Types

Working with several additional graph types will give you a close-up look at how easy it is to create additional graphs or to change the type for the existing graph. In this section you will use the current data series to create a line graph and a stack-bar graph. Then you will create a pie chart with a subset of this data. Follow these steps to create the three additional graphs:

1. Select Type Line.

2. Select View to display a graph like the one shown in Figure 8-13.
   Notice that different symbols are used for each series shown on the graph. The legend is automatically changed from the hatch patterns to these symbols.

3. Press any key to return to the Graph menu.

4. Select Name Create, type **Sls_line**, and press ENTER.

5. Select Type Stack-Bar.

6. Select Options Titles Second, press ESC to remove the existing title, type **Total Company Sales**, and press ENTER.

Figure 8-13.   *Displaying the same data with a line graph*

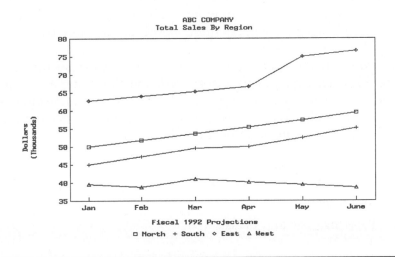

You can use this technique when you want to change any of the current graph specifications.

7. Select Quit and View to display a stack-bar graph.
   Notice that the legend is automatically changed back to the hatch patterns.

8. Press any key to return to the Graph menu.

9. Select Name Create, type **Sls_sbar,** and press ENTER.

10. Select Reset to produce this display:

11. Select Graph.
    This will eliminate all the previous graph settings.

12. Select A, type **B5.B8**, and press ENTER.

13. Select X, type **A5.A8**, and press ENTER.

14. Select Type Pie.

15. Select Options Titles First, type **ABC COMPANY**, and press ENTER.

16. Select Titles Second, type **January Sales by Region**, and press ENTER.

17. Select Quit View to view a graph like the one in Figure 8-14.

18. Press any key, select Quit, move your cell pointer to A12, and make these entries:

   A12: 1
   A13: 102
   A14: 3
   A15. 4

With Release 2 or higher, you can use these codes to change the appearance of the graph. First create a range with the same number of value entries as the range shown on the graph.

Figure 8-14. *A pie chart*

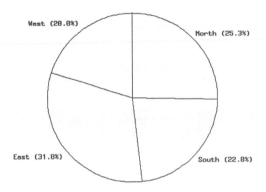

Numbers 0 to 7 are used, each representing a unique hatch pattern. Adding 100 to any one of these entries will explode that piece from the pie (that is, split it off from the pie sections that remain joined).

These values will show as Currency, since that is the Global format. This will not affect their impact on the graph; however, if you find the dollar signs ($) confusing, you can eliminate them with Range Format General.

19. Select Graph B, type **A12.A15**, and press ENTER.

20. Select View.

If you are using Release 2 or higher, notice how the new graph shown in Figure 8-15 differs from the previous one. It is much easier to read and emphasizes the South's contributions.

21. Press any key to return to the Graph menu.

22. Select Name Create, type **Jan_pie**, and press ENTER.

23. Select Quit to return to READY mode.

Figure 8-15. *A pie chart with shading and a slice exploded*

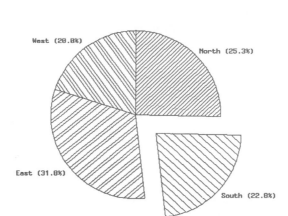

Saving a Graph

Several aspects of graphs must be saved. You must save the graph definition if you plan to use the graph the next time you work with the current worksheet. Since 1-2-3 cannot print a graph, you must also save the graphic or print image for printing with the PrintGraph or Allways program.

Saving the Worksheet File

After you have created one or more graph definitions, you will want them to be available the next time you work with the current worksheet. To save these graph definitions, save the worksheet file to disk after defining the graphs. Do the following to save the graphs for the Profit file:

Select File Save, type **Profit,** and press ENTER.

Saving the Graph Image

When you save the worksheet file you do not automatically save the graphic or print image for the current graph. In order to save this image so that you can print it with the PrintGraph or Allways program, you must select Graph Save. This command saves the file under the name that you specify and adds the filename extension of .PIC to distinguish the file from a worksheet file.

To save multiple graphs for later printing, you must save each one as the current graph, even though the graphs are all defined on the same worksheet. For each graph, choose Graph Name Use, followed by Save.

Follow these steps to save the graphs created for the Profit worksheet:

1. Select Graph Save, type **Jan_pie**, and press ENTER.
    Since you exited the Graph menu to save the worksheet, you must now reenter it. The current graphic image was not saved along with the graph definition stored in the worksheet file. Although you are using the same name as you used for the graph specifications on the worksheet, the step you just took creates a unique file. The file that is created with this instruction will be named JAN_PIE.PIC as it is stored on disk.

2. Select Name Use, point to Sls_bar, and press ENTER.
    The bar graph you created will now be the active graph. When you perform another graph save, this is the image that will be saved.

3. Press any key, select Save, type **Sls_bar**, and press ENTER.
    This will save the graphic image of the bar graph you created.

4. Select Name Use, point to Sls_line, and press ENTER.
    The line graph you created will now be the active graph.

5. Press any key, select Save, type **Sls_line**, and press ENTER.

6. Select Name Use, point to Sls_sbar, and press ENTER.
    The stack-bar graph that you created will now be the active graph.

7. Press any key, select Save, type **Sls_sbar**, and press ENTER.

8. Select Quit to exit the Graph menu.

9. Select Quit Yes.

Depending on how you entered 1-2-3, Quit will return you either to DOS or to the Lotus Access System. If quitting takes you back to DOS you can enter **LOTUS** to place yourself in the Lotus Access System. The following examples assume that you are in the Lotus Access System and are ready to learn how to print the graphs.

Printing a Graph

As mentioned, you can use the Lotus PrintGraph program to obtain a printed copy of your graphs. Before you can use this program, you must have previously saved the graph in a .PIC file. PrintGraph also must be configured for your system. This should have been completed when 1-2-3 was configured in the installation process. If not, return to Install to add the necessary information to the PrintGraph program. This process is described in Appendix A, "Installing 1-2-3 and WYSIWYG."

You can also print graphs using the Allways or WYSIWYG add-ins, which are supplied with Releases 2.2 and 2.3 and can be purchased for use with Releases 2 and 2.01. These add-ins offer additional advanced features that you can also use to print your worksheets. These features are covered in Chapter 12, "WYSIWYG and Other Add-Ins." For now, you can use PrintGraph to print your graphs with its extensive printing features.

The Lotus Access System, which you will use to select the PrintGraph option, is shown here for Release 2.3:

The PrintGraph menu for Release 1A is very different from the Release 2.3 menu shown in Figure 8-16. Despite this difference, the features are very similar. It is just that the definition of the various settings is covered by the selection Settings in Release 2.3 but by two different selections (Options and Configure) in Release 1A. This chapter emphasizes the Release 2.3 selections for completing PrintGraph tasks; but even if you are using a lower release, these descriptions should help you make the correct selections.

Figure 8-16.   *The PrintGraph menu in Release 2.3*

```
Copyright 1985, 1991 Lotus Development Corp. All Rights Reserved.        MENU

Select graphs to print or preview
Image-Select  Settings  Go  Align  Page  Exit
    GRAPHS     IMAGE SETTINGS                    HARDWARE SETTINGS
    TO PRINT   Size               Range colors  Graphs directory
               Top       .395     X                E:\123R23
               Left      .750     A             Fonts directory
               Width    6.500     B                E:\123R23
               Height   4.691     C             Interface
               Rotation  .000     D                Parallel 1
                                  E             Printer
               Font               F
               1  BLOCK1                        Paper size
               2  BLOCK1                           Width     8.500
                                                   Length   11.000

                                               ACTION SETTINGS
                                               Pause  No    Eject  No
```

Selecting Graph Files

Before you can print a graph you must have a copy of it saved as a .PIC file (the type of file that 1-2-3 uses when you select Graph Save). This file must be in the directory shown on the main PrintGraph menu screen under "Graphs directory." If this description of the directory location for your graph files does not match the location of your .PIC files, you must change the directory.

Changing Directories

To make this change, enter Settings Hardware to activate this menu:

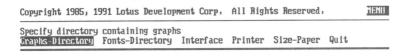

```
Copyright 1985, 1991 Lotus Development Corp. All Rights Reserved.        MENU

Specify directory containing graphs
Graphs-Directory  Fonts-Directory  Interface  Printer  Size-Paper  Quit
```

The graph directory has a default setting of A:\. This means that 1-2-3 will expect to read your graph files from drive A. If you have graph files stored on another drive, you need to change the graphs directory setting. Check the current setting for your graph files now; if a change is required, follow these steps:

1. Select Settings Hardware Graphs-Directory.

2. Type the pathname for your graph files.

   For example, if your graph files are stored on drive C in the directory \123graphs, you would type this entry:

   C:\123graphs

3. Press ENTER to finalize the new setting.

4. Select Quit twice to return to the main menu.

Selecting Graphs to Print

The Image-Select option on the main PrintGraph menu allows you to select graphs from the directory listed under "Graphs directory" on the right side of the main PrintGraph screen. Once you select Image-Select, the names of the graph files in this directory will be displayed for you, as shown in Figure 8-17. A highlighted bar will rest on the first filename in the list. The arrow keys will let you scroll through the list of filenames, moving the highlighted bar through the list until you find a file that you wish to print.

To mark a file for printing, position the highlighted bar on the filename and press the SPACEBAR. If you change your mind, press the SPACEBAR again to undo the selection. After you select the first file you can move the highlighted bar up and down in the list to select as many additional files

Figure 8-17. *PrintGraph menu for selecting images to print*

```
Copyright 1985, 1991 Lotus Development Corp,  All Rights Reserved,        POINT

Select graphs to print

    GRAPH FILE  DATE      TIME    SIZE
    ----------------------------------        Space bar marks or unmarks selection
    JAM_PIE     02-08-91  11:28    1918       ENTER selects marked graphs
    PIE         02-08-91  11:28    1918       ESC exits, ignoring changes
    SLS_BAR     02-08-91  11:28    1918       HOME moves to beginning of list
    SLS_LINE    02-08-91  11:28    1918       END moves to end of list
    SLS_SDAR    02-08 91  11:20    1918       ↑ and ↓ move highlight
                                                List will scroll if highlight
                                                moved beyond top or bottom
                                              GRAPH (F10) previews marked graph
```

8

as you like. 1-2-3 will even remember the order in which you made your selections and print the graphs in that sequence.

If you are uncertain what a graph file contains, you can move the highlighted bar to the filename and press F10. (You may have to change the fonts directory first if it is not in drive A.) 1-2-3 will recreate the chosen graph on your screen for you to review. When you have finished viewing the graph, you can press ESC to return to the selection screen to make additional selections. Once you have marked all the graphs, press ENTER to select the graphs you want for printing. Use these steps to select the graph files created in this exercise:

1. Select Image-Select.

2. Use the highlighted bar and move to JAN _ PIE. Press the SPACEBAR to mark the graph with a #.
   Once it is marked, you can make additional selections.

3. Move the highlighted bar to SLS _ SBAR and press the SPACEBAR.

4. Move the highlighted bar to SLS _ BAR and press the SPACEBAR.

5. Move the highlighted bar to SLS _ LINE and press F10 to view the graph.

6. Press ENTER to return to the menu, and then press the SPACEBAR.

Controlling the Settings

The PrintGraph program has a wide variety of settings that allow you to tailor the printing of a graph. Many of these settings are advanced features, best explored only once you have mastered the basics. This section presents the basic settings that you can work with to make PrintGraph respond to your needs. The following menu shows the various aspects of the graphic process that can be changed when you select Settings from the main PrintGraph menu:

Copyright 1985, 1991 Lotus Development Corp. All Rights Reserved.   MENU

Select graph size, fonts, and colors
Image   Hardware   Action   Save   Reset   Quit

Image Settings

The Image settings allow you to alter features such as size, color, and fonts. Although these features are nice to have available because you can use the default settings, they are not relevant to the basic set of skills you are initially trying to develop.

Hardware Settings

You have already explored one hardware setting change: the change to the directory for your graph files. You can also alter the directory where the fonts are stored. The fonts affect the type of printing used for labels throughout the graph. To access these fonts you must be sure that the font files are in the directory shown at the right side of the main PrintGraph menu. If they are not there, you can change this display by using the command Graphs Settings Hardware Fonts-Directory and typing a new directory name.

Interface and Printer Type

The proper interface and printer type must show on the PrintGraph menu in order for your printer or plotter to produce graphs correctly. Eight different interface options are available, although the first two are used most frequently because they represent standard parallel and serial interfaces. The first option, 1, represents a standard *parallel connection,* which is the most common way of connecting a printer to your system. The second represents a *serial connection,* which is commonly used to connect a plotter to your system. The default value for this setting is 1, which represents a standard parallel interface. If your output device is a plotter, you may need to change this setting to serial. However, consult with your dealer or other knowledgeable source before making these changes.

If you have installed PrintGraph to operate with a variety of printers, the Hardware Printer setting may require frequent change. Each time you want to use a different printer, select PrintGraph Settings Hardware Printer and the output device you want to use for your graphs. If your current setting is blank or needs to be changed, follow these steps:

1. Select Hardware Printer.

2. Select the correct output device from the list of options specified during the Install process. Press ENTER and select Quit.

If no options are displayed it means that you did not install Print-Graph. If the printer type you wish to select is not displayed as an option, return to Install to correct the problem.

Saving Changes

All the changes you make to the settings are temporary; unless you save them, they will apply only to the current session. When you want to retain the new setting values for subsequent sessions, you must store them in the file PGRAPH.CNF (GRAPH.CNF in Release 1A). To make the new settings permanent, you must select Save from the Settings menu to store the settings in the PGRAPH.CNF file. Do the following to save your changes:

Select Save and Quit to return to the main menu.

Unlike other Save operations, here you do not need to enter a filename. 1-2-3 always uses the same file.

Printing the Graphs

Once you have made all the selections, printing the graph is quite simple. 1-2-3 will begin printing the graphs you have chosen with Image-Select when you choose Go from the PrintGraph menu. Pressing the CTRL and BREAK keys simultaneously will stop the printing if you need to interrupt the process. However, the printer will not stop right away; it will continue to print the lines that have already been transmitted to it. Follow these steps to print the graphs you selected earlier:

1. Check to ensure that your printer is both on and online.
2. Select Go.
3. Once all the graphs have been printed, select Exit.

If you are printing a color graph to a plotter, PrintGraph prompts you to press a key when the pens it lists are loaded before printing a graph. If you have set the Page Eject option to Yes, the printer will advance to the next page after each graph is printed. If you have set the Eject option to No, the printer will use all the space on a page for graphs before advancing the paper. The Pause option allows you to change the paper when a graph is completed. The setting for Pause must be Yes when you want to make this change for a device like a plotter. PrintGraph will continue the printing process until it has completed all the selected graphs, unless you choose to intervene with CTRL-BREAK.

Review

- 1-2-3 can create seven different graph types from your worksheet data. It can create bar, line, pie, stack-bar, XY, HLCO, and mixed graphs.

- 1-2-3 can plot up to six series of data in a graph.

- A graph can contain legends to identify the data ranges, grid lines, and titles that enhance its appearance.

- A worksheet has only one current graph at a time. Once you name a graph, you can make a different graph current and still be able to use the named graph at a later time.

- You can save the graph settings by saving the worksheet.

- You can save the graphic image with Graph Save to save the graph to a file that PrintGraph, Allways, or WYSIWYG can use.

- PrintGraph can print 1-2-3 graphs with a variety of print enhancements. If you prefer you can use the Allways or WYSIWYG add-in packages supplied with Release 2.2 or 2.3 of 1-2-3.

Commands and Keys

Entry	Action
F10 (GRAPH)	Displays the current worksheet
GA	Graph A assigns worksheet data to the A data range
GB	Graph B assigns worksheet data to the B data range
GC	Graph C assigns worksheet data to the C data range

Entry	Action
GD	Graph D assigns worksheet data to the D data range
GE	Graph E assigns worksheet data to the E data range
GF	Graph F assigns worksheet data to the F data range
GX	Graph X assigns worksheet data to the X data range
GG	Graph Group assigns worksheet data to all data ranges
GT	Graph Type selects the current graph type
GNU	Graph Name Use makes a named graph the current graph
GNC	Graph Name Create makes the current graph a named graph
GS	Graph Save saves the graphic image to a .PIC file
GV	Graph View views the current graph
GOTF	Graph Options Titles First provides the first line title for the current graph
GOTS	Graph Options Titles Second provides the second line title for the current graph
GOTX	Graph Options Titles X-Axis provides the title for X axis in the current graph
GOTY	Graph Options Titles Y-Axis provides the title for Y axis in the current graph
GOL	Graph Options Legend assigns legends to the A through F data ranges
GOGH	Graph Options Grid Horizontal displays horizontal grid lines in the current graph

Entry	Action
GOGV	Graph Options Grid Vertical displays vertical grid lines in the current graph
GOGB	Graph Options Grid Both displays horizontal and vertical grid lines in the current graph
GOGC	Graph Options Grid Clear removes grid lines in the current graph
GOQ	Graph Options Quit returns to the Graph menu
GOB	Graph Options B&W displays current graph in black and white (monochrome)
GOC	Graph Options Color displays current graph in color

PrintGraph Command	Action
I	Image-Select selects the graphic images to print
SHG	Settings Hardware Graphs-Directory selects the directory containing the graph files
SHF	Settings Hardware Fonts-Directory selects the directory containing the font files
SHI	Settings Hardware Interface selects the communications port to the printer
SHP	Settings Hardware Printer selects the printer to use for printing
SS	Settings Save saves the settings made with the Settings menu
G	Go prints the selected graphs
E	Exit leaves PrintGraph

8

9

Data-Management Basics

All the work you have done with 1-2-3 up to this point has been concerned with calculating some type of numeric result. This is the typical application for the 1-2-3 program. However, 1-2-3 also has other features—features that are oriented more toward the management of information than toward calculations. These data-management features are a special group of commands that provide capabilities for the design, entry, and retrieval of information, with or without additional calculations. You can use these commands to keep track of information about your suppliers, clients, or employees.

Since this is a new area of 1-2-3 for you, the first step is to learn some new terms. A *database* is a collection of all the information you have about a set of things. These things can be customers, employees, orders, parts in your inventory, or anything else. If you created a database of employee information, you would place the information about each of your employees in it. All the information about one employee would be in one *record* of the database. A record is composed of all the pieces of information you want to record about each thing in the set, such as one employee. These individual pieces of information in the record are referred to as *fields*. Fields to include in each record in an employee database might contain name, job classification, salary, date of hire, and social security number. Every time you design a new database, you need to decide what fields will be included in each record.

A 1-2-3 database is a range of cells on the worksheet. The database can be in any area of the worksheet you want, but you must put the fields' names in the top row of the range. The records in the database, which contain data for each field, go in the rows beneath the field names.

Creating a Database

To create a new database, first create a list of the fields you plan to use, and then estimate the number of characters required for each field. To make this estimate, total the characters required to store one record in the database. Then estimate the number of records that you will place in the database, and multiply this number by the size of one record to get an estimate of how much memory is required for the database. Next, load 1-2-3 and select Worksheet Status to see how much memory is available. If the total you need exceeds the amount of memory available, another alternative is required—for example, splitting the database into two sections. Try this process for the employee file you will create.

1. Take a piece of paper and write down this list of field names:

   Last Name
   First Name
   SS#
   Job Code
   Salary
   Location

2. Write the size of the field next to each field name.
   For this example, use 12 characters for the last name, 12 for the first name, 11 for the social security number, 4 for the job code, 8 for the salary, and 3 for the location. This makes a total of

50 characters for one record. (If you want your estimate to be more exact, add 4 for each field since 1-2-3 uses 4 characters to store information about each cell.)

3. Estimate the number of records you plan to eventually enter into the database and multiply this number by the size of one record.

   For this example, 100 records is the estimate. Multiplying 100 by 50 results in a product of 5000. This should be well within the limit of any system. However, for those occasions when it is larger, take a look at how to verify this calculation:

4. Select Worksheet Status and check the amount of available memory.

The amount of memory shown in the worksheet status display in Figure 9-1 is 244,000 bytes—more than enough to accommodate 5000 characters, plus some extra for special options such as formatting. If the amount of available memory exceeds the size requirements of the database, it is safe to proceed. When the size of the database is larger than available memory, you must develop an alternative plan before beginning data entry. One possibility is to disable the Undo feature since it uses half of the available memory.

Choosing a Location

Any area of the worksheet can be used for a database. Normally, when your worksheet serves a dual purpose (for both calculations and a database), place the database below the calculations so it can expand easily. If nothing else is stored on the worksheet, row 1 is as good a starting location as any other.

Entering Field Names

Whatever area you select for your database, record your field names across the top row. Always choose *meaningful names;* they will be used again to invoke the data-management features. Meaningful names should be *self-documenting*—that is, they should help clarify what you are doing. Each field name must be contained within a single cell. Field names that span

9

Figure 9-1. *Using the Worksheet Status command to check available memory*

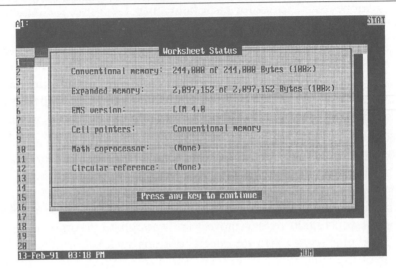

two cells are not acceptable; neither are spaces at the end of a field name. Spaces or special characters in the cell immediately beneath the field name can also cause a problem with some of 1-2-3's data-management features.

To enter the field names in the chosen area, simply type them in their respective cells and adjust the column widths.

1. Enter the field names for the employee database in these cells now:

A1:	Last Name
B1:	First Name
C1:	"SS#
D1:	Job Code
E1:	"Salary
F1:	Location

    Pay special attention to the spelling of field names. When you use the field names in later tasks, they must match exactly if the job is to be completed properly.

2. Move the cell pointer to column A and select Worksheet Column Set-Width, type **12**, and press ENTER.

3. Repeat step 2 for columns B, C, and E. If you are using Release 2.2 or above, you can select Worksheet Column Column-Range Set-Width to set the width for columns A through E to 12 and Worksheet Column Reset-Width for column D.

These entries should create a display like this:

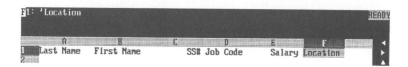

The label entries require a width equal only to the number of characters in the field. The Salary field has been estimated at 8 digits; however, 12 is allowed in the column width for the addition of a dollar sign, a comma, a decimal point, and one extra space to separate the entry from the adjacent fields.

Entering Data

Now that you have entered the field names, you can begin entering the data beneath them. The first record should be entered immediately beneath the field names. Each record will occupy one row; do not skip any row as you begin to enter records.

Make sure that the data you enter in each field is the same type. If a field contains value entries, the entries in all records for this field should contain value entries. If you do not have all the data for a record, you can leave the field blank as long as you do not leave the entire row blank. Except for these few simple guidelines, everything is exactly the same as when entering data in the worksheet environment.

You will need to complete the data entry for the database used throughout the rest of this chapter. The normal procedure for entering records in a database is to enter a complete record at once; however, since it might be easier to complete the entries in one column before moving to the next one, the directions in this chapter are written from that perspective. You can either work from the screen display shown in Figure 9-2 or follow these explicit directions to complete the entries:

1. Place these entries in the Last Name field:

A2:	Larson	A7:	Lightnor
A3:	Campbell	A8:	McCartin
A4:	Campbell	A9:	Justof
A5:	Stephens	A10:	Patterson
A6:	Caldor	A11:	Miller

2. Make these entries in the First Name field:

B2:	Mary	B7:	Peggy
B3:	David	B8:	John
B4:	Keith	B9:	Jack
B5:	Tom	B10:	Lyle
B6:	Larry	B11:	Lisa

Figure 9-2.   *The employee database*

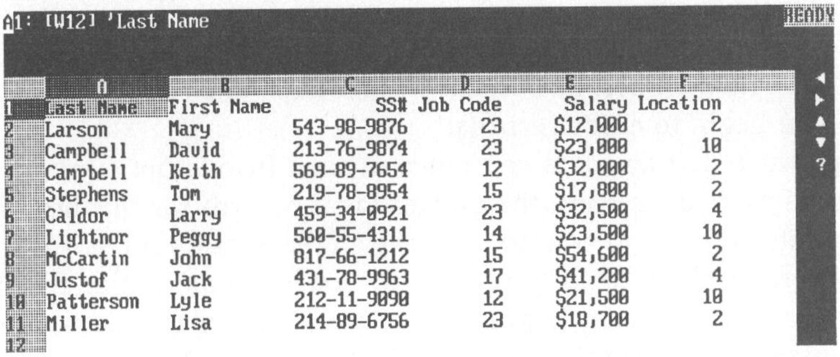

A1: [W12] 'Last Name						READY
	A	B	C	D	E	F
1	Last Name	First Name	SS#	Job Code	Salary	Location
2	Larson	Mary	543-98-9876	23	$12,000	2
3	Campbell	David	213-76-9874	23	$23,000	10
4	Campbell	Keith	569-89-7654	12	$32,000	2
5	Stephens	Tom	219-78-8954	15	$17,800	2
6	Caldor	Larry	459-34-0921	23	$32,500	4
7	Lightnor	Peggy	560-55-4311	14	$23,500	10
8	McCartin	John	817-66-1212	15	$54,600	2
9	Justof	Jack	431-78-9963	17	$41,200	4
10	Patterson	Lyle	212-11-9090	12	$21,500	10
11	Miller	Lisa	214-89-6756	23	$18,700	2
12						

3. Make the following entries in the SS# field:

C2:	'543-98-9876	C7:	'560-55-4311
C3:	'213-76-9874	C8:	'817-66-1212
C4:	'569-89-7654	C9:	'431-78-9963
C5:	'219-78-8954	C10:	'212-11-9090
C6:	'459-34-0921	C11:	'214-89-6756

Notice that a single quotation mark was used at the beginning of each of these entries. The social security numbers must be labels because they include the hyphen character (-). If you forget to start these entries with a label indicator, a negative number will appear in the cell. You will then need to edit the cell entry and insert the label indicator at the beginning.

4. Enter the following job codes:

D2:	23	D7:	14
D3:	23	D8:	15
D4:	12	D9:	17
D5:	15	D10:	12
D6:	23	D11:	23

5. Move the cell pointer to E2, select Range Format Currency, type **0**, press ENTER, move the cell pointer to E11, and press ENTER.

6. Make the following salary entries:

E2:	12000	E7:	23500
E3:	23000	E8:	54600
E4:	32000	E9:	41200
E5:	17800	E10:	21500
E6:	32500	E11:	18700

9

7. Enter the following location codes:

F2:	2	F7:	10
F3:	10	F8:	2
F4:	2	F9:	4
F5:	2	F10:	10
F6:	4	F11:	2

This completes the entries required to create a database with ten records.

Making Changes

Making changes to entries in the database is no different from making changes in the worksheet data you use. You have two good choices: Retype any entry to replace it, or use the F2 (EDIT) technique to make a quick correction. To feel at home with making changes, just as if you were still making worksheet entries, carry out the following steps to change the salary and social security number for Mary Larson:

1. Move the cell pointer to C2, press the F2 (EDIT) key, and move with the LEFT ARROW key until the cell pointer is under the 7. Press the DEL key, type **4**, and press ENTER to correct the SS#. The social security number now reads as 543-98-9846.

2. Move the cell pointer to E2, press F2 (EDIT), and press the HOME key. Next, press the DEL key, type **2**, and press ENTER. The salary now reads as $22,000.

Sorting the Database

1-2-3 provides Sort features that can alter the sequence of the records in your database to any sequence you need. If you decide that you would like an employee list in alphabetical order, 1-2-3 can do this for you. If you decide that you want the records in order by job code, salary, or location, 1-2-3 can make this change easily. You will find 1-2-3's sort commands easy to work with, and you will be amazed at how rapidly 1-2-3 can resequence your data.

All the commands that you will need to specify the sort are located on the menu shown in Figure 9-3. You can activate this menu by selecting Data Sort. The settings sheet, which appears below the menu in this figure, allows you to see at a glance the selections you have already made. You will always want to check the accuracy of the entries shown on this sheet before selecting Go to start the sort operation.

Defining the Location

The first step in resequencing your database is to tell 1-2-3 where the data is located. When you are sorting data, 1-2-3 is not interested in the

Figure 9-3. *The Data Sort menu and dialog box*

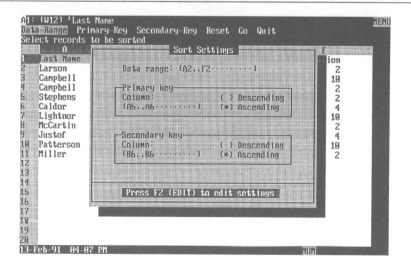

field names, only in the data values that you expect it to sort. If you accidentally include the field names in this range, 1-2-3 will sort them just as if they were intentionally included as data values.

In defining the area to be sorted, you have the choice of defining some of the records or all of them. Always include all the fields, even if you want to exclude some of the records. This is because excluded fields remain stationary and do not remain with the other portion of the record to which they belong, thus jeopardizing the integrity of your file. It is therefore a good idea to save the file before sorting in case you accidentally exclude some of the field names. Having Undo enabled is another safeguard, although it will only be effective in reversing the result of a Sort operation if you do so before entering another command. Follow these steps to tell 1-2-3 where the employee records are located:

1. Select File Save, type **EMPLOYEE**, and press ENTER.

2. Select Data Sort.

3. Select Data-Range to produce this display:

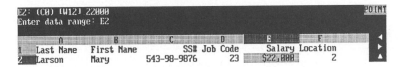

4. Press the HOME key. Press the DOWN ARROW key.

    This will position you in A2, right below the first field name. If you had sorted this database previously, you would have had to press ESC first to free the beginning of the range before moving the cell pointer.

5. Type a period and press the END key followed by the DOWN ARROW key. Press the END key followed by the RIGHT ARROW key.

    At this point the database range should be highlighted like the one shown in Figure 9-4. You can, of course, use the mouse to make your selection.

6. Verify that the range you wish to sort is highlighted and press ENTER.

Figure 9-4. *Highlighting the range to sort*

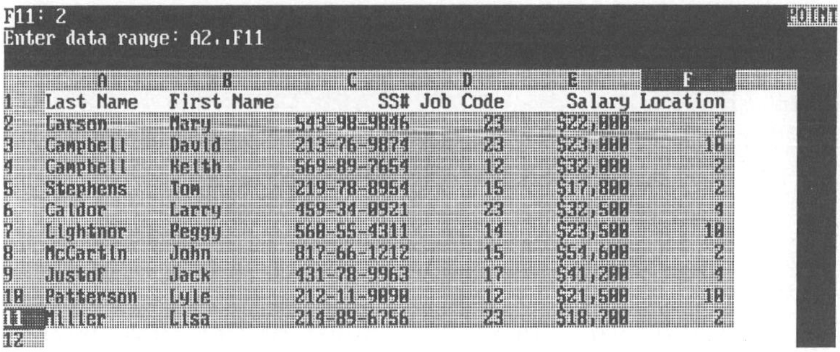

Defining the Sort Sequence

You can sort your data in sequence by any of the database fields. If you sort by the contents of column D, the database will be in sequence by job code. If you sort by column C, social security number will determine the sequence. Whichever field you choose to sort by, you will also have to decide whether you want the entries to be sequenced from highest to lowest (descending) or lowest to highest (ascending).

1-2-3 refers to the field that determines the sequence of the records after the sort as the *primary key*. It also allows you to establish a *secondary key*. This secondary key, which is optional, is a precaution against duplicates in the primary key. 1-2-3 ignores the secondary key even when you specify one, except where the primary key contains duplicate entries. In that case, the secondary key is used to break the tie.

Choosing a Primary Key

There are three ways to specify the sort sequence. One is to select Data Sort Primary-Key and point to a cell that contains an entry for the field that will control the order of the records. Another is to type the address of this cell. The third way will work if you have named the first cell in each of the data-entry columns. An easy way to apply these names is to select Range Name Label Down and specify the range of labels that represent the field names. If you use this approach you can press F3 (NAME) when prompted for a field or a column and select from the list of range names provided. 1-2-3 will display the cell address of the entry on the settings sheet and follow it with the name assigned to the range. The first time the data is sorted, the named cell may be shuffled to a record other than the first record, but this will not affect later use of it because the sort accepts any of the entries with a field. Regardless of the method chosen for specifying the cell, the next prompt you will see asks for the sort order, for which A and D are the only acceptable choices. An A represents ascending sequence and a D represents descending sequence. When 1-2-3 asks for the sort order, a default choice is on the screen. If you want to use it, just press ENTER.

Follow these steps to see the Data Sort Primary-Key command in action:

1. Select Primary-Key to create this prompt:

2. Move the cell pointer to C2 and press ENTER.
   This selects the social security number as the primary sort key.

3. Type **D** to create the following display:

4. Press ENTER to request descending sequence.

5. Select Go to activate the sort and change the sequence of the records to match Figure 9-5.
   Just defining the sort key does not change the data sequence. You must select Go to tell 1-2-3 that you are ready for the sort to take place.

Figure 9-5. *Records in SS# sequence*

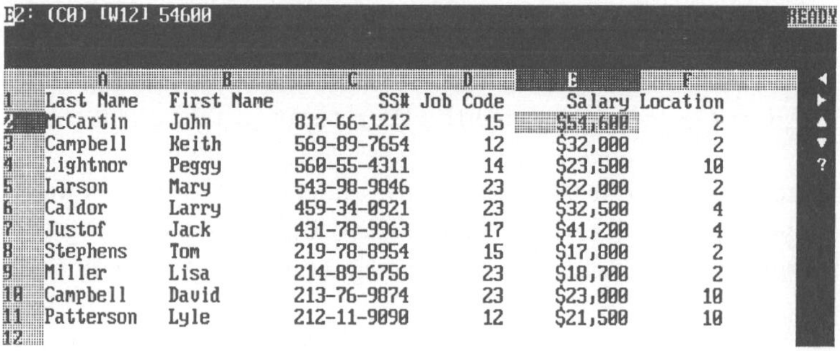
E2: (C0) [W12] 54600 READY

	A	B	C	D	E	F
1	Last Name	First Name	SS#	Job Code	Salary	Location
2	McCartin	John	817-66-1212	15	$54,600	2
3	Campbell	Keith	569-89-7654	12	$32,000	2
4	Lightnor	Peggy	560-55-4311	14	$23,500	10
5	Larson	Mary	543-98-9846	23	$22,000	2
6	Caldor	Larry	459-34-0921	23	$32,500	4
7	Justof	Jack	431-78-9963	17	$41,200	4
8	Stephens	Tom	219-78-8954	15	$17,800	2
9	Miller	Lisa	214-89-6756	23	$18,700	2
10	Campbell	David	213-76-9874	23	$23,000	10
11	Patterson	Lyle	212-11-9090	12	$21,500	10
12						

Choosing a Secondary Key

The secondary key is the tie breaker. It resolves duplicate entries and determines which one of the duplicates should be listed first, based on the value of the secondary field. In situations like the last example where social security number was the controlling sequence, a secondary key is not needed. Since the social security number field does not contain legal duplicates, there is no need for a tie breaker. On the other hand, if you want to sort the employee file by last name, a secondary key is appropriate since last names sometimes are duplicated.

The process for specifying the secondary key is the same as the process for specifying the primary key, except that you select Data Sort Secondary-Key. Try this feature by sorting the employee database in name order, following these steps:

1. Select Data Sort Reset.

   This cancels the current settings for the data range and for the primary and secondary sort keys.

2. Select Data-Range, type **A2.F11** or select these cells with your mouse, and press ENTER.

3. Select Primary-Key, type **A2**, press ENTER, type **A**, and press ENTER.

   The top cell in the Last Name field was selected as the sort key.

4. Select Secondary-Key, type **B2**, press ENTER, type **A**, and press ENTER.

9

The top cell in the First Name field was selected as the secondary key. This key will be used to resolve the tie only when more than one employee has the same last name. In that case, the First Name field will determine which record is placed first.

5. Select Go to resequence the data to an alphabetical name list.

There is no need to quit the Sort menu. Selecting Go to execute the sort will place you back in READY mode after the data has been resequenced. The Quit option is available for occasions when you want to exit the menu without performing the sort.

When you save the worksheet with File Save, 1-2-3 will save the sort specifications you just entered. The next time you use the worksheet you can execute the sort and change only those options that are different. Be especially careful when updating the data range if you add more fields to the end of the database. If you do not adjust the range, the new fields will remain stationary while the rest of the record is shifted to a new row.

Searching the Database

As your database grows, it becomes increasingly important to review the information it contains selectively. Once the employee file contains 500 records, it becomes extremely time-consuming to locate all the records that have a job code of 23 by scanning the Job Code column visually.

1-2-3 gives you a way to work with information in your database selectively by means of *exception* or *selective reporting* capabilities. This means you will have a method of selectively presenting information that falls outside of a norm you establish. The selective reporting feature can also provide an easy way to clean up the database or to create reports in response to unexpected requests.

Working with 1-2-3's selective reporting feature requires that you enter your specifications for record selection on the worksheet. These specifications are known as *criteria* and must be entered on the worksheet before invoking 1-2-3's commands. Once the criteria are entered, you must make various menu selections.

All the commands required for working with 1-2-3's selective reporting feature are found in the Data Query menu, which follows:

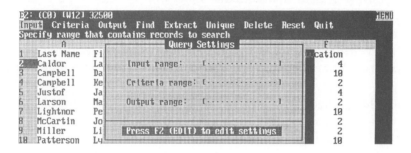

Like the Sort menu, the Data Query menu is "sticky"; in most situations, you will have to make more than one selection from the menu before 1-2-3 will complete your task, and you will have a settings sheet on the screen to keep track of the selections you have made if you are using Release 2.2 or above. You will want to check this sheet carefully after making your entries. A common mistake is to choose the same area of the worksheet for more than one of the selections; this is never correct.

Since the Data Query feature has a number of steps, the best approach is to look at each step and then try a few examples. You will begin by exploring the rules for entering your criteria on the worksheet.

Entering Criteria

You enter criteria on the worksheet to tell 1-2-3 which records you want to work with. 1-2-3 will ignore records that do not match these criteria when you ask the Data Query feature to perform a task with the database.

The first step in creating criteria is choosing a blank area on the worksheet in which to enter them. The rules for entering criteria differ, depending on whether you are working with label data or value data. Regardless of which type of data you want to enter, the criteria will represent the field name you are attempting to match in the existing records. If you want to match the Job Code field, type **Job Code** in the blank area that you chose. You must enter the field name exactly as it is in the database; that is, with identical spelling. You will then place the criteria specification immediately beneath this field name.

9

Value Data Criteria

You can enter two different types of criteria for matching records when you use a field that contains value entries. One type is *exact entry match criteria,* which places a value that could occur in the field beneath the field name. If you want to search for all records with a 23 in the Job Code field, all you need to do is type **23** beneath the Job Code entry in the criteria area. Make the following entries to set up the exact match criteria:

1. Move the cell pointer to D1, select Copy, press ENTER, select A13, and press ENTER.

   Copying the field name instead of retyping the field name prevents you from accidentally entering an entry that is different from the field name at the beginning of the database table. When 1-2-3 is looking for an exact match such as in this example, a slight difference between the text in the criteria area and the database table will prevent 1-2-3 from locating the records you want.

2. Move to A14, type **23**, and press ENTER to create the criteria entry shown below:

These entries do not select any records. They only enable you to use the Data Query commands to select the records you want. Before moving on to the remaining steps, look at the other types of criteria that are available. In fact, you can set up examples of some of these on the worksheet. You can make multiple-criteria entries in different locations on the worksheet as long as you use them one at a time.

The other type of value criteria is a *comparison formula.* This can be more powerful than exact entry match criteria; it not only performs an exact match but can also identify records whose values are less than, greater than, and not equal to an established value. The variety of logical operators that can be used to express these conditions is shown in Table 9-1.

Table 9-1. *Logical Operators for Building Criteria Formulas*

=	Equal
>	Greater than
>=	Greater than or equal to
<	Less than
<=	Less than or equal to
<>	Not equal to

Although not required because 1-2-3 does not care what field name you use when entering formula criteria, it is worth entering the correct field name on the worksheet at the top of the criteria area to help document the basis of your selection.

After the field name, the next entry is the formula. The formula is designed to compare the first value in a field against another value. For example, to select records where the salary was greater than \$25,000 you could enter the formula +E2>25000. You must use E2 as the cell reference in this formula because you must use the first value in a field. You can use column C for this criteria by following these directions:

1. Move the cell pointer to E1, select Copy, press ENTER, select C13, and press ENTER.

   Actually, any field name would work equally well. Salary is the recommended entry, however, because it clarifies which field you are using in the comparison.

2. Move to C14, type **+E2>25000**, and press ENTER.

Do not be alarmed that your entry displays a 1 rather than the formula. The 1 means it is true—E2 is greater than 25,000. If you are intent on seeing it display as you entered it, you can select Range Format Text on the cell. However, that is not really necessary.

Label Data Criteria

There are both similarities and differences between the value and label criteria. Exact match entries work the same way as value entries do. You can place a field name in the criteria area and place the label entry you are looking for immediately beneath it. 1-2-3 is not concerned with differences in either capitalization or alignment between the two entries.

Wildcard characters are a new option with label entries. You can make a partial entry and use the asterisk (*) to tell 1-2-3 that you do not care which characters come at the end of the entry as long as the characters that you have specified match. For example, to find all the records where the last name begins with "C," you would enter **Last Name** for the field name in the criteria area and immediately beneath it you would enter **C***. To find all the records where the last name starts with "Camp," you would enter **Camp***. Enter a sample for this type of criteria:

1. Move the cell pointer to A16, type **Last Name**, and move the cell pointer to A17 to finalize.

2. Type **Camp*** and press ENTER.

In Releases 2 and higher, there is one additional type of label criteria, which uses string formulas. Since this is an advanced topic, we will only address the use of the label criteria you have already entered.

The Data Query Input Command

You must tell 1-2-3 where your data is stored before it can search the database for the information you need. In this case, you must include the field names in the range that you provide, since they are an integral part of identifying the information you want to select.

The command by which you specify the location of the database is Data Query Input. After you select this command, you can point to your data range or type the required cell references as a range address. In both cases the field names must be included. You can select the employee database with these steps:

1. Select Data Query Input.

2. Press HOME to move the cell pointer to A1, type **.** and press the END key followed by the DOWN ARROW key, and then press the END key followed by the RIGHT ARROW key.

    The database area should be highlighted as shown in Figure 9-6. Notice that the field names are included in this area.

3. Press ENTER to finalize.

The menu will remain on the screen for additional selections, such as the criteria location and the type of selection you want performed.

Accessing Stored Criteria

1-2-3 uses criteria to determine which records from the database will be used to fill your request. You have already entered several sets of criteria on the worksheet. Now you need to choose one set that 1-2-3 can use to check each record in the database. 1-2-3 will ignore records that do not meet these criteria.

To define the location of your criteria on the worksheet, select Data Query Criteria. Earlier than Release 2.2, the command was Data Query Criterion. Remember that the criteria must already be stored on the

Figure 9-6. *Selecting the area for Data Query Input*

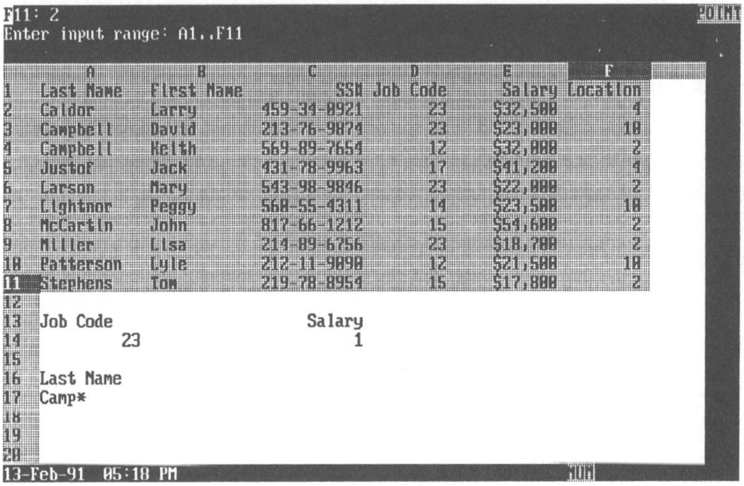

worksheet from the READY mode before you can use this command effectively. First use the criteria that searches all the records to find those that contain a job code of 23. Follow these steps:

1. Select Criteria.
2. Move the cell pointer to A13, type ., press the DOWN ARROW key once, and press ENTER.

Now all you need to do is tell 1-2-3 to highlight records that match the criteria.

Finding and Extracting Matching Records

1-2-3's Data Query Find command highlights records that match the criteria you have defined. If there are multiple entries that match, the records are highlighted one at a time. 1-2-3 begins at the top of the database, highlighting the first record that matches, and lets you use the arrow keys to move to other records that match the criteria. If the number of fields exceeds the width of the screen, you can also use the arrow keys to view other fields within a highlighted record. You cannot move to records that do not match the criteria; the highlighted bar automatically skips over them.

You completed the preliminary steps for Find when you entered your criteria on the worksheet and then defined its location as well as the location of the data. Now, whenever you select Find, the criteria that was defined and referenced with Criteria will be used. The data referenced with the range input will be searched for matching records. Because the preliminaries have been completed, only one step is needed to highlight the first record.

1. Select Find to produce a display like this:

A2: [W12] 'Caldor					FIND
	A	B	C	D	E	F
	Last Name	First Name	SS#	Job Code	Salary	Location
1						
2	Caldor	Larry	459-34-8921	23	$32,500	4
3	Campbell	David	213-76-9874	23	$23,000	10
4	Campbell	Keith	569-89-7654	12	$32,000	2
5	Justof	Jack	431-78-9963	17	$41,200	4

Notice that the first record containing a job code of 23 was classified as matching the criteria, and that it is currently highlighted.

2. Press the DOWN ARROW key to move to the next record with a job code of 23.

3. Press the UP ARROW key to move back to the previous record.

4. Press ESC to return to the Data Query menu.

The Find operation is useful when you need to answer a question quickly or take a quick look at someone's record. You can specify the criteria to have these records selectively highlighted for you. The problem with Find is that the data does not stay on the screen. Often when you move to the second record, the first record disappears from view (the database is probably larger than your small example). The *Extract* operation can solve this; it permits you to selectively copy fields from the database to a new area on the worksheet. As you extract this information, you can also use the fields in any sequence in the output area you are building.

To use Extract, you must complete a preliminary step from READY mode. This step involves constructing an output area in a blank area of the worksheet. You create the output area by placing the field names you wish recorded in this area at its top. Any sequence is acceptable as long as the names are an exact match with the ones in the top row of the database in terms of spelling, capitalization, and alignment.

Setting Up an Output Area

You must choose a location for the output of the Extract command and prepare it to receive data. One approach is to leave some blank rows at the bottom of the database and place the output area beneath this area. This way you will not find yourself moving the output area as the database expands. Another approach is to place the output area to the right of the database so you do not need to worry about the amount of expansion that will be required. Once you have selected the location, enter the names of the fields you want copied from matching records. Remember, you will not need to include every field, and the fields you choose do not need to be placed in the same sequence as those in the database. You may want to copy the field names to the output area from above the database. This strategy eliminates all possibilities of a difference in spelling, capitalization, or alignment. Complete this task now for the employee file by following these steps.

1. Select Quit to return to READY mode.
   You cannot build the output area from the Data Query menu. You must exit it and return after you have completed the needed cell entries.

2. Move the cell pointer to A41, type **First Name**, and move the cell pointer to B41 to finalize the entry.

3. Type **Last Name** and move the cell pointer to C41.

4. Type **″Salary** and move the cell pointer to D41 to finalize.

5. Type **Job Code** and press ENTER.

This is all that is required to set up the output area like the following:

You are ready to take a look at the remaining menu commands required to complete the Extract operation. The first command you need is Data Query Output so that you can tell 1-2-3 where the output area is located. You can define the row containing the field names you just entered as the output area. This would be row 41 in the current example. Be aware that 1-2-3 will use all the rows from this point to the end of the worksheet to write matching records. You can also select the row containing the field names and an appropriate number of rows beneath it. If you choose the latter approach, the output area you choose must be large enough to contain all the selected records or you will get an Error Message rather than the results you are looking for.

Performing the Extract

Once you have completed the preliminaries you have done the difficult work. Now all that is required is selecting Extract from the menu. Try this now with your data:

1. Select Data Query Output. Move the cell pointer to A41, type . and press END, press the RIGHT ARROW key, and press ENTER.

2. Select Extract.

3. Select Quit to return to READY mode.

Move the cell pointer so you can view the entries that have been copied to the extract area. They should look like the ones shown below:

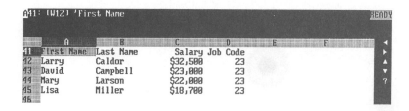

More Examples

You entered more than one set of criteria as you looked at some of the ways that criteria could be entered in worksheet cells. You can try an extract with the remaining two sets of criteria, using just a few easy steps. First use the criteria that selects records where the salary entry is greater than $25,000, and then use the criteria that selects records where the last name begins with "Camp."

Follow these steps:

1. Select Data Query Criteria, type **C13.C14**, and press ENTER.

This is where you stored the criteria to select records by the Salary field. You can use the same input area and the same output area as in your previous request without making another entry.

2. Select Extract to produce the list shown here:

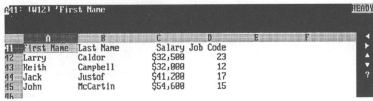

3. Select Criteria, type **A16.A17,** and press ENTER.

   This will use the criteria you entered earlier, which selects last names that begin with Camp*. If you choose to point to this criteria rather than typing the range address, press ESC first.

4. Select Extract to produce the data shown below:

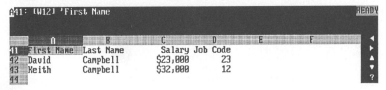

5. Select Quit to return to READY mode.

Special Features

Now that you have completed the basics of data management, we will look at some of 1-2-3's data-management features. These include a short-cut approach to executing a Query operation, referencing the database with a range name, and the powerful database statistical functions.

Shortcuts

There is a short-cut approach to reexecuting a Data Query command. However, it requires that certain conditions be met. The first condition is that the database be the exact same size and in the exact same location as when the last query was executed. The second condition is that your criteria must be the same size and shape as when the last query was executed. They can have new values or check new fields, as long as the location of these criteria is the same. The third condition is that if you are performing Extract operations, the output area must be the same size and shape as in the last query. The fourth and last condition is that you must be performing the same Data Query operation. If you performed an Extract last time, you must perform an Extract this time. If all of these conditions are met you can reexecute the last Query operation by pressing F7 (QUERY).

Try this by carrying out the following directions to update the criteria:

1. Move the cell pointer to A17, type **L***, and press ENTER.

2. Press F7 (QUERY), and then press PGDN twice to produce the display shown below:

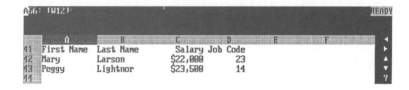

This is a handy feature if you need to perform multiple Query operations. You only need to use the menu the first time. Then you can type new values in the criteria area if you wish, and press F7 (QUERY) to have 1-2-3 use the new criteria.

Naming the Database

Using a name rather than a range address to refer to the database can provide flexibility. 1-2-3 permits you to assign a name to a range of cells. If you expand this range of cells by inserting blank rows or columns in the middle, the range referenced by the name will be expanded automatically. If a built-in function or formula references the name rather than an address, the built-in function is automatically adjusted for any change in the range.

9

You can assign names with the Range Name Create command, which was first introduced in Chapter 2, "Defining Your Calculations." Try it now with the employee database by following these steps:

1. Select Range Name Create, type **EMPLOYEE**, and press ENTER.
2. Press ESC and then HOME. Type . and then press END followed by DOWN ARROW, END followed by RIGHT ARROW, and ENTER.

You will now be able to reference the range A1..F11 by the name EMPLOYEE. If you insert blank rows or columns in the middle of your database and make entries, the reference to EMPLOYEE will make these available immediately.

Database Statistical Functions

The database statistical functions are a special category of built-in functions that are designed to work exclusively in the data-management environment. Like other built-in functions, they are prerecorded formulas that can perform calculations for you with a minimum of work on your part. Unlike other built-in functions, they operate on a database and require that you establish criteria for which records are to be included in the calculations they perform.

All the database statistical functions have the same format for their arguments. They are patterned after the following:

@DFUNCTION (database,offset in database,criteria location)

The first argument in all these functions is the location of the database. The range that you use to identify this location should include the field names as well as the data. The second argument, the offset, is the column number of the field that you want used in the calculations. This column number is always one less that what you would expect with the ordinary way of counting. 1-2-3 refers to the first column in the database as column 0 and increments this by one for each column to the right. Since you have no control over 1-2-3's procedures, you will have to adjust your way of thinking when using these functions. The last argument is the location of the criteria. These criteria are defined in the same way as the ones you used with Extract and Find in the Data Query menu. You must record them on the worksheet before you include their location in the function. Putting a few of these to work will clarify exactly how you work with them.

Using @DAVG

The @DAVG function allows you to compute the average for a field in a selected group of database records. You can use this function to determine the average salary for employees with a job code of 23. You can use the criteria you entered for the Data Query feature. Just follow these steps:

1. Move the cell pointer to A21. Type **Average Salary for Job Code 23:** and move the cell pointer to D21 to finalize your entry.
2. Type **@DAVG(EMPLOYEE,4,A13.A14)** and press ENTER.

Notice that the database reference uses the range name, EMPLOYEE, which includes the field names, all records, and all fields. The offset is 4 because you are referring to the fifth column and 1-2-3 starts with column 0 rather than column 1. The criteria location uses the entries in A13 and A14 to select the records whose salary entries will be included in the average. The results follow:

Using @DSUM

The @DSUM function follows the same pattern as the @DAVG function. If you want to total one of the fields in the database for all records with a job code of 23, you can use it without entering criteria again. Follow these steps:

1. Move the cell pointer to A22. Type **Total Salaries for Job Code 23:** and move the cell pointer to D22 to finalize your entry.

2. Type **@DSUM(EMPLOYEE,4,A13.A14)** and press ENTER.

The results of this calculation follow:

Using @DCOUNT

The @DCOUNT function is used to selectively count the number of non-blank entries in records that match your criteria. It follows the same pattern as the other database functions and operates on the entries in the column specified by the offset.

You can use this function to count the number of employees with a job code of 23. Follow these steps to enter the function:

1. Move the cell pointer to A23. Type **Number of Employees in Job Code 23:** and move the cell pointer to D23 to finalize your entry.

2. Type **@DCOUNT(EMPLOYEE,3,A13.A14)** and press ENTER.

The results of this calculation follow:

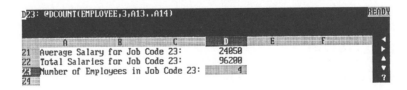

The Count operation is performed on the Job Code field. This will effectively give you a count of the records coded as job code 23. If the Job Code field were blank, the records could not be selected as matching the criteria for job code 23; therefore the @DCOUNT function does not count records that do not match.

Using @DMIN

The @DMIN function searches for the minimum value in the column specified. Only records that match your criteria are eligible for this minimum comparison. This provides a convenient way to determine the lowest salary paid to an individual in location 2 or the lowest salary paid to someone with job code 23. This time you will change the criteria and then enter the formula to determine the lowest salary in location 2. Follow these steps:

1. Move the cell pointer to E13 and type **Location**.

2. Move the cell pointer to E14 and type **2**.

3. Move the cell pointer to A24 and type **Minimum Salary for Location 2:**. Then move the cell pointer to D24 to finalize your entry.

4. Type **@DMIN(EMPLOYEE,4,E13.E14)** and press ENTER to produce these results:

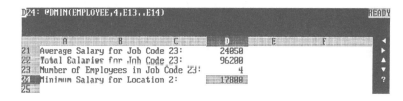

Review

- You can create a database with 1-2-3 by using a tabular area on the worksheet. Your first step should be comparing your storage needs with the available memory in your computer.

- Field names are placed one per cell across the top row of the table. Rows beneath the field names are used for the data in the database records.

- You can resequence the records in a 1-2-3 database with the Data Sort command. The records are specified as the data range for the sort. Primary and secondary keys can be selected to control the sequence of the records. Once your specifications are defined, the Go option will sort the records.

- 1-2-3's Data Query command allows you to select records of interest in the database. You can highlight matching records with the Find option or copy them out to a new area on the worksheet if you set up an output area and then use Extract. Only records that match your criteria or specifications are highlighted or copied.

- The database statistical functions are @ functions that work with the records in a 1-2-3 database and the criteria you have established to select records of interest. You can obtain a total, average, minimum, or maximum, and you can perform other statistical computations on a selected group of your records with these functions.

Commands and Keys

Entry	Action
F7 (QUERY)	Repeats the most recent Query operation
DQC	Data Query Criteria defines for 1-2-3 the specification you have entered on the worksheet

Entry	Action
DQE	Data Query Extract writes copies of records meeting the specifications in the criteria area to the output area
DQF	Data Query Find highlights records matching the criteria
DQI	Data Query Input defines for 1-2-3 the database records for the Query operation
DQO	Data Query Output defines the output area for a Data Query Extract operation
DSD	Data Sort Data-Range defines the records to be sorted
DSG	Data Sort Go performs the Sort operation
DSP	Data Sort Primary-Key defines the primary sort sequence for 1-2-3
DSS	Data Sort Secondary-Key defines the secondary sort sequence for 1-2-3
@DAVG	Computes an average of a specified field in the records matching your specifications
@DCOUNT	Computes a count of the non-blank entries in a specified field for the records matching your specifications
@DMIN	Determines the minimum value in a specified field in the records matching your specifications
@DSUM	Computes the sum of a specified field in the records matching your specifications

9

10

Advanced File-Management Techniques

By now you are probably an expert at the basic file-management features for saving and retrieving your worksheet files. These commands are the workhorses of the file commands because they play a central role in every worksheet session. A number of other file-management commands are used less commonly but provide some powerful options that you will want to incorporate into your set of skills.

In this chapter you will learn to use the 1-2-3 combine features, which let you combine an entire file or a range of data with the file currently in memory. With Release 2.2 and above you can also combine information from several files into one worksheet with the file link features. This new method is easier and less error prone because you can even update the links for shared network files at any time with the File Admin Link-Refresh command. These new techniques allow you to bring data into memory from disk without wiping out the current entries in the worksheet, as File Retrieve does. Together, these new commands provide ways to increase productivity by letting you reuse existing data rather than having to reenter it. The commands also let you consolidate the numbers in individual worksheets to compute a total automatically.

Combining Files

The File Retrieve command has a Worksheet Erase command built right into it. Every time you select File Retrieve, the file in memory will be replaced by the contents of the file you are bringing in from the disk. In many cases this is exactly what you need. But in others, you might prefer to retain the current contents of memory and bring information into memory from disk to add to the current data. The File Combine command provides this capability and performs the Release 2.2 file link features covered later in the chapter. You will want to review the File Combine command capabilities and then contrast them with the file linking ability covered later.

In this section you will examine each of the File Combine menu options separately in order to understand the functions they serve. These components will then be joined in examples to help you understand their sequence and their relationship to the File Combine menus.

The Combine Operation

There are many applications for the File Combine command. This feature has three options, with a menu like this:

The first option copies data from disk to an area of the worksheet and replaces the contents of that area with what is on the disk. This option would be useful for adding a list of account names that are stored in a file.

The second option adds the data on the disk to the data already in memory. Each value in the file will be added to a corresponding value in the current worksheet. The corresponding value is determined by the cell pointer location at the time the command is invoked. This option would let you automate the consolidation of sales or expenses for all the units within a company to produce a total company report.

The third option is subtraction. This option could be used to remove the results for a subsidiary from the total company reports.

You have two options when combining a file with the current worksheet: You can combine everything in the file, or you can combine the contents of a range name. The option you choose depends on whether or not the file contains data you want to combine.

Using an Entire File

When you combine an entire file, everything in the file will be placed within the current worksheet. Which combining method to use depends on which selections you make. Figure 10-1 shows a list of account names that are stored in a file named ACCOUNTS. You can create this file by entering each of the account names and saving the file as ACCOUNTS. Then erase the screen and start the new worksheet.

Figure 10-1.   *Account names*

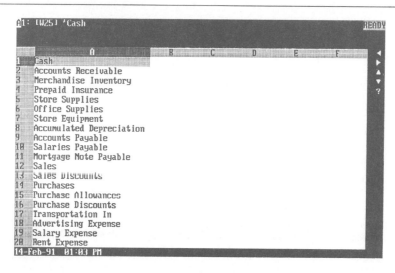

```
A1: [W25] 'Cash                                                    READY

                      A           B      C      D      E      F      ◄
   1  Cash                                                          ►
   2  Accounts Receivable                                          ▲
   3  Merchandise Inventory                                        ▼
   4  Prepaid Insurance                                            ?
   5  Store Supplies
   6  Office Supplies
   7  Store Equipment
   8  Accumulated Depreciation
   9  Accounts Payable
  10  Salaries Payable
  11  Mortgage Note Payable
  12  Sales
  13  Sales Discounts
  14  Purchases
  15  Purchase Allowances
  16  Purchase Discounts
  17  Transportation In
  18  Advertising Expense
  19  Salary Expense
  20  Rent Expense
 14-Feb-91  01:03 PM
```

10

Figure 10-2.   *Worksheet requiring account names*

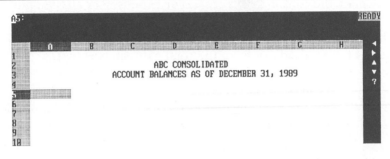

The current worksheet shown in Figure 10-2 can use the list of names displayed in Figure 10-1. The result of combining ACCOUNTS with the current worksheet is shown in Figure 10-3. The accounts were put just where they were needed by the placement of the cell pointer in A5, then the Combine operation was invoked by selecting File Combine Copy Entire-File, and the file ACCOUNTS.WK1.

Figure 10-3.   *Worksheet with account names added*

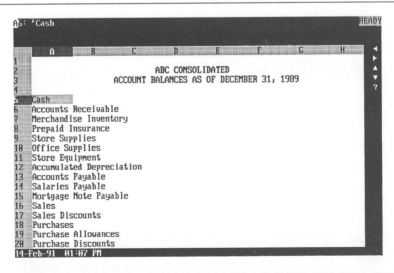

Using a Range

You were introduced to range names in Chapter 2, "Defining Your Calculations." Ranges of cells can be assigned range names for a variety of reasons. For example, names can be added to improve the readability of formulas. They can also be used to let you combine less than an entire file with the current worksheet.

If you want to transfer numbers to another worksheet, you can use the Range Name command in the sending file, save that file, and use the File Combine command with the Named/Specified-Range option to obtain the data you need in a receiving file. While you can combine ranges by providing range addresses instead of range names, range names are easier to remember than range addresses, which prevents mistakes.

To try this follow these steps:

1. Select Worksheet Column Set-Width, type **18**, and press ENTER.

2. Complete these entries:

A3:	Sales - Product 1
A4:	Sales - Product 2
A5:	Sales - Product 3
B2:	"Jan
B3:	1200
B4:	4400
B5:	5400
C2:	"Feb
C3:	1500
C4:	5600
C5:	7800
D2:	"Mar
D3:	1100
D4:	7800
D5:	9900
E2:	"Qtr1
E3:	@SUM(B3.D3)
E4:	@SUM(B4.D4)
E5:	@SUM(B5.D5)

3. Move the cell pointer to E2 and select Range Name Create.

10

You are including the label Qtr1 in this range in order to see how the label is handled.

4. Type **Total** and press ENTER.

5. Move the cell pointer to E5 to produce the display in Figure 10-4.

6. Press ENTER.

Both the label and formulas are now named Total. Later, if you use this named range with File Combine, the combination method you select will determine whether the current value of the formula or the formula itself is used. The command you select will also determine whether the label at the top of the formulas is used. This will be more clear after you have examined the options for combining in more detail.

7. Select File Save, type **1ST_QTR**, and press ENTER.

8. Move the cell pointer to D3.

9. Select File Xtract Values.

This command will allow you to specify a range and will save the values in those cells to another file.

10. Type **QTR1VALU** and press ENTER to indicate the name of the new file.

11. Move the cell pointer to E5 so that the range will be E3..E5.

12. Press ENTER to finalize. 1-2-3 will write the current values to A1..A3 in QTR1VALU.

Figure 10-4.   *Naming a range to use later with File Combine*

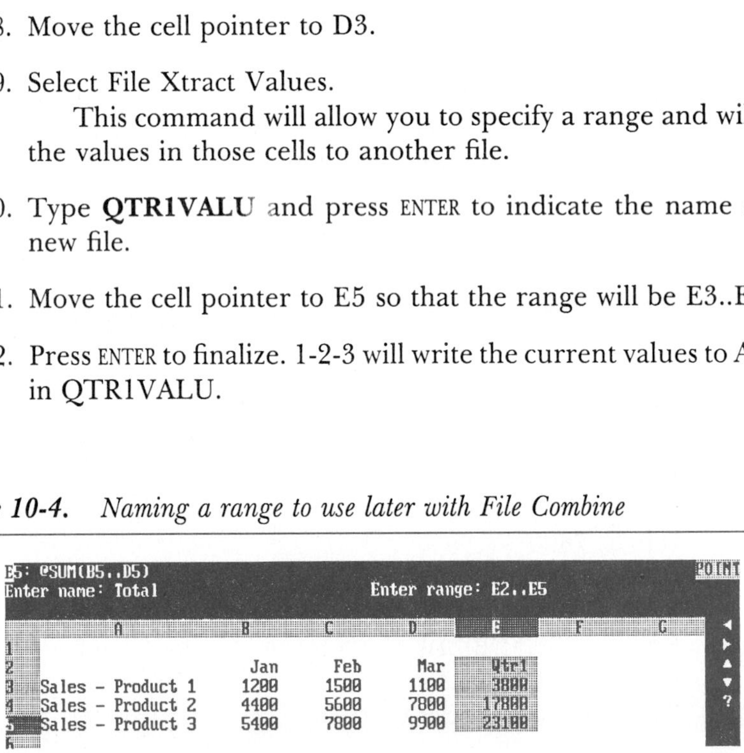

Methods for Combining

There are three different methods for combining data in a file with the current contents of memory. Each method has a completely different effect on the current worksheet, so be certain that you understand each one clearly before using these features on your own applications. It is also recommended that you save the current worksheet before you begin. That way, if you use the wrong method, you can retrieve the worksheet from disk and try again.

You will need to build a new worksheet model to use with the Combine options. Follow these directions:

1. Move the cell pointer to B2, select Range Erase, move the cell pointer to E5, and press ENTER.

   This is a short-cut approach to creating the new model, since you need the same entries and width for column A.

2. Make these worksheet entries:

B2:	"Qtr1
C1:	Sales Summary by Quarter
C2:	"Qtr2
D2:	"Qtr3
E2:	"Qtr4
F2:	"Total
F3:	@SUM(B3.E3)

3. Select Copy, press ENTER, move the cell pointer to F4, type a period (.), move to F5, and press ENTER.

The model shell is now ready to receive data from the various quarters and looks like the worksheet in Figure 10-5.

The Combine options provide the perfect solution because they do not destroy the current model as you bring the quarter totals in from other files. The data that you will be bringing in must be on disk, either as a range in a complete model or as an extract file that contains only the data you need. The next three sections cover the File Combine commands for copying, adding, and subtracting file data.

10

Figure 10-5.   *Worksheet before File Combine*

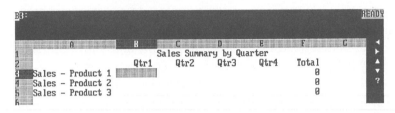

File Combine Copy

The File Combine Copy command is used when you have data stored on disk, and you want to replace a section of the current worksheet. To bring this data into the current worksheet, position the cell pointer carefully; this is what will control the placement of the data. Use the values you stored in QTR1VALU for this example. Follow these directions:

1. Move the cell pointer to B3.

2. Select File Combine Copy.

3. Select Entire-File.

4. Type **QTR1VALU** and press ENTER to produce the results shown in Figure 10-6.

Figure 10-6.   *Copying data to the worksheet with File Combine Copy*

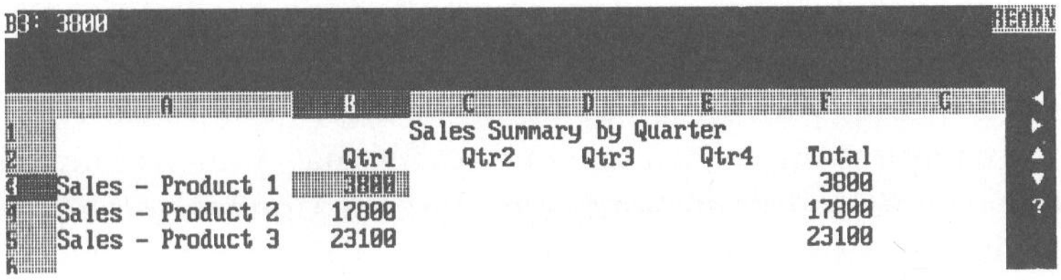

Notice that each of the values in this small file is placed on the model and the entries are included in the total.

If you had tried to bring in the information without extracted values, the formulas in the model would have presented a problem. Although everything would appear the same at first glance, a close up look would reveal problems. The entry placed in Qtr1 would have incorrect cell references in an @SUM formula. A CIRC indicator would also appear at the bottom of your screen. CIRC indicates a formula with a reference to the cell containing the formula (that is, a formula reference to itself) and can cause serious problems in a model. In most cases, this problem is resolved by editing the formula and correcting the cell addresses the formula uses.

Another problem to be on the lookout for is incorrect cell pointer placement or a lack of knowledge of the exact contents of an extract file or a range. If you were to position the cell pointer in the wrong place and use the File Combine command, you could wind up with results like the one shown in Figure 10-7. Notice how everything has shifted by one row, making the model useless.

File Combine Add

When you use the File Combine Add command, values will be added to the existing values. Which values are added is determined by cell pointer position and placement of the file values within the file. If the worksheet cells are blank, the only difference between Copy and Add is that Add ignores labels. Follow these steps to try the new command:

Figure 10-7. *Misjudging cell pointer's position for File Combine*

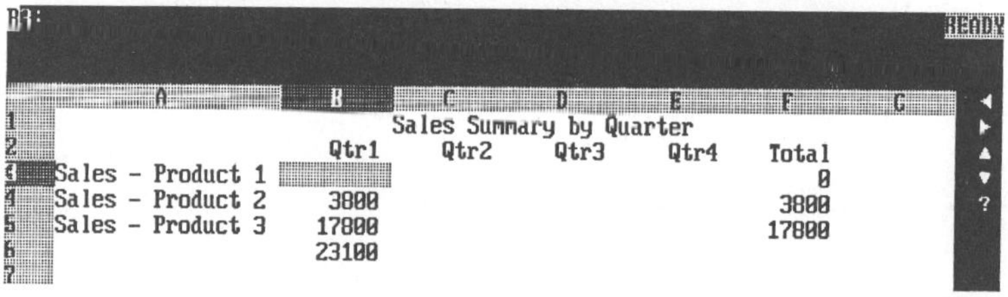

1. Move the cell pointer to B3, select Range Erase, move the cell pointer to B5, and press ENTER.

2. Move the cell pointer to B2.

   You will be using the named range Total in the 1ST_QTR file this time. Since the label Qtr1 is included in the range, you need to move the cell pointer to B2 so that the first value in the file will be matched with B3.

3. Select File Combine Add Named/Specified-Range.

4. Type **Total** and press ENTER.

5. Type **1ST_QTR** and press ENTER to produce the results shown in Figure 10-8.

   Try this again to see if it really adds.

6. Select File Combine Add Named/Specified-Range.

7. Type **Total** and press ENTER.

8. Type **1ST_QTR** and press ENTER. Move the cell pointer to B3 to see the value 7600 in B3, as in Figure 10-9.

You can see that each of the numbers in the current worksheet doubled, as the numbers on the file were added to the current worksheet again.

Figure 10-8. *Copying data to the worksheet with File Combine Add*

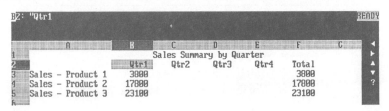

Figure 10-9. *Adding a range to the worksheet twice*

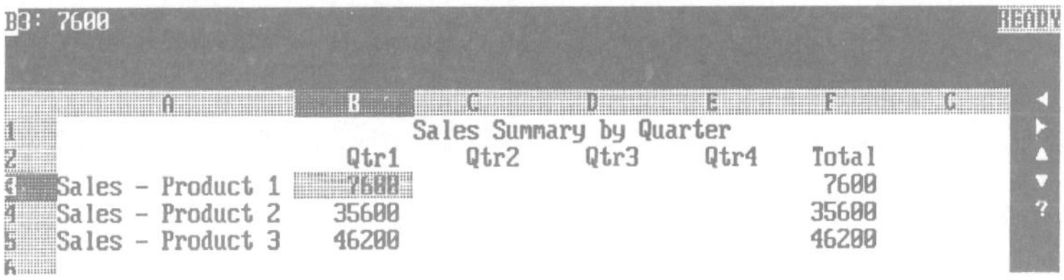

File Combine Subtract

The File Combine Subtract command is the exact opposite of the Add option. It subtracts the values stored on disk from the current worksheet cells. This command depends on the cell pointer location and the offset within the file that controls which numbers will be subtracted from which entries. You can try this by subtracting the last entry you added to the worksheet, following these steps:

1. Select File Combine Subtract Entire-File.
   Since you will use the QTR1VALU file, leave the cell pointer in B3, since there is no need to have the cell pointer in B2. This file does not have a label before the numeric values the way the named range did.

2. Type **QTR1VALU** and press ENTER to produce the results shown in Figure 10-10.

Figure 10-10. *Subtracting data from the worksheet with File Combine Subtract*

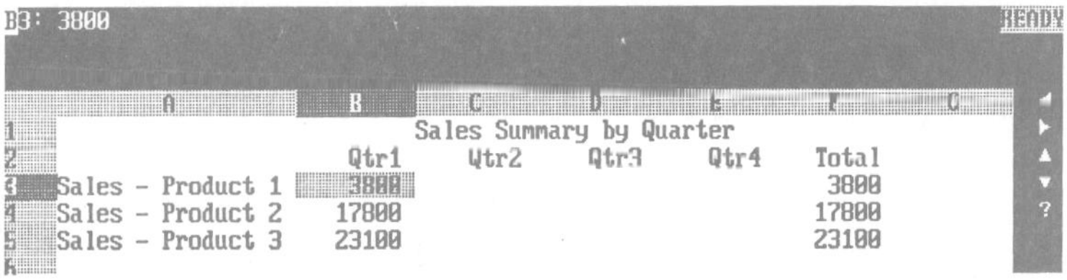

Each of the entries returned to the original values as the Subtract operation was completed.

3. Select File Save, type **QTRTOTAL**, and press ENTER to save this new file.

Using Links to Incorporate Data

The File Combine commands provide a set of tools for using data from other worksheets in the current one. Data from other files that is combined with the current worksheet is not automatically updated when there are changes in the original files from which you obtained the data. When you use the File Combine command to reference data in other worksheet files, you must repeat the File Combine commands every time you use the worksheet to ensure that the data is still current.

If you are using Release 2.2 or above, however, you have another way of updating the worksheet data. This update is accomplished by establishing links to data in other worksheet files. 1-2-3 will update the links that you establish every time you retrieve the file containing the links. If you are working on a network, and other users may be updating the values of the data your worksheet is linked to, Releases 2.2 and above even provide a command to refresh the links. All you need to do is select File Admin Link-Refresh.

As an example of the file link feature, the summary worksheet that you create to combine expenses can contain formulas that reference the totals in the supporting worksheets. The summary worksheet is referred to as the *target file* because it will contain data stored in the other files. The files that contain the data are referred to as the *source files* because they are the source of the data you need. If the data in a source file changes, 1-2-3 changes the cells that reference the data in the source file each time you retrieve the target file that contains the links or select the File Admin Link-Refresh command.

Releases 2.2 and above support a one-to-one link between worksheet cells. A one-to-one link is established when one cell in the target file obtains the value of a single cell in a source file. When a cell in the target file references the value of a cell in a source file, the cell cannot include other functions or formula operators; it must be a simple cell reference.

The Viewer add-in (Release 2.3) makes it easier to create links. You will be able to see the contents of your worksheets while you make selections with the Viewer.

Using the File Links

To include a value from another file, you must specify the worksheet file from which you want to obtain the value as well as the worksheet cell address or range name. If the file is not on the current drive or in the current directory, you will need to specify this information along with the filename. If the filename has an extension other than .WK1, as in .WKS for a link to a Release 1A worksheet, you must specify the filename extension. The filename must also be enclosed in a set of double angle brackets, as in + << BUDGET.WK1 >> A2, which links the current cell in the target file worksheet to cell A2 in the BUDGET worksheet.

Follow these easy steps to establish a link from the current cell to a cell in a source file worksheet:

1. Type **+** to tell 1-2-3 that you are starting a formula.

2. Type **<<** to enter the left side of a set of angle brackets. Use the less-than symbol (**<**) to create these brackets.

3. Enter the filename.

   Although 1-2-3 does not require you to include the directory name or the file extension unless you are using a directory other than the current directory or an extension other than .WK1, you may want to develop the habit of entering it anyway. Then you will not need to worry about which directory is current when you establish the link. 1-2-3 assumes that the file has a .WK1 extension unless you provide another extension.

4. Enter the right side of the set of angle brackets by typing **>>**. Use two greater-than symbols to create these brackets.

5. Enter a reference to the cell that contains the value you want to link to, such as B10.

   This reference can be entered as a cell address or a range name. If the range name is assigned to more than one cell, 1-2-3 uses the cell in the upper left corner of the range.

6. Press ENTER to finalize the entry.

10

1-2-3 finds the value in the source file worksheet and displays the current value in the cell containing the link in the target file worksheet.

A cell that references an external worksheet cell cannot include other formula features of 1-2-3. Thus, + <<BUDGET.WK1>>A2* <<BUDGET.WK1>>B3 would not be an acceptable entry. Nor can the external worksheet cell reference be an argument for a function in the cell, so @PMT(<<FINANCE.WK1>>A3,B3,C7) would not be acceptable. If you try using a file link with other formula features, 1-2-3 places the worksheet in EDIT mode and prompts you to fix the error.

If you are using a worksheet with file links in a network environment, you may want to confirm that file links are using the most up-to-date values of the cells in the other worksheets. This is necessary because other users may be updating entries in the source file while you are working in the target file. Before printing or making decisions based on the information in the target file, you may want to refresh the links to data in the source file. To do so, select File Admin Link-Refresh. This command checks all external file links. If any have changed, 1-2-3 updates the value in the current worksheet.

Consolidating quarterly sales data provides a practical application for the use of external file links. Follow these steps to create a consolidated worksheet using file links:

1. Select File Retrieve, type **1ST_QTR**, and press ENTER.

   This contains the first quarter of data that you want to consolidate. Notice that the data that you will include in the consolidation is stored in E3, E4, and E5. You can use this worksheet as the basis for the second quarter's data.

2. Complete these entries:

B2:	"Apr
B3:	1400
B4:	6000
B5:	8900
C2:	"May
C3:	1100
C4:	5600
C5:	7600
D2:	"Jun

> D3:   1300
> D4:   6400
> D5:   8000
> E2:   "Qtr2 *type in, or edit cell and replace 1 with 2.

These entries produce the result shown in Figure 10-11.

3. Select File Save, type **2ND_QTR**, and press ENTER to save this new file. Notice that the data that you will include in the consolidation is stored in E3, E4, and E5.

4. Select File Retrieve, type **QTRTOTAL**, and press ENTER.

5. Select Range Erase, select B3..B5, and press ENTER.

    Since you can use external file references instead of the File Combine commands, you will want to remove the old data first.

6. Enter + <<**1ST_QTR**>>**E3** and press ENTER. The formula looks like this:

1-2-3 adds .WK1 to the filename for you. The value 3800 is the one that the 1ST_QTR.WK1 file has stored in E3. If the values

Figure 10-11.   *Worksheet containing second-quarter data*

```
B2: "Qtr2                                                    READY

              A           B         C         D         E      F      G
1
2                         Apr       May       Jun      Qtr2
3    Sales – Product 1    1400      1100      1300      3800
4    Sales – Product 2    6000      5600      6400     18000
5    Sales – Product 3    8900      7600      8000     24500
6
```

10

in 1ST_QTR.WK1 later change, 1-2-3 will use the updated value when you retrieve this file. Since this external file link is a formula, you can use the Copy command to copy it for the other products.

7. Select Copy, press ENTER, move to B4, type a period (.), move to B5, and press ENTER to copy the formula from B3 to B4..B5.

   Notice how 1-2-3 automatically adjusts the cell reference in the formula as you copy it. You cannot copy the formula to the next column because the second-quarter column uses a different worksheet file, making it easier to type the external reference in the correct way than to edit it.

8. Move to C3, enter **+ <<2ND_QTR>>E3**, and press ENTER.

   1-2-3 adds .WK1 to the filename for you. The value 3800 is the one that the 2ND_QTR.WK1 file has stored in E3. If the value in E3 in 2ND_QTR.WK1 later changes, 1-2-3 will use the updated value when you retrieve the file. Since this external file link is a formula, you can use the Copy command to copy it for the other products.

9. Select Copy, press ENTER, move to C4, type a period (.), move to C5, and press ENTER to copy the formula from C3 to C4..C5. The worksheet now looks like the one in Figure 10-12.

The real advantage of using file links instead of the File Combine commands becomes apparent when the data changes. To see the effect of changing the data, follow these steps:

Figure 10-12.   *External file links to obtain data from another worksheet*

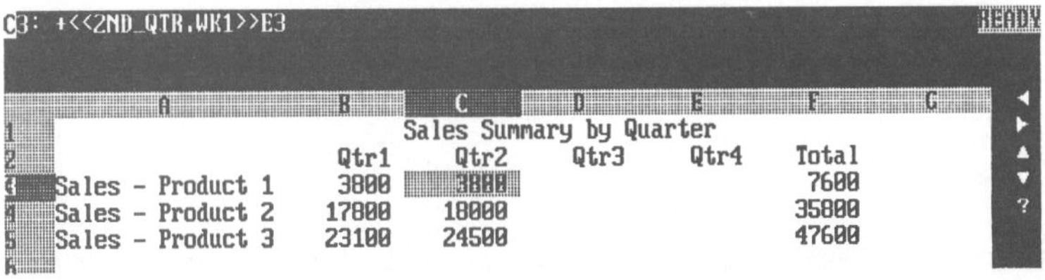

1. Select File Save, press ENTER, and select Replace to save the QTRTOTAL file.

2. Select File Retrieve, type **2ND_QTR**, and press ENTER.

3. Move to D3, enter **1700**, and press ENTER.

   The new value automatically updates the Product 1 total in E3. If you used the File Combine commands to consolidate data, the consolidated data would not contain the updated number. If you create a file link between the consolidated worksheet and the supporting worksheet, 1-2-3 will update the values for you.

4. Select File Save, press ENTER, and select Replace to save the 2ND_QTR file.

5. Select File Retrieve, type **QTRTOTAL**, and press ENTER. The worksheet looks like the one in Figure 10-13.

In the new worksheet, 1-2-3 updated the file links when you retrieved the file.

External File Links

As you develop models with external file links, it can become difficult to remember all the source files to which a worksheet is linked. To quickly remind you which files the current worksheet uses, 1-2-3 has the File List Linked command. When you select this command for the QTRTOTAL file, 1-2-3 displays this result:

This screen lists the files to which QTRTOTAL is linked. From this display, you can press ENTER to return to the worksheet.

You can also use the File Admin Table Linked command to create a table of the links to the current file in an empty area of the worksheet. The first step is determining an empty area of the worksheet that is at least four columns wide and contains enough rows to list all the current links plus a couple of extra rows. Once you have determined the area you are going to

10

Figure 10-13. *File links refreshed to show updated data*

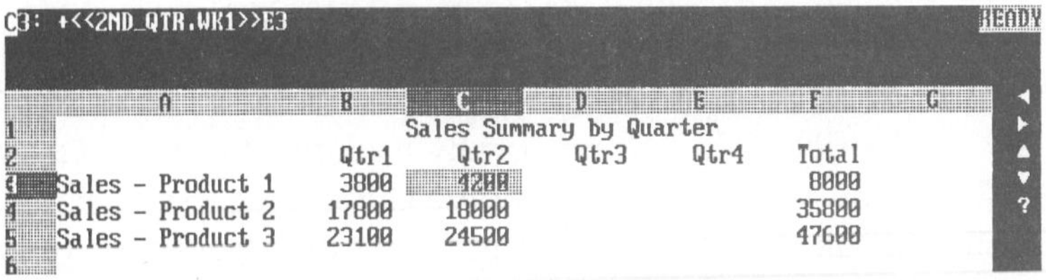

use, you can invoke the command and highlight the cells for the table. 1-2-3 will write the current file path and filename in the first column and include additional information such as date, time, and file size.

Using the Viewer Add-In (Release 2.3) for Links

Release 2.3 comes with a Viewer add-in that allows you to build links while looking at the contents of any of your worksheet files. You do not have to guess at the correct filename or the location of the information that you want if you attach the Viewer add-in and invoke it while building your link. You can use the current worksheet, but you will need to attach the add-in before you can try this:

1. Select Add-In or press ALT-F10.

2. Select Attach, then select VIEWER.ADN.

   This step causes 1-2-3 to use a small part of your system's memory for the Viewer add-in. It will be available whenever you choose to invoke it unless you detach the add-in or end your 1-2-3 session. You can assign the add-in to a key combination with ALT and one of the function keys listed, or you can invoke it by using the Add-In Manager menu.

3. Select 7 to assign the add-in to ALT-F7, then select Quit to exit the Add-In Manager menu.

4. Move the cell pointer to E3, select Range Erase, then press ENTER to erase the one cell.

5. Type a **+**, then press ALT-F7 to invoke the Viewer add-in and select Link. A list of files similar to the list in Figure 10-14 will appear.

6. Use the DOWN ARROW key until 1ST_QTR is highlighted. Use the RIGHT ARROW key to move to the worksheet data, highlight E3, then press ENTER.

   This will establish the link for you.

7. Select File Save, press ENTER, and select Replace to save the file.

Review

- You can combine the values of a range or entire worksheet file into the current worksheet file with the File Combine command. You must be careful where the cell pointer is when you perform this command because the cells copied into the current worksheet have the same relative distance to the cell pointer's position as they have in their original file to the upper left corner of the range or worksheet. The Combine option lets you copy (incoming data replaces current worksheet data), add (incoming num-

Figure 10-14.   *Building a link with the Viewer add-in*

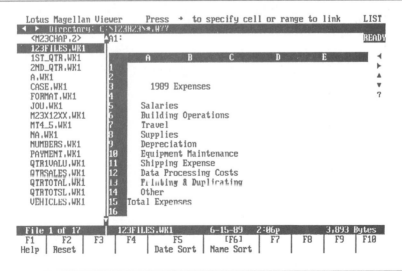

bers are added to the current worksheet data), or subtract (incoming numbers are subtracted from the current worksheet data).

- Worksheets created in Releases 2.2 and above can contain external file links, which return the value of a cell in another worksheet. Cells containing an external file link have a **+**, the filename in double angle brackets (<< >>), and the cell address or range name of the cell in the target file worksheet. The links are updated when you retrieve a file or when you select the File Admin Link-Refresh command. If you have Release 2.3, you can use the Viewer add-in to look at the worksheet that you are linking while you build the link.

Commands and Keys

Entry	Action
FAL	File Admin Link-Refresh refreshes external file links
FCA	File Combine Add adds range or worksheet data from another file to the current worksheet
FCC	File Combine Copy copies a range or worksheet from another file to the current worksheet
FCS	File Combine Subtract subtracts range or work-sheet data from another file to the current worksheet

11

Creating 1-2-3 Macros

Many 1-2-3 users are intimidated by macros. They have heard about the failures that others have experienced when attempting to use them. But this failure can be avoided; in fact, if you use the step-by-step approach presented in this chapter, you will have no need for concern. There is no reason why you cannot be just as successful with macros as you are with 1-2-3's Range Format and File Save commands.

In their simplest form, macros are nothing more than a way to automate the selections you have been making from 1-2-3's menus. These macros are referred to as *keyboard alternative macros*. In their most complex form, macros provide an entire programming language with the special 1-2-3 command language instructions. Attempting to use the most sophisticated form of macros without mastering the keyboard variety is a little like practicing diving before you have learned to swim. If you jump in at the deep end of the pool without knowing how to swim to the edge, you will be well over your head and doomed to failure. Clearly, using the command language macros before mastering the keyboard alternative variety is asking for problems; why, then, do so many new users use this approach? Fortunately, the material in this chapter introduces the material in a logical sequence to help you avoid this problem.

This chapter will introduce you to a step-by-step approach to the creation of keyboard alternative macros that can ensure your success. You will learn how to enter menu selections and special keyboard entries in worksheet cells for later execution. You will learn 1-2-3's rules for naming macros and how you can execute the macro instructions you have stored. You will also learn how to use Release 2.3's Learn feature to significantly reduce the effort involved in the creation of keyboard alternative macros. You will create several ready-to-use macros, which will be your foundation for creating macros that fit your particular needs. Since macros are based on a series of building blocks, you will need to learn something about each of the building blocks before creating a macro. In this chapter you will be introduced to the building blocks and then combine them in your first macro example, before making your entries.

Keyboard Alternative Macros

Keyboard alternative macros are nothing more than a column of label entries that have a special name assigned to them. The contents of the label entries are the sequence of 1-2-3 keystrokes that you want 1-2-3 to execute for you. Once the keystrokes are entered in the column of worksheet cells, you will use the Range Name Create command to assign a name to the top cell in the macro. You can use \ and a single letter for the macro name or use a longer entry up to the 15 character limit for range names. If you choose \ and the single letter, you can execute the macro by holding down the ALT key and the letter used in the macro name or by pressing ALT-F3 (RUN) and selecting the name from the list of macro names. If you use the longer entry option for the name, your only alternative is to press ALT-F3 (RUN) and select the macro name. When you save the worksheet on which you entered the macro, you save the macro for later use with the worksheet on which it was entered. If you were to use the macro on another worksheet, you would have to reenter it, use the File Combine command covered in Chapter 10, or use the more sophisticated Macro Library option covered in more advanced books on 1-2-3.

11

Keyboard alternative macros provide a wealth of time-saving features. You can use them to automate printing, formatting, or any other 1-2-3 task that can be handled with menu selections. After you have learned the basics, you will want to examine the tasks you execute repeatedly. The more frequently a task is performed, the greater the potential payback of automating it with macro instructions. Some users find that data-management tasks such as sorting and extracting are the most important to automate; other users give printing or formatting the highest priority because they use these commands most frequently. Although the macros in the remainder of the chapter have widespread application, only you can decide which tasks offer you the greatest payback when automated.

Macro Basics

The secret to creating macros that run correctly the first time you try them is having a structured approach that you use consistently for each new macro you create. At first glance the steps recommended here might seem unnecessarily time-consuming; however, you will find that they guarantee immediate success and thereby save debugging time.

The first step to successful macros is to lay out a road map of where you want to go with the macro. Whether you type the macro entries or use the Learn feature's recorder to place them on the worksheet, you need to test the instructions that you hope will get you there. If you are not using the recorder, you may want to test the instructions before entering them on the worksheet. After the instructions are stored on the worksheet you will need to name them. Documenting the workings of the macro is an often overlooked step, but it can guarantee continued trouble-free execution. Complete this step for every macro. Only then will you be ready to try your new macro. You can examine each of these steps more closely in the sections that follow.

If you are typing the macro entries, the only way to guarantee first-try success for every macro is to try the 1-2-3 instructions that you want to store in a macro and to monitor their effect on the worksheet. This happens automatically when you use the Learn feature because 1-2-3 is executing and recording the instructions as you enter them. Write each command on a piece of paper as you enter it. If the results meet your needs, you can enter the keystrokes you have written on your sheet of paper as a series of label entries on the worksheet. If the commands do not perform the required tasks, you can alter them and try again. Once you discover the correct combination of menu requests, you have a guarantee (if you enter them carefully) that they will function. You have already tried these commands and ensured their correct operation before recording them.

The other objective of this planning phase for the macro is to ensure that you have not forgotten any of the requirements. Planning is required if you use the recorder approach as well, because you must understand the path of the specific commands that you will need.

Recording Menu Selections

You will want to select an out-of-the-way location on the worksheet for recording your macro commands. With Release 2, 2.01, or 2.2, put them at the far right side of the worksheet.

To prevent 1-2-3 from executing the menu commands you want to record, begin the macro sequence with an apostrophe so that it is treated as a label. Indicate each request for the menu with a slash, and record each menu selection as the first letter of the selection. To record the keystrokes necessary to obtain a worksheet status display, type **'/ws** or **'/WS** in the cell. Case is never important when you are entering menu selections.

In addition to entering the menu selections, you sometimes have to indicate that the ENTER key would be pressed if you were entering the command sequence from the keyboard. In a macro, this key is represented by the tilde mark (~). When you are entering data other than menu selections, such as a filename or a range name, enter the names in full. For example, to record the keystrokes necessary to retrieve a file named Sales, you would enter **'/frSales~** in the macro cell.

Menu selections should always be recorded with the first letter of the selection. Typing the full name of the command is not a substitute for the first letter and will cause errors in the macro. While it is possible to select commands by pointing to the menu selections through the successive use of the RIGHT ARROW key, followed by the use of the ENTER key, this should be avoided in macros. In subsequent releases of the product, Lotus might alter the sequence of the menu selections, causing the cursor-movement method to fail. However, you can be assured that the first letters of the selections are not likely to change. This guarantees that your macros will be compatible with future releases of the 1-2-3 product.

Recording Special Keys

There are a number of special keyboard keys, such as the function and arrow keys, that you will want to include in your macros. These keys and the macro keywords that stand for them are shown in Table 11-1. Notice that all the special keywords are enclosed in curly brackets or braces ({ }). You will find it easy to remember most of these words; they are the same words you probably connect with the special keys—for example, EDIT represents F2. The only thing you will need to remember is to use the braces like this: {EDIT}. Without the braces, 1-2-3 will not recognize the entry as a special key.

There are several special keys that cannot be represented in a macro. The NUM LOCK key has no representation and must be turned on by the operator if a macro requires it. The use of the SCROLL LOCK key follows the same procedure, since it too cannot be represented. CAPS LOCK also has no representation, although this is less important than the other two keys; you will be able to control capitalization if you are requested to input directly during a macro. If macro instructions include cell entries for other parts of the worksheet, you will get to choose whether to make these entries upper- or lowercase when building the macro. The case you choose will be maintained when the macro is executed.

Moving the Cell Pointer

When you are creating a macro, movement of the cell pointer to the right will be represented by {r}, {RIGHT}, or {right}. The Learn feature uses the abbreviated form shown first. The Learn feature records every press of a key even if the same key is pressed multiple times, as in {u}{u}{u} to represent pressing the UP ARROW key three times. When you type the entries you can enter {UP 3}, or {U 3} as a shortcut.

Table 11-1. *Special Keys in Macro Commands*

Cursor-Movement Keys	Keywords
UP ARROW	{UP} or {U}
DOWN ARROW	{DOWN} or {D}
RIGHT ARROW	{RIGHT} or {R}
LEFT ARROW	{LEFT} or {L}
HOME	{HOME}
END	{END}
PGUP	{PGUP}
PGDN	{PGDN}
CTRL-RIGHT ARROW	{BIGRIGHT}
CTRL-LEFT ARROW	{BIGLEFT}

Editing Keys	Keywords
DEL	{DEL}
INS	{INS}
ESC	{ESC}
BACKSPACE	{BACKSPACE} or {BS}

Function Keys	Keywords
F1 (HELP)	{HELP} Releases 2.2 and 2.3
F2 (EDIT)	{EDIT}
F3 (NAME)	{NAME}
F4 (ABS)	{ABS}
F5 (GOTO)	{GOTO}
F6 (WINDOW)	{WINDOW}
F7 (QUERY)	{QUERY}
F8 (TABLE)	{TABLE}
F9 (CALC)	{CALC}
F10 (GRAPH)	{GRAPH}
ALT-F7 (APP1)	{APP1} Releases 2.2 and 2.3
ALT-F8 (APP2)	{APP2} Releases 2.2 and 2.3
ALT-F9 (APP3)	{APP3} Releases 2.2 and 2.3
ALT-F10 (APP4 or ADD-IN)	{APP4} Releases 2.2 and 2.3

Case is never important for the special macro words, although uppercase will be used throughout this chapter. Movement to the left is {LEFT}, movement down is {DOWN}, and movement up is {UP}.

In Release 1A, moving the cursor up three cells was represented by {UP}{UP}{UP}. In Release 2 there is a short-cut approach that lets you enter this same instruction as {UP 3}.

When you are working from the keyboard, the effect of the HOME key depends on whether you are in READY mode or EDIT mode. This is also true in the macro environment. If you record {HOME} in a macro, its effect will depend on what you are having the macro do for you. If you have placed 1-2-3 in EDIT mode, the instruction will take you to the left side of the entry in the current cell; otherwise, it will place you in A1.

The END and arrow key combinations are supported in macros. You can enter {END}{RIGHT} to have the cell pointer moved to the last occupied cell entry on the right side of the worksheet. To specify paging up and down, you can use {PGUP} and {PGDN}.

Function Keys

With the exception of the function keys to run macros, all function keys can be represented by special macro keywords. To use F2 (EDIT), you would enter {EDIT}. The F5 (GOTO) key is another key that is used frequently. To record the fact that you want the cell pointer moved to D10, you would make this entry in a macro:

{GOTO}D10~

Notice that the cell address you want the cell pointer moved to is placed outside the braces and is followed by a tilde (~). Remember that the tilde represents the ENTER key and is required to finalize the request, just as you would press ENTER to finalize if you were executing the command directly.

Other keys required frequently are F6 (WINDOW) and F9 (CALC). As you might expect, {WINDOW} is the macro representation for F6 and {CALC} is the macro representation for F9. The remaining function keys are shown in Table 11-1.

Edit Keys

In addition to F2 (EDIT), which places you in the EDIT mode, there are several keys that are used frequently when you are correcting cell entries. The ESC key can remove an entry from a cell and can delete a menu default, such as a previous setup string. This option allows you to cancel the default and make a new entry. ESC is used in a macro just as it is outside a macro except that braces are required. The entry would therefore be {ESC}.

To delete a character to the left of the cell pointer while in EDIT mode, or to delete the last character entered, use either {BS} or {BACKSPACE} in your macro. To delete the character above the cell pointer from EDIT mode, use {DEL} or {DELETE}. For example, you could create a macro that requests a change in the label prefix to center justification. The sequence of entries in a macro would be

{EDIT}{HOME}{DEL}^~

This is exactly the same sequence of keys that you would press if you were typing the request to be executed directly, rather than storing the keystrokes in a macro.

In Release 2, repeat factors can also be used with these keys. That is, {DELETE 4} is equivalent to pressing the DELETE key four times. {BACKSPACE 7} will delete seven characters to the left of the cell pointer on the edit line.

Creating the Macro

As you may recall, we promised you not the fastest path to macro entry but the fastest path to a macro that would run correctly the first time you tried it. Your first step in creating a macro will be to make a plan and to try your plan before recording your first keystroke. This step is the critical one if you want to ensure success. You may wonder why you are not using the Learn feature in your initial efforts. You will find that making your own entries will provide a much better understanding of the process.

Planning the Macro

If you are thinking of creating a macro, you must have a task that you want to automate. For your first example, you will automate a request for formatting, based on the assumption that you need to format data as Currency frequently and would like to create a macro that will save you a few keystrokes. Your first step is to ask yourself which 1-2-3 commands you normally use to handle this task. The answer should be the Range

11

Format Currency command sequence. Also ask yourself if you want the macro to specify the number of decimal places and the range for formatting or whether you want the operator to complete the instruction from the keyboard. For your example, the number of decimal places will be supplied but the range will be controlled by the operator at execution.

Once your decisions are made, you will want to test the series of instructions you plan to use before typing them. If you are using 1-2-3's Learn feature, covered later in this chapter, you can use your trial run to capture the keystrokes. Either way, you will need some test data on the worksheet before beginning. Follow these directions for creating test data to see if the formatting commands and subsequent macro function correctly:

1. Make the following worksheet entries:

   A1: 2
   A2: 5
   A3: 4
   A4: 9
   A5: 7
   C6: 8
   C7: 9
   C8: 3

   There is nothing special about these entries. They are just a few numbers that will be stored in the default format of General and that will provide practice entries for formatting. Copy them across the worksheet to create additional entries.

2. Move the cell pointer to A1, select Copy, and press the END key followed by the DOWN ARROW key. Press ENTER, move the cell pointer to B1, type a period (.), move the cell pointer to F1, and press ENTER.

3. Move the cell pointer to C6, select Copy, move the cell pointer to C8, and press ENTER. Move the cell pointer to E6, type a period (.), move the cell pointer to F6, and press ENTER to create this display:

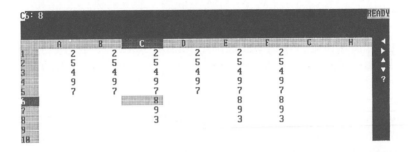

This provides a little variety in the length of the column of numbers you will be formatting with your macro once it is created. Now you are ready for a trial run of the instructions you plan to enter.

4. Move the cell pointer to A1.

This is the first cell you will format. The movement of the cell pointer could be incorporated in the macro, but it would eliminate some of the macro's flexibility and is probably not desirable.

5. Enter **/** and write a slash on the piece of paper on which you are recording the keystrokes from the trial.

6. Select Range and write "R" on the piece of paper.

7. Select Format and write "F" on the piece of paper.

8. Select Currency and write "C" on the piece of paper.

9. Type **0** and write "0" on the piece of paper.

10. Press ENTER and write a tilde (~) on the piece of paper.

Notice how every keystroke that you enter, whether it is from the menu or just a keyboard entry, should be written on the piece of paper. Most beginners would skip steps 5 through 10. This is the very cause of failure in their macros. Once you become a 1-2-3 expert and have all the menu selections committed to memory, there is no problem with skipping the writing. But until you reach that point, the importance of these steps cannot be over-emphasized.

11. Press ENTER again to record the range selection. However, do not write this down; you are leaving the range selection up to the user when the macro is executed.

12. Select File Save, type **NUMBERS,** and press ENTER.

This will save a copy of the numeric entries in the NUMBERS file. You can retrieve it at a later time to practice with this or other macros.

Making Entries
The macro entries you need to make are written on your sheet of paper. All you need to do now is record these entries on the worksheet. You can record them all in one cell or you can split them into more than one cell—as long as the cells are contiguous in a column on the worksheet. With such a short macro it will not make much difference, but as your macros become longer, you may want to split them well before you reach the 240-character limit for a cell entry. Keeping the length of an individual cell entry to a minimum will allow you to document each step in the macro.

Normally you would place your macro to the right side of the worksheet. Since this is your first macro, however, you will want to keep it in view as it executes, so place it below the entries in column B. Follow these steps to record the macro keystrokes you have written on your sheet of paper:

1. Move the cell pointer to B10.

2. Type **'/r** and then move the cell pointer to B11.
   The apostrophe is used to prevent immediate execution of your entries. The slash represents the request for the menu and the "R" is used to invoke the Range commands (the "R" can be either lower- or uppercase).

3. Press the DOWN ARROW key, type **fc0 ~**, and press ENTER.

These entries tell 1-2-3 that you want to use the Format option and have selected Currency with 0 decimal places as the format you want to use.

This is all that is required for entering any macro. The only mandatory step that remains is naming the macro.

Naming the Macro

Now that you have recorded all the keystrokes, you are ready to name the macro. Before doing this you will want to position the cell pointer on the top cell in the macro, as this is the only cell that you will name. You will use the Range Name Create command that you were introduced to in earlier chapters to apply the name to this cell. You must assign a name of not more than 15 characters, or a special name consisting of a backslash and a single letter, to the cell. The backslash identifies your entry as a macro name, which will allow you to execute the macro with the ALT key and the letter used in the macro name. This naming convention lets you create 26 unique, quickly executable macros on one worksheet, since 1-2-3 does not distinguish between upper- and lowercase letters in a macro name.

If you follow the recommendation of positioning the cell pointer before you begin, the process is quite simple. You will only need to press ENTER after typing the name to have the name applied to the macro. Saving a macro after you name it will save both the macro entries and the name, so they will be available when you use the worksheet.

Follow these steps to name the formatting macro you just entered.

1. Move the cell pointer to B10.
2. Select Range Name Create.
3. Type **\c** and press ENTER twice.

This will apply the name to the current cell.

Theoretically, you can now execute the macro; however, it is best to document it first. If you do not take the time to document your work now, you will never do it; later, it will be difficult to remember what name you chose for the macro and what each step accomplishes unless you document it.

Documenting the Macro

You will want to develop a few easy documentation rules for yourself so that your documentation is always stored in the same place. A good strategy to use for documentation is to place the macro name in the cell immediately to the left of the top cell in the macro. If the macro is named \a, you would enter '\a in this cell. The apostrophe is required to prevent the backslash from being interpreted as a repeating label indicator and filling your cell with the letter "a."

A good area to use for documenting the macro is the column of cells to the right of the macro instructions. Depending on the length of the macro instructions, this documentation may extend one or more cells to the right of the macro column. Entering a brief description of every command can make the purpose of the macro much clearer when you go back to examine it at a later time.

Follow these steps to document the formatting macro:

1. Move the cell pointer to A10, type **'\c** and press ENTER.

2. Move the cell pointer to C10, type **request Range command**, and press ENTER.

3. Move the cell pointer to C11, type **select Currency format with 0 decimal places**, and press ENTER.

The macro is now ready to execute with the instructions in the next section.

Executing the Macro

Once you have entered and named a macro, you can use it whenever you wish. Whenever you have a macro that requires the cell pointer to be positioned in a certain cell, you will need to put the cell pointer there before you execute the macro. The cell pointer does not need to be on the macro itself in order to execute it. After you have positioned your cell pointer, you can execute the macro by holding down the ALT key and, while the key is pressed, pressing the letter key you used in your macro name. The macro will begin executing immediately. Follow these instructions to try your new formatting macro:

1. Move the cell pointer to B1.

2. Press the ALT key and, while holding the key down, type **c**, and then release the ALT key.

    This causes the macro to execute. This particular macro requests formatting and ends in time for you to complete the range that should be formatted.

3. Move the cell pointer to B5 and press ENTER.

The entries in B1..B5 should now be formatted as Currency with 0 decimal places. You will want to try this again to see how flexible the macro is.

4. Move the cell pointer to C1 and press the ALT key and type **c**. Move the cell pointer to C8 and press ENTER to create this display:

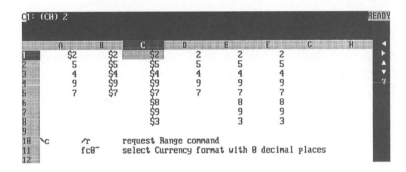

This time the entries in C1..C8 are formatted. This same macro can format one cell or a large range of cells. Try the macro several more times with the remaining numeric entries on the worksheet.

5. Select File Save, press ESC, type **FORMAT**, and press ENTER to save this example.

6. Select Worksheet Erase Yes to clear the worksheet from memory.

The Learn Feature

If you have Release 2.2 of 1-2-3, you can use the Learn feature of the package to record keyboard alternative macros rather than typing them. This approach offers a couple of major advantages. First, you can try out your plan for a macro and have 1-2-3 record your entries. If you make a few mistakes, you do not need to start over because you can edit the entries that 1-2-3 places on the worksheet with the same techniques you have used for changing any entry. Second, when you have 1-2-3 record the keystrokes you do not need to remember the keywords that 1-2-3 uses for the function keys and other special keys. All you need to do is press the proper key and 1-2-3 will record it in the macro cells correctly.

11

Release 2.01 also has a Learn feature as part of the optional Value Pack. The Lotus HAL package also has a capability that allows you to record 1-2-3 keystrokes. Each of these works a little differently than Release 2.3 and is not compatible with Release 2.3. You will need to consult the documentation for these other products if you want to use their features rather than the Learn feature of 2.3.

To use 1-2-3's Learn feature you must follow several steps. First you must tell 1-2-3 where to record the keystrokes. Then you must start the recording and remember to stop it when you are finished. You can try out this procedure with a macro that will correctly format three date entries. First, place the date entries on the worksheet using the @DATE function covered in Chapter 7:

1. Type **@DATE(89,7,15)** in A1 and then press the DOWN ARROW key.

2. Type **@DATE(90,4,15)** in A2 and then press the DOWN ARROW key.

3. Type **@DATE(89,5,30)** in A3 and then press the DOWN ARROW key.

Now you are ready to explore the Learn feature.

Specifying a Range

Just as you selected an out-of-the way location for macros when you typed them, you will normally want to choose the same type of location when 1-2-3 is recording them. To specify this range, select Worksheet Learn. 1-2-3 prompts you for a learn range. Highlight the range you wish to use. You can move the cell pointer to the beginning of the range, type a period, and move to the end of the range to highlight all the cells in the range.

When you press ENTER, 1-2-3 remembers this location as an area in which it can record your keystrokes when you ask it to start recording for you.

For the date macro you want to record, follow these steps to specify a range:

1. Select Worksheet Learn Range.
   The other two menu selections under Learn are used to erase a learn range that you no longer need or to cancel the definition of a learn range.

2. Move the cell pointer to E1, type a period (.), and move the cell pointer to E9.

> Your screen should look like the one in Figure 11-1. In this example, a location that would allow you to see the entire example at one time was selected rather than an out-of-the-way location.

3. Press ENTER to finalize your selection.

Activating Learn

Just as a telephone answering machine does not begin recording your messages until you attach the unit to your phone and turn it on, 1-2-3 does not begin recording keystrokes until you start the Learn feature and its recorder by pressing ALT-F5 (LEARN). Since this action tells 1-2-3 to immediately begin recording keystrokes, you should position your cell pointer where you want to begin working with worksheet data in the macro before doing this.

For the current worksheet follow these steps:

1. Move the cell pointer to A1 by pressing the HOME key.

2. Press ALT-F5 (LEARN).

> 1-2-3 will place a LEARN indicator in the bottom line of your screen to let you know that it has started to record your keystrokes. This indicator will remain until you press ALT-F5 (LEARN) again.

3. Select Range Format Date 1 to select Date format 1.

Figure 11-1.   *Specifying a learn range*

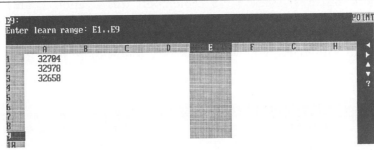

4. Press the DOWN ARROW key twice to highlight the range of the three dates, and press ENTER.

     You will not see 1-2-3 record anything in the learn range yet, as it is always a step behind in writing the information to the worksheet.

5. Select Worksheet Column Set-Width, type **10**, and press ENTER.

     Notice that when you start entering this new command, 1-2-3 writes the previous command to the worksheet.

6. Press ALT-F5 (LEARN) to stop recording.

     The LEARN indicator is removed from the bottom of the screen, but a CALC indicator appears. This indicator is there because 1-2-3 has not as yet placed the last instruction recorded in the learn range.

7. Press F9 (CALC) and the last instruction will be added. Your screen will look like this:

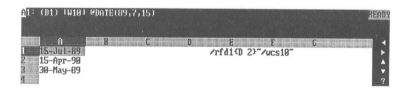

8. Move the cell pointer to D1, type **format_3dates**, and press ENTER.

9. Select Worksheet Column Set-Width and type **14** to widen the column.

10. Select Range Name Labels Right to use this entry to name the top cell in the macro. Press ENTER.

     The Range Name Labels Right command allows you to specify a columnar range of labels and applies those labels as names for the cells to the immediate right of each cell in the range.

11. Type three more date numbers as shown here:

   A5:   @DATE(89,12,31)
   A6:   @DATE(90,6,8)
   A7:   @DATE(90,4,2)

12. Move the cell pointer to A5 and try the macro by pressing ALT-F3
    (RUN). Highlight the name of the macro as shown in Figure 11-2
    and then press ENTER.
       1-2-3 will format the cells as dates, as shown in Figure 11-3.

Creating Another Macro

Now you have created your first two macros, but you haven't begun to
experience the variety that macros can offer. You can follow the instructions in this section to create another macro. This practice should help you
improve your skill level with macro instructions.

Creating a Print Macro

Print macros are useful because print must be created from most
worksheets periodically. In addition, by adding instructions in a print
macro you can add any special form feeding, range printing, headers,

Figure 11-2.   *Running the macro*

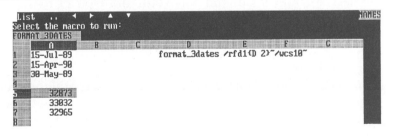

Figure 11-3. *Result of the macro*

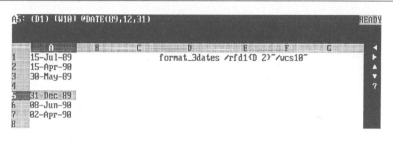

footers, borders, or extra copies. Make these entries to provide a few lines of data to print:

1. Select Worksheet Erase Yes Yes, select Worksheet Column Set-Width, type **15**, and press ENTER.

2. Place these entries on the worksheet:

   A1:   Name
   A2:   John Smith
   A3:   Bill Brown
   A4:   Karen Hall
   A5:   Janice Gold
   B1:   Salary
   B2:   25600
   B3:   45300
   B4:   18900
   B5:   42500
   C1:   Location
   C2:   Dallas
   C3:   Chicago
   C4:   Dallas
   C5:   Chicago

Your worksheet should look like this:

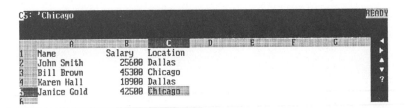

Now you are ready to create a print macro. It will print two copies of the data you just entered on the worksheet.

3. In cell F2: type '**\p** and then continue making these entries to create the macro:

G2:	'/pp	H2:	Invoke print printer command
G3:	rA1.C5˜	H3:	Specify range
G4:	g	H4:	Begin printing
G5:	pa	H5:	Page and align
G6:	g	H6:	Print a second copy
G7:	pa	H7:	Page and align
G8:	q	H8:	Quit the print menu

4. Move the cell pointer to G2, select Range Name Create, type **\p**, and press ENTER twice. If you prefer, you can also move the cell pointer to F2 and use the Range Name Labels Right command to name the top cell in the macro code.

   Make sure your printer is on for the next instruction.

5. Press ALT and type **p** to execute the macro and print the worksheet.

Special Topics

There are many macro options — so many, in fact, that complete books are written on the subject. This chapter cannot cover all possible options, but it can show you a few of particular interest that go beyond the simpler keyboard alternatives to add command language ability, minus all the complexity. In this section you will take a look at a few of the special options, as well as at several command language instructions.

Automatic Macros

1-2-3 has a unique feature that lets you create an automatic macro. Every time a worksheet containing an automatic macro is retrieved, 1-2-3 immediately executes the macro without requiring you to press any keys, as long as Worksheet Global Default Autoexec has not been set to No.

There are numerous applications for a macro that executes as soon as you retrieve the worksheet file containing it, once you begin to use the advanced command language features. For now, there are still a few applications for an automatically executing keyboard macro. For example, you might want to create a worksheet in which the input area is immediately erased. This means that even if the file is saved with previous data, the slate will be wiped clean with each new retrieval and you will be ready for data input.

The only difference between an automatic macro and one that you must execute is the name that you assign to it. An automatic macro must be named \0 (zero).

Command Language Enhancements

You have already become acquainted with the keyboard alternative macros. The command language instructions make up a complete programming language for 1-2-3 instructions. However, you can look at just a few that can add power to your macros. The macro instructions in this section are the Release 2 versions of the instructions.

If you are using Release 1A and you plan to use the command language instructions extensively, you will want to acquire an upgraded version of 1-2-3 in order to have access to a full set of commands.

Each of the special command language commands uses braces around the keyword entry for the command, as in {QUIT}, the command that ends a macro. Some of the command language commands also use arguments similar to the built-in functions' use of arguments. These arguments refine the use of the command to a specific situation. They look something like this:

{BRANCH End}

This command will cause the macro to begin executing the instructions stored at the range named End. Notice that the command language argument is also enclosed within the braces.

Branching Within a Macro

The {*BRANCH*} command allows you to change the flow of execution within a macro to another location on the worksheet. This location can be specified as a cell address or a range name. The format of the command is {BRANCH *location*}. This command is seldom used alone; normally, it is combined with a condition test that will cause the macro to branch only if a certain condition is true.

This command does not alter the location of the cell pointer. It is not related to the command {GOTO}, which is designed to position the cell pointer rather than to alter the flow of execution of a macro.

Adding a Counter

A *counter* will permit you to count the number of times that you have executed a group of instructions. This is the typical use for a counter; to use it in that way, however, you must combine it with other instructions in this section. For now, you will find out how counters are established; then, later in this section, you will see how it is combined with other instructions to create a macro that executes certain instructions repetitively. As you learn more about the macro, you will find that 1-2-3 has a {FOR} instruction that automatically initializes a counter and increments it for you. You may want to use this option later; when beginning to work with macros, however, you will find it more beneficial to establish your own counter so you can understand exactly what is happening.

A counter can be a cell address or a range name that you have assigned to a cell address. Once you decide on a location to use for a counter, you should reserve the location's use for this counter.

The {*LET*} command is used to set the value for a counter. When used in a macro with repetitive processing, {LET} must be used in two different ways: first, to initialize the value of the variable at the start of the macro, and second, to increment the variable each time you process the repetitive instructions within the macro. To use A1 as a counter and initialize it to zero, you could use this instruction at the beginning of the macro:

{LET A1,0}

To increment this counter within a macro after completing an iteration of the processing, you could use this instruction:

{LET A1,A1 + 1}

This instruction is written to work regardless of the current value of A1, as long as it contains a value entry.

The two instructions affecting the value of the counter might be incorporated in a macro that performs repetitive processing, like this:

```
\m       {Let A1,0}
Top      ...
         {LET A1,A1 + 1}
         ...
End      {QUIT}
```

You would enter the instructions to be executed repetitively in the section between Top and End. Top represents the beginning of the repetitive section. End marks the first instructions following the section that would be executed repetitively. Naturally, other instructions must be added to control the flow of execution.

Adding a Condition Check

Just as the @IF function is one of the most powerful built-in function tools, the {IF} macro instruction is one of the most powerful command language instructions. It serves a similar purpose because it also allows you to deal with logical conditions. Its power is far more extensive because it lets you perform any other macro instruction, depending on the result of the condition test. It is not limited to controlling the value of a single cell the way that @IF is. In fact, the {IF} command is normally combined with {BRANCH} to completely change the execution flow within a macro.

Any condition can be tested. In macros where you have established a counter to control processing, the condition that is normally checked is the value of the counter. If the condition tested is true, the command on the same line as the {IF} will be executed. You might find a line like this within a macro:

{IF A1 > 10}{BRANCH End}

This line checks the value of A1. If A1 is greater than 10, the macro will branch to the range named End and execute the macro instructions it finds at that location.

Accepting Keyboard Input

There are several commands that let you accept data from the keyboard while a macro is executing. The simplest of these is {?}. When a macro encounters this special entry, it suspends execution and waits for input from the keyboard. When the operator presses ENTER, the macro continues where it left off.

You can use this feature to create a macro that removes the repetition involved in entering a series of built-in functions. You can supply the variable portion of the function and have the macro automate the entry of the portion that does not vary.

A macro like this enters the date for you; all you need to supply is the year, month, and day:

	X	Y	Z
1	\d	@DATE(	Start date function
2		{?}	Wait for year to be input
3		,	Add comma after year
4		{?}	Wait for month to be input
5		,	Add comma after month
6		{?}	Wait for day to be input
7		)~	End function and finalize with ENTER
8		/rfd1~	Format entry as a date

Make sure that you place an apostrophe in front of the entries in X1, Y1, Y3, Y5, Y7, and Y8 to ensure that the contents of these cells are interpreted as labels.

If you like, you can enter this macro and give it a name. The following section provides a version of this same macro that is a bit more sophisticated. It incorporates several advanced macro features into the macro and creates a macro that will enter ten dates. You will use a slightly different strategy with this macro and document each instruction immediately after entering it. This will help you understand what each step is doing.

11

Building a Date-Entry Macro

This section combines the advanced features just discussed in a working macro example. It uses the concept of a counter, branching, and keyboard input all in one macro, since it is common to include multiple advanced instructions in a macro. Follow these directions to enter the macro:

1. Select Worksheet Erase Yes Yes, move the cell pointer to J1, select Worksheet Column Set-Width, type **23**, and press ENTER. Type **{LET A1,0}** and move the cell pointer to K1.

2. Type **Initialize A1 to 0 as a counter** and move the cell pointer to J2.

3. Type **{IF A1 = 10}{BRANCH End}** and move the cell pointer to K2.

4. Type **Check for max value in the counter** and move the cell pointer to J3.

5. Type **{LET A1,A1 + 1}** and move the cell pointer to K3.

6. Type **Increment counter** and move the cell pointer to J4.

7. Type **'@DATE(** and then move the cell pointer to K4.
   The apostrophe is required to prevent 1-2-3 from interpreting @ as a value entry in the cell.

8. Type **Enter first part of function** and move the cell pointer to J5.

9. Complete the remaining entries like this:

J5: {?}	K5: Pause for the entry of the year
J6: ,	K6: Enter the comma separator
J7: {?}	K7: Pause for the entry of the month
J8: ,	K8: Enter comma separator
J9: {?}	K9: Pause for the entry of the day
J10:)~	K10: Generate close and finalize
J11: {DOWN}	K11: Move the cell pointer down one cell
J12: {BRANCH Top}	K12: Begin Loop again

J13: {UP}{END}{UP}		K13:	Move to the top of the date column
J14: '/rfd1		K14:	Invoke date entry
J15: {END}{DOWN}~		K15:	Expand format range
J16: '/wcs12~		K16:	Widen column
J17: {QUIT}		K17:	End macro after 10 entries and format

The {QUIT} command is the only one that has not been discussed. It is used to end the execution of a macro just as a blank cell will do. Using {QUIT} rather than a blank cell makes it clearer that you intend the macro to end at that point.

10. Enter these labels in the cells specified:

> I1:   '\z
> I2:   Top
> I13:   End

Move the cell pointer to I1. The macro should now match Figure 11-4.

11. Select Range Name Labels Right, expand the range to I13, and press ENTER.

   The Range Name Labels Right command saves you from having to use the Range Name Create command three times. It assigns the labels in the range you specify to the entries in the cells immediately to the right of the cell containing the label.

12. Move the cell pointer to D1 and press and release ALT-Z to execute the macro.

You can enter anything you want for the year, month, and day for each date as long as the entries are valid and you press ENTER after each entry. Figure 11-5 shows one set of date entries that was completed with the macro.

Figure 11-4. A macro to enter dates

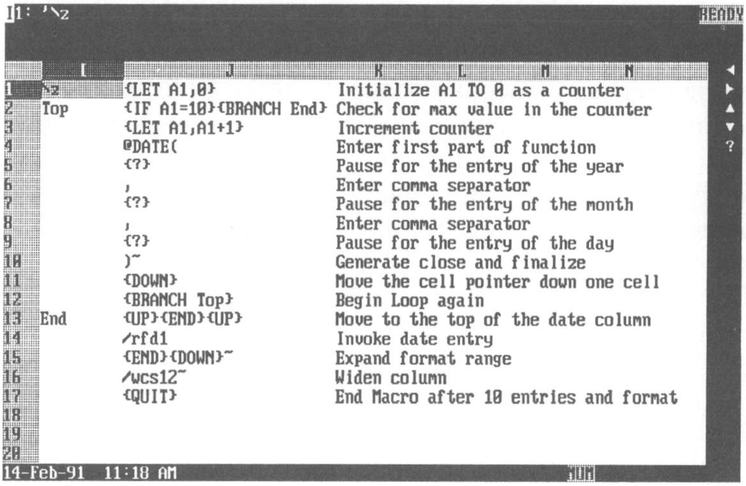

```
I1: '\2                                                            READY

           I         J                    K    L    M    N
1   \2        {LET A1,0}            Initialize A1 TO 0 as a counter
2   Top       {IF A1=10}{BRANCH End} Check for max value in the counter
3             {LET A1,A1+1}         Increment counter
4             @DATE(               Enter first part of function
5             {?}                  Pause for the entry of the year
6             ,                    Enter comma separator
7             {?}                  Pause for the entry of the month
8             ,                    Enter comma separator
9             {?}                  Pause for the entry of the day
10            )~                   Generate close and finalize
11            {DOWN}               Move the cell pointer down one cell
12            {BRANCH Top}         Begin Loop again
13  End       {UP}{END}{UP}        Move to the top of the date column
14            /rfd1                Invoke date entry
15            {END}{DOWN}~         Expand format range
16            /wcs12~              Widen column
17            {QUIT}               End Macro after 10 entries and format
18
19
20
14-Feb-91  11:18 AM                                              NUM
```

Debugging Macros

The debugging process involves testing and correcting macros to ensure that you are obtaining the desired results. One of the most common mistakes users make in creating keyboard macros is forgetting to enter the tilde mark to represent each time the ENTER key is pressed. When you add command language commands to a macro, you do not have the ability to test it completely before entering it.

Figure 11-5. Dates entered with the macro

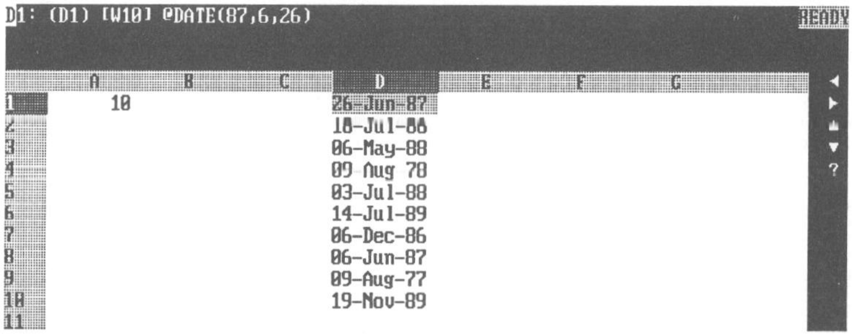

```
D1: (D1) [W10] @DATE(87,6,26)                                    READY

        A       B       C       D       E    F    G
1              10                26-Jun-87
2                                18-Jul-88
3                                06-May-88
4                                09 Aug 78
5                                03-Jul-88
6                                14-Jul-89
7                                06-Dec-86
8                                06-Jun-87
9                                09-Aug-77
10                               19-Nov-89
11
```

1-2-3 has a STEP mode that executes a macro one keystroke at a time. This allows you to follow its progress and spot the area of difficulty if problems are encountered. In Release 2.2, pressing the ALT and F2 keys simultaneously will turn on the STEP mode. In Release 2, pressing the SHIFT and F2 keys simultaneously will turn on the STEP mode. In Release 1A, pressing the SHIFT key plus the F1 key activates the STEP mode. Since this is a toggle process, holding the keys down too long will toggle the STEP mode into the off position again. When this mode is operational, you will see the word STEP at the bottom of your screen, as shown in Figure 11-6.

When the STEP mode is on, any macro you invoke will be executed one step at a time. You will press the SPACEBAR each time you are ready for the next keystroke. In Release 2.2, 1-2-3 displays its location in the macro. It shows the current cell address within the macro and its contents, and even uses a small highlight to mark the current keystroke. This information is displayed on the bottom line of the screen. The menu selections invoked will display in the control panel to provide information on the operation of the macro. You will not be able to input direct commands

Figure 11-6. *Placing the macro in STEP mode*

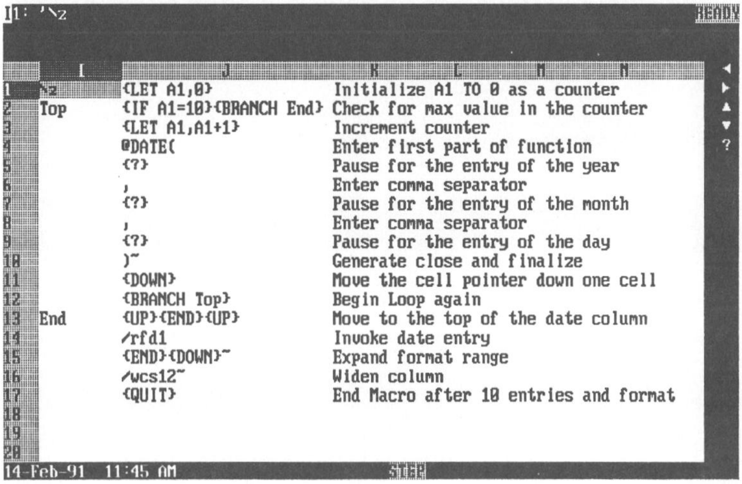

while the macro is executing. SST will appear at the bottom of the screen while the macro is executing. In Release 2.2, SST only appears when the macro is waiting for input.

To stop a malfunctioning macro, press the CTRL and BREAK keys simultaneously. This cancels the macro operation immediately and presents an error indicator at the upper right corner of the screen. Pressing ESC will return you to READY mode so you can make the necessary corrections to your macro.

Follow these instructions to try a macro in STEP mode:

1. Select File Retrieve, type **Y** to retrieve without saving, type **FORMAT**, and press ENTER.

2. If you are using Release 2.2 or 2.3, press the ALT and F2 keys. If you are using Release 2, press the SHIFT and F2 keys. If you are using Release 1A, press the SHIFT and F1 keys.

3. Move the cell pointer to F1, press ALT, and type **c**.

4. Press the SPACEBAR to execute a keystroke.

5. Continue pressing the SPACEBAR until you are asked to supply the range to format.

6. Press the END key followed by the DOWN ARROW key, and press ENTER.

7. Execute step 2 again to toggle the STEP mode into the off position.

8. Select Worksheet Erase Yes Yes.

Review

- 1-2-3's keyboard alternative macros allow you to perform repetitive tasks with ease. You can type the keystrokes in a cell or use 1-2-3's Learn feature to record them. Once they are named you can execute all the keystrokes with one request.

- To record function keys and special keys, you must use 1-2-3's keywords enclosed in braces ({ }). To record menu selections, use the first character in each command name. To record entries, type them as you would without a macro.

- Macros are entered in a group of contiguous cells in a column of the worksheet. If you are typing the entries, each one must be a label entry.

- You can use two different methods for naming macros. In both cases, only the top cell in the macro is named. Your selection will determine how you can execute the macro. If you use \ and a single letter, you can press ALT and type the letter to execute the macro. If you use a regular range name, you will need to use F3 (RUN) to execute the macro.

Commands and Keys

Entry	Action
ALT-*letter*	Executes a macro
ALT-F2	Enables STEP mode
ALT-F3	Executes a macro
ALT-F5	Enables Learn feature
RNLR	Range Name Labels Right applies names to cell immediately to the right
WL	Worksheet Learn specifies a learn range for 1-2-3

12

WYSIWYG and Other
Add-Ins

The output devices connected to most computers are able to support features that just a few years ago were only available to publishers with access to sophisticated typesetting equipment. These features have come to be called desktop publishing.

The Print menus in 1-2-3 and its PrintGraph program create professional-looking output but do not fully use the desktop publishing features of your printer. Separate add-in programs have been provided with Releases 2.2 and 2.3 to add these features to 1-2-3. Add-ins are not automatically part of 1-2-3's feature set until they are attached. After attaching an add-in, you can invoke it at any time, and its features will be accessible from menus in much the same way that regular 1-2-3 menu commands are. The add-in that adds desktop publishing features to 1-2-3 Release 2.3 is called WYSIWYG. (Allways was designed for similar use with Release 2.2.) Although WYSIWYG is a separate program, a copy of it is included with every copy of 1-2-3 Release 2.3. To install WYSIWYG you will need a hard disk and a minimum of 128K of memory above the requirements of 1-2-3. WYSIWYG can also be used with earlier versions of 1-2-3 since it was originally designed and sold as a separate add-in.

WYSIWYG is a little different than other add-ins since once you attach it, it is always available. It is not necessary to use the add-in menu to invoke WYSIWYG. Any time you want to use WYSIWYG you can press the : from READY mode. You will soon rely on its features so much that you will begin to think of them as an integral part of 1-2-3.

The Allways add-in that preceded WYSIWYG with Release 2.2 must be invoked each time you use it. You can either use Add-In Invoke or you can assign it to a hot key such as ALT-F7 that will invoke it for you automatically once it is attached.

With both Allways and WYSIWYG you can use as many as eight different fonts per printout to change the size and appearance of characters. A set of soft fonts is provided with these add-ins. This means that you have definitions of these characters stored on disk and can use these fonts with either laser or dot matrix printers. You can also continue to use the "native" fonts that your printer has built into it or that you have added by installing a cartridge.

You can boldface or underline individual cells and ranges. You can use shading lines and boxes to highlight important information in a report. You can adjust the width of one or more columns or change the height of rows. You can also print graphs and text on the same page with flexible sizing options, if your printer is capable. Menus similar to the 1-2-3 menus and immediate changes in the appearance of your worksheet (making what you see on the screen what you will get on your printer) make these add-ins simple to master. You will be able to use the exercises in this chapter whether you are working with WYSIWYG and 1-2-3 Release 2.3 or Allways and an older release of 1-2-3. After a little practice you will feel like an expert with whichever add-in you choose.

In this chapter the exercises will present some of the basic features of WYSIWYG. In the few instances where different instructions are needed for Allways, they will also be provided. Before starting to work with either add-in, you will look at some of the basic procedures for using add-ins. You already used the Viewer add-in in Chapters 4, "Working with Files," and 10, "Advanced File Management Techniques," and you will build on that knowledge in this chapter. As you work through the WYSIWYG or Allways exercises, you will learn more about spreadsheet publishing concepts as well as the specific add-in procedures necessary to apply them. You will also have an opportunity to try your newly learned add-in skills with the Auditor add-in supplied with Release 2.3.

Working with Add-Ins

12

1-2-3 add-in programs are separate programs that have been designed to attach to 1-2-3 through its Add-In Manager. These add-ins can be attached to 1-2-3 to allow them to function without removing 1-2-3 or the current worksheet from memory. Because these add-ins have additional memory requirements, you may not be able to leave Undo enabled unless you have expanded memory on your system.

Attaching an Add-In

When an add-in program is attached to 1-2-3, you define how you want to invoke the features of the add-in. You can invoke it through menu selections or through a short-cut feature known as a *hot key*. When the hot-key option is chosen, you select one of the allowable function keys at the time you attach the add-in. To execute a hot-key add-in, you press the ALT key in combination with the function key selected at the time of attachment. WYSIWYG is an exception since it is always available once it is attached. (Remember, all you need to do is type : from READY mode to display the WYSIWYG menu.)

If you are using Release 2.2 or above, you will want to disable the Undo feature before attaching WYSIWYG or Allways if you only have conventional memory in your machine. Select Worksheet Global Default Other Undo Disable Quit. Then use the following steps to attach WYSI-WYG or Allways after following the installation instructions that appear in Appendix A:

1. Select Add-In. 1-2-3 displays this Add-In Manager menu:

2. Select Attach.
   This invokes the Add-In Manager and displays a menu listing the names of all the add-in files in 1-2-3's directory.

3. Highlight the name of the add-in you wish to attach as shown here:

If you are working with Release 2.2, you could choose ALL-WAYS.ADN or MACROMGR.ADN.

4. Press ENTER.

5. Type **7** to assign the add-in to the ALT-F7 key combination, or type **N** to avoid assigning a key to the add-in.

6. Select Quit to return to READY mode.

WYSIWYG affects the screen appearance, and its features are available when you type a colon (:). If you want to use the features of Allways immediately, select Invoke. If you want to use WYSIWYG, type **:**, or move the mouse to the control panel and click the right mouse button to switch between the 1-2-3 and WYSIWYG menus.

1-2-3 assigns the hot key ALT-F10 to the Add-In Manager menu when it is not assigned to an add-in program. When you press this hot key, 1-2-3 displays the Add-In Manager menu just as if you had selected Add-In. Once you assign an add-in to a function key, the number does not appear as an available option the next time you select Add-In Attach.

Invoking an Add-In

When add-ins are attached, most need to be invoked by selecting Invoke from the Add-In Manager menu, or by their hot keys if they have been assigned. If you attempt to invoke an add-in before attaching it, its name will not appear in the list of add-in options after you select Invoke from the Add-In Manager menu. If no add-ins are attached, an error message at the bottom of the screen will indicate that. Remember, WYSIWYG does not require this step although Allways does.

12

To invoke an add-in with a hot key assigned, press ALT and the function key assigned. To invoke an add-in without a hot key assigned, follow these steps:

1. Select Add-In from the main menu.

   Alternatively you can press ALT-F10 if this key combination is not already being used as a hot key for an add-in.

2. Select Invoke.

3. Highlight the name of the attached add-in you wish to invoke (for this example, ALLWAYS.ADN) and press ENTER.

   When Allways is invoked, it displays its opening screen then shows the screen as it will print (see Figure 12-1).

4. You can return to 1-2-3 by pressing ESC.

Detaching an Add-In

Once an add-in is attached, it will remain attached even if you deactivate it by returning to 1-2-3. This means that you can activate it again and again, whenever you want. It also means that some of your

Figure 12-1. *The Allways opening screen*

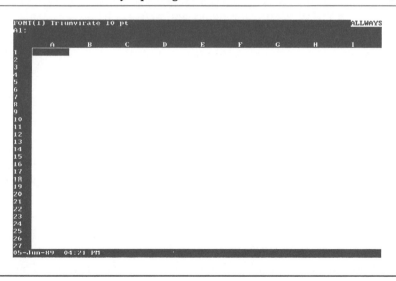

computer's memory is allocated to the add-in. If you know you are not going to use the add-in again, the best approach is to eliminate its attachment to 1-2-3. This can be accomplished in two ways.

For one add-in, select Detach from the menu for the Add-In Manager. To eliminate all the attachments for add-in with one command, select Clear from the Add-In Manager menu. Any remaining add-ins are detached when you quit 1-2-3.

If you are using Release 2.3, you can remove the attachment for WYSIWYG and reattach it by following these steps:

1. Select Add-In.

2. Select Detach, highlight WYSIWYG, and press ENTER. Then, select Quit.

3. Press : and notice that this combination no longer invokes WYSIWYG. Press ESC.

4. Select Add-In.

5. Select Attach.

6. Highlight WYSIWYG.ADN in the list of selections and press ENTER.

7. Type **N** to avoid attaching WYSIWYG to any key.

8. Select Quit to return to READY mode in 1-2-3. Figure 12-2 shows the WYSIWYG display when you activate it.

Using the WYSIWYG and Allways Features

WYSIWYG and Allways provide support for printing worksheet data and 1-2-3 graph images. The worksheets and graphs are created by using menu selections covered in earlier chapters. Rather than printing the worksheet with the Print commands covered in Chapter 6, you can invoke WYSIWYG or Allways and enhance the worksheet entries before printing them.

Unlike PrintGraph, WYSIWYG and Allways do not require that you exit 1-2-3 to start another program when you want a printout of a graph.

Figure 12-2. *WYSIWYG screen after activating it with a colon (:)*

12

In addition, WYSIWYG and Allways can print a graph on the same page as text entries from a worksheet program, and these add-ins allow you to change fonts, the range of worksheet cells occupied by the graph, and colors.

Because WYSIWYG and Allways provide desktop publishing features, they have many options that deal with page layout. In 1-2-3 itself, page layout options are limited and affect every entry on the sheet instead of individual cell entries. Many features of WYSIWYG and Allways, like the Range Format commands in 1-2-3, are oriented toward changing the appearance of a range of worksheet cells. There are many more options with WYSIWYG and Allways, however. Before looking at the menu commands necessary for a full implementation of these features, you will want to enhance your understanding of the general concepts that apply to using desktop publishing features.

Changing a Worksheet with WYSIWYG or Allways

In Chapter 6, you learned that 1-2-3's Print menus offered a few features to control the layout of the page. By defining margins and specifying different print ranges you learned that you had some control over page appearance. The use of printer setup strings allowed you to pass a message (for instance, for formatting various rows within the document) to your printer at the beginning of the Print operation. Although these features added flexibility to page appearance, there were many restrictions, such as the inability to use a particular print feature for an entry within a row if the worksheet had multiple entries within the row. WYSIWYG and Allways make 1-2-3 users' presentations more sophisticated without changing the 1-2-3 worksheet data in any way.

After you attach WYSIWYG (activated by typing :), the worksheet in memory will be presented with the WYSIWYG menu at the top. If you are using Allways (invoked with ALT-F10, selecting Invoke, highlighting ALLWAYS, and pressing ENTER; or with a hot key such as ALT-F7 if you assigned one), the worksheet currently in memory will then be presented on the Allways display. Although it is the same information found on the worksheet, it looks a little different in WYSIWYG or Allways because the display simulates the appearance of the information on a printed page.

Once you invoke WYSIWYG or Allways, the worksheet becomes frozen. Although you can change the worksheet's appearance, you cannot update values in the worksheet. If you need to change a worksheet value, you must return to 1-2-3. Even though you cannot change any of the entries stored in worksheet cells when WYSIWYG or Allways is active, you can make significant changes to the appearance of the information. Like 1-2-3, WYSIWYG and Allways have a menu that displays at the top of the screen. With Allways you must type a slash (/) to activate this menu.

When you activate WYSIWYG the following menu is presented:

The Allways add-in provided with 1-2-3 Release 2.2 has a similar menu (activated with a slash):

Menu selections are made by entering the first letter of the desired selection or by highlighting the desired selection and pressing ENTER to complete the selection. You can also use your mouse to make a menu selection if you are using WYSIWYG. You will notice a mode indicator in the upper right corner that tells you what is happening at any given moment. As in 1-2-3, you can invoke the Help feature by pressing F1.

Commands in the Format menu selection will allow you to change fonts and use boldface, underlining, and other features. In contrast to 1-2-3, WYSIWYG and Allways will display the text on the screen as it will print. Also, format changes will appear in the top line of the control panel as you move the cell pointer around on the worksheet. The entries are not coded like 1-2-3's but are spelled out.

Another difference between the menu selections in WYSIWYG or Allways and 1-2-3 is that you will not find a File selection to save and retrieve files. The selections you make with these add-ins will be saved if you return to 1-2-3 and save your 1-2-3 file. WYSIWYG will store your formatting settings to a file with the same name as the worksheet but with an .FMT extension. Allways will store your formatting settings to a file with the same name as the worksheet it formats and an .ALL extension. Since there is no way you can end these add-ins without returning to 1-2-3, this should help you remember to save your changes. When you retrieve your 1-2-3 file at another time, all of your WYSIWYG or Allways changes will be available when you work with the add-in.

Unlike 1-2-3, Allways (though not WYSIWYG) has a set of *accelerator keys* that are shortcuts you can use to request selections. These are shown as follows:

ALT-B	Boldface On/Off
ALT-G	Grid lines On/Off
ALT-L	Lines Outline/All/None
ALT-S	Shading Light/Dark/Solid/None
ALT-U	Underline Single/Double/None

ALT-1	Font 1 (Triumvirate 10 point)
ALT-2	Font 2 (Triumvirate Italic 10 point)
ALT-3	Font 3 (Triumvirate 14 point)
ALT-4	Font 4 (Triumvirate 20 point)
ALT-5	Font 5 (Times 10 point)
ALT-6	Font 6 (Times Italic 10 point)
ALT-7	Font 7 (Times 14 point)
ALT-8	Font 8 (Times 20 point)

Changing Fonts

The selection of fonts for your entries will alter the typeface and the size of the characters. The term *typeface* refers to the style of print characters. These characters may be somewhat plain or they may have embellishments at the ends of the lines constructing each letter. Fonts without embellishments are referred to as *sans serif* fonts. Fonts with embellishments are known as *serif* fonts.

Figure 12-3 shows the default fonts shipped with WYSIWYG. Note that the last font actually changes the symbols as well as the style.

Figure 12-4 shows the default fonts that are shipped as part of the Allways package. These are the fonts that you see initially when you select a font for your worksheet. You can use any of the many fonts that come with Allways and WYSIWYG in addition to any of the fonts that your printer or a cartridge provides.

The fonts shipped with WYSIWYG and Allways are soft fonts, which means that they are defined by the software and do not require the

Figure 12-3.   *Sample of fonts available in WYSIWYG*

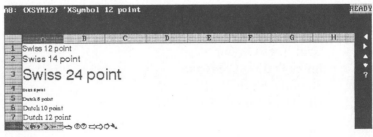

12

Figure 12-4. *Sample of fonts available in Allways*

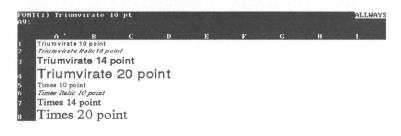

insertion of font cartridges in your printer. You may be able to buy other fonts on cartridges or disks from your printer manufacturer or other outside companies. Once your printer has access to a particular font, the characters of the font are created by a grid pattern of wires inside your printer. This grid can create any graphic pattern by using or not using any of the wires. Although WYSIWYG and Allways will support the use of font cartridges for your printer, there are many fonts included with the package. The four default fonts with WYSIWYG are called Swiss, Dutch, Courier, and XSymbols.

The size of the characters is another important component of a font. Size is measured in points in WYSIWYG and for laser printers in Allways. Each point is 1/72 of an inch. Normally 10- or 12-point fonts are used for regular spreadsheet entries. Headings may use 12- or 24-point fonts and fine print may be displayed with a 5- or 7-point font. For dot matrix printers, Allways measures character size in pitch, which is the number of characters per inch.

Using Different Fonts

You can use as many as eight fonts on any single output created with WYSIWYG or Allways. The fonts available at any one point are part of a selectable font set. For different worksheets you might have a different set of fonts. The first font in any set is always the font used as the default, which means that it will be used for all entries unless you select a different font with the Format Font command or an Allways accelerator key. When you format part of the worksheet to use a different font, the column may need to be resized to fit all of the characters. When worksheet entries are printed with the default font, you do not have to change the column width because the add-in defines the column width according to the size of the default font.

To look at the application of different fonts for a worksheet, you will want to complete the entries shown in Figure 12-5. Figure 12-6 displays the actual WYSIWYG screen showing the same worksheet data. Follow these step-by-step directions:

1. Select Worksheet Global Format **,** (comma), type **0**, and press ENTER.

2. Move the cell pointer to C2, type **ABC COMPANY**, and press the DOWN ARROW key.

3. Type **Unit Sales By Region** and move the cell pointer to A6.

4. Complete the following entries:

A6:	Tires	C9:	60
A7:	Radios	D5:	"East
A8:	Tuners	D6:	3400
A9:	Sky-views	D7:	1109
B5:	"North	D8:	870
B6:	1200	D9:	55
B7:	750	E5:	"West
B8:	850	E6:	980
B9:	70	E7:	1502
C5:	"South	E8:	1050
C6:	650	E9:	120
C7:	690	F5:	"Total
C8:	675	F6:	@SUM(B6..E6)

Figure 12-5.   *Worksheet for demonstrating add-in features*

Figure 12-6. *WYSIWYG screen showing worksheet from Figure 12-5*

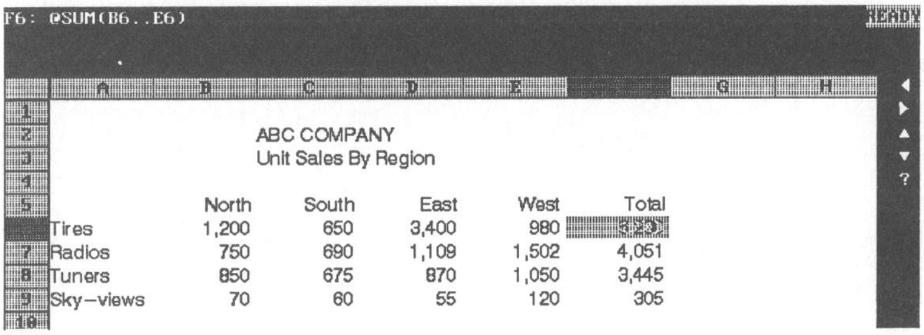

5. With your cell pointer on F6, select Copy, press ENTER, move the cell pointer to F7, and type **.** (period). Move the cell pointer to F9 and press ENTER to complete the Copy operation.

6. Move the cell pointer to C2 by pressing the F5 (GOTO) key, typing **C2**, and pressing ENTER.

7. If you are using Allways, invoke your add-in according to the directions provided earlier in the chapter.

8. Type a slash (/) to activate the Allways menu or type a colon (:) to invoke WYSIWYG and its menu.

9. Select Format Font to tell the add-in that you want to use a different font for a range.
   Eight font selections that are part of its font set will display.

10. Select Swiss 14 point if you are using WYSIWYG, Triumvirate 14 if you are using Allways. The add-in will prompt you for the range you want to format with this font.

11. Move the highlight to C3 to expand the range, and then press ENTER. Your screen will show the range in the new format. Figure 12-7 shows the change in the WYSIWYG screen. Notice that the entire entries for C2 and C3 are displayed in the new font, including the portions that borrow space from cells in column D. The control panel also shows your font selection.

Figure 12-7. *Changing the font size to e. .e text*

```
C2: (SWISS14) 'ABC COMPANY                                              READY
```

	North	South	East	West	Total
Tires	1,200	650	3,400	980	6,230
Radios	750	690	1,109	1,502	4,051
Tuners	850	675	870	1,050	3,445
Sky-views	70	60	55	120	305

ABC COMPANY
Unit Sales By Region

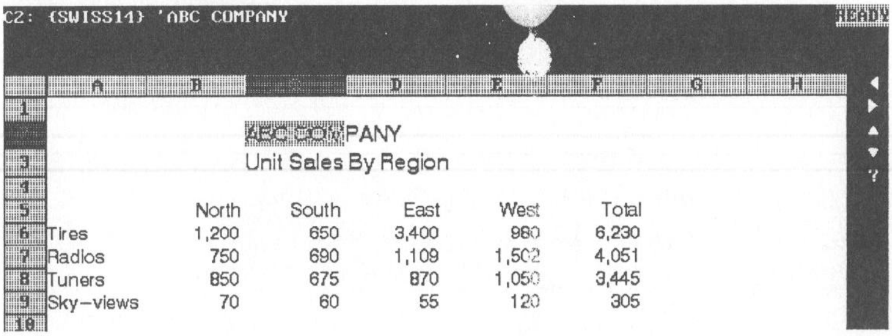

Changing the Font Set

When you first install WYSIWYG or Allways, your font set is created from eight of the soft fonts (the default font set) provided with the add-in. You also have the ability to replace any of these default fonts with fonts directly supported by your printer or another soft font. If you have a printer that supports font cartridges, you can tell the add-in which of these fonts you will be using and they will also be available for your selection.

To replace an existing font, follow these steps:

1. Activate the menu with a / or :, depending on which add-in you are using.

2. Select Format Font.

3. In Allways, highlight the font you want to change and select Replace.

4. Highlight the font that you wish to use as the replacement, and press ENTER.

5. Highlight the font size in Allways, or type the font size in WYSIWYG that you wish to use as the replacement, and press ENTER.

6. Select Quit. (Select Quit a second time in WYSIWYG.)

To configure WYSIWYG or Allways to use printer cartridges, follow these steps:

12

1. Activate the menu.

2. Select Print Config 1st-Cart in WYSIWYG or Print Configuration Cartridge in Allways.

3. Highlight the desired cartridge in the list and press ENTER.

4. Select Quit to leave the Configuration menu. (Select Quit a second time in WYSIWYG.)

The cartridge fonts will now be included in the list of fonts to select from when you replace a font. In WYSIWYG, they will be listed after you select Other.

Other Formatting Options

In addition to changing fonts, you can alter the appearance of cell entries in other ways. For a range as small as one cell or as large as all your spreadsheet entries, you can use single or double underlining, color selections, shading, and an outline around each cell. You can also use boldface anywhere in a row of the worksheet.

Adding Boldface

Practice changing point size and adding boldface to text in the following exercise. Try these steps with the worksheet you have created:

1. Select the range A6..A9. The selected range is highlighted.
   In Allways you select a range by typing a period and highlighting the range; in WYSIWYG, press F4 (ABS), highlight the range and press ENTER.

2. Type / or : to activate the menu for the add-in.

3. Select Format Font Dutch 10 point for WYSIWYG or Times 10 point for Allways.

4. Activate the add-in's menu.

5. Move the cell pointer to A5 and select Format Bold Set. Next, move the cell pointer to F5 and press ENTER. The old font is still displayed except that it is in boldface. Your screen will look like the one in Figure 12-8.

Figure 12-8.   *Worksheet after changing fonts and adding boldface*

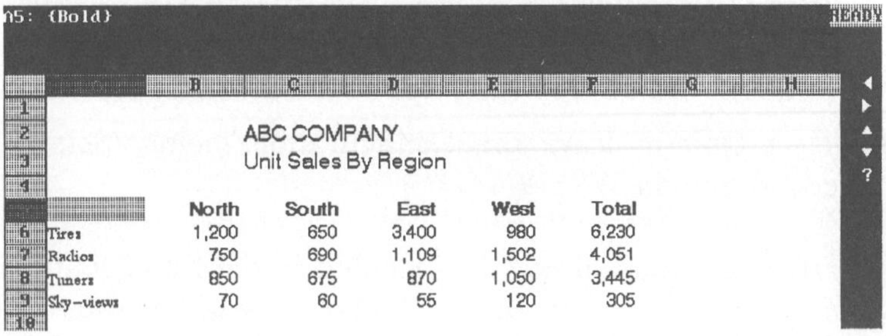

Adding Lines

You can add lines at any side of a cell or a range of cells. If you use the outline feature, you can completely outline all the walls of each cell in a range.

If you are discussing eliminating the Sky-views product line, you may want to outline the entries in that row. Move the cell pointer to B9 and then follow these steps.

1. Select Format Lines Outline.

2. Move the cell pointer to F9 and press ENTER.
   A box is drawn around the outer edges of the range.

Your screen will look like the one in Figure 12-9 with a selection of Outline in WYSIWYG or Allways. (With a selection of All, each cell in the range would be boxed.)

Removing a Format Option

You can remove any format that you add to a worksheet range. The Format Reset command strips away any format changes made and displays the entries in Font 1 format.

To eliminate the outline around the Sky-views entries, follow these steps:

Figure 12-9.   *Outline added to worksheet range*

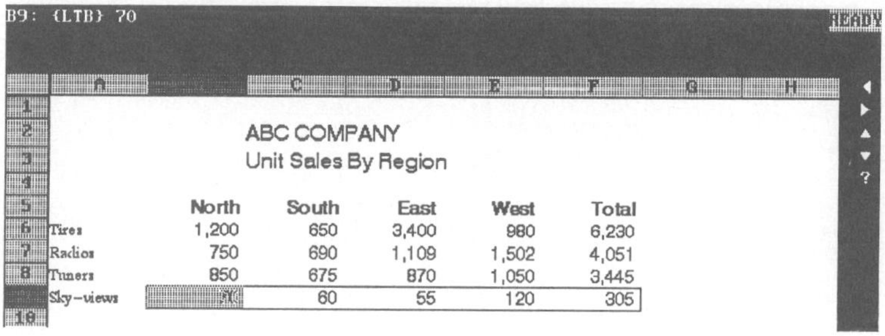

1. Select Format Reset with the cell pointer still in B9.

2. Expand the range by moving the cell pointer to F9 and pressing ENTER.

Adding Shading

You can add three levels of shading to one or more cells in the worksheet. WYSIWYG and Allways support light, dark, and solid black shading levels. The Format Shade command will add shading to a preselected range or prompt you to select a range to format.

To use light shading on numbers in the Total column, follow these steps:

1. Move the cell pointer to F6.

2. Activate the add-in's menu.

3. Select Format Shade Light.

4. Move the cell pointer to F9 and press ENTER.

Your screen will look like the one in Figure 12-10 if you are using WYSIWYG. If you are using Allways, your screen will be similar but not identical.

Figure 12-10.   *Range formatted for light shading*

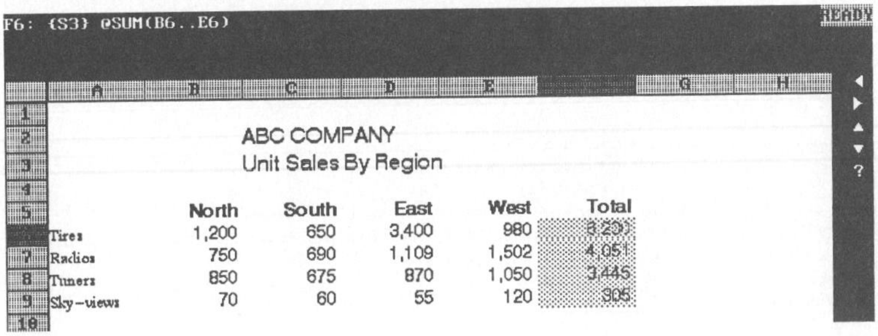

Adding Underlining

You can underline text with either single or double underlining. Single underlining differs from a line at the bottom of the box in that it is only added for the length of the cell entries, not the entire cell width. Double underlining underlines the entire cell's width. To underline the titles at the top of the screen, follow these steps:

1.   Move the cell pointer to C2.

2.   Activate the add-in's menu.

3.   Select Format Underline Single.

4.   Move the cell pointer to C3 and press ENTER.

Your screen will display underlining beneath the entire entries in C2 and C3. If you decide to remove the underlining but want to leave other format changes such as the font intact, use the Format Underline Clear command.

Changing Column Widths and Row Heights

You can change the width of a column in the WYSIWYG or Allways display and printout. Row height is normally adjusted for the font size selected but can also be changed to a custom height. To change the

12

column width, use the Worksheet Column Set-Width command to specify a size. The row height is changed with the Worksheet Row Set-Height command.

In Allways, the column width can be adjusted more precisely than in 1-2-3. The columns are measured in terms of the number of characters of the default font that will display in the column. You can change to fractional sizes like 11.42 if you wish to accommodate the exact width needed for a different font. In WYSIWYG, the Worksheet Column Set Width command has the same effect and follows the same rules as 1-2-3's Worksheet Column Column-Range Set Width command.

To change the column width for column A, follow these steps:

1. Move the cell pointer to column A.

2. Activate the add-in menu.

3. Select Worksheet Column Set-Width.

4. Press the RIGHT ARROW five times and press ENTER. Press ENTER in WYSIWYG to select column A to change.

To reset the column width to 1-2-3's width in Allways or the default global column width in WYSIWYG, select Worksheet Column ResetWidth with the add-in menu active.

Row heights are uniform initially, but as you select different fonts, WYSIWYG and Allways automatically adjust the height to properly display the data. You can establish a specific height for a row by selecting Worksheet Row Set-Height, selecting a range of rows to change, and pressing the DOWN or UP ARROW key to visually set the row height. Try this now by moving to row 5 and entering the command. To reset the row height so that it adjusts automatically, select Worksheet Row Auto.

Label Alignment

WYSIWYG allows you to change the alignment of labels with Text Align. Always does not have an option for changing the label alignment. You must return to 1-2-3 and change the label prefix to alter the label alignment.

Allways displays labels differently than 1-2-3 or WYSIWYG do. In 1-2-3, labels that are centered or right-aligned but exceed the width of their cells will be left-aligned. This is not true in Allways because Allways will allow these entries to spill over to adjacent cells, displaying part of a centered label to the right of its cell and part to the left.

If you return to 1-2-3 and change the label prefixes at the front of C2 and C3 to carets, and then invoke Allways again, you will see that your labels are centered.

Changing the Page Layout

You can change several options that control what a printed page of your output will look like. With the Print Layout Page-Size command (Layout Page-Size in Allways), you can select one of the standard sizes that the add-in supports or enter your custom requirements. You can also change the margins or add a header or a footer. Follow these steps for a look at the options:

1. Activate the add-in menu.

2. Select Print Layout Page-Size (Layout Page-Size for Allways) and look at the list of options.

3. Press ESC to leave the current choice unchanged, although it would be possible to select another size of paper for a special need.

4. Select Margins from the Layout menu. You could select and enter a new number for any margin.

5. Select Top, type **2**, and press ENTER.

6. Select Quit to exit the Margin menu.

7. Select Quit once in Allways, or twice in WYSIWYG to exit the Layout and Print menus.

Printing a Worksheet

Once you have made all the changes you need, you can print the document. You must print it from the add-in to see the enhancements you have made in the worksheet. All of the options for printing can be accessed by selecting Print. You can define any size range you wish and can print this range, with all its enhancements, to the printer or to a file. You can also choose to print more than one copy of the selected range.

To specify the print range, select Print Range Set, highlight the desired range, and press ENTER. You can use the Print Range Clear command to eliminate a print range.

Try this now with the current worksheet:

1. Activate the add-in menu.

2. Select Print Range Set.

3. Press the HOME key to move to A1.

4. Type . and then press the END key followed by the HOME key to move to the last non-blank cell on the worksheet.

5. Press ENTER.

6. Select Go from the menu to print a copy.

Changing the Print Settings

WYSIWYG and Allways have print settings that allow you to further customize your output. You can use these options to print multiple copies of your output or to print a selected range of pages.

To print two copies of output, follow these steps:

1. Select Print Settings Copies.

2. Type **2** and press ENTER.

3. Select Quit twice to exit the add-in's menu.

To print a selected range of pages, follow these steps:

1. Select Print Settings Begin.

2. Type the number of the first page you wish to print and then press ENTER.

3. Select End, type the number of the last page you want to print, and press ENTER.

4. Select Quit.

Adding Graphs to the Display

WYSIWYG and Allways support the display of graphs created in 1-2-3 by placing these graphs in ranges of the worksheet. The add-ins automatically size each graph for the size of the selected range. You will be able to print the graphs on the same page as worksheet text because the add-ins use the same Print commands to print a worksheet whether it consists of worksheet entries, graphs, or a combination of both.

To display a graph on the worksheet, you will need to have a copy of the desired 1-2-3 graph saved as a .PIC file on disk. These graph files are created with 1-2-3's Graph Save command once a graph is displayed in 1-2-3. Once you have stored the graph files on disk in 1-2-3, displaying them in the add-in is as simple as selecting Graph Add and choosing the name of the .PIC file. In WYSIWYG, you have additional options for adding current and named graphs from the current worksheet, and for adding Metafile and blank graphics.

To add a couple of graphs to the current display, follow these steps.

1. Press ESC until you return to the READY mode.

2. Select Graph to invoke 1-2-3's Graph menu. Select Type Bar.
   You will create two graphs—a bar graph and a pie chart. If you have never created a 1-2-3 graph before, you will want to be sure to look at the details in Chapter 8.

3. Select Group, highlight A6..E9, press ENTER, and select Column-wise so that 1-2-3 divides the range into data series according to columns.
   If you are using Release 1A, 2, or 2.01, you must select each range individually. Select X to specify the X range, highlight A6..A9, and press ENTER. Select A to specify the A range, highlight B6..B9, and press ENTER. Select B to specify the B range, highlight C6..C9, and press ENTER. Select C to specify the C range, highlight D6..D9, and press ENTER. Select D to specify the D range, highlight E6..E9, and press ENTER.

4. Select Save, type **BAR1**, and press ENTER.
   You could have added legends and titles to the graph with the techniques used in Chapter 8, but instead you will have a quick graph to use with Allways or WYSIWYG without any further entries.

12

5. Select Reset Graph to clear the bar graph specifications.

6. Select Quit to leave the Graph menu. Enter the numbers **1** through **4** in G1..G4 to use later for establishing hatch-mark patterns.

    This step must be completed while you are in READY mode.

7. Select Graph Type Pie.

8. Select A, highlight B6..B9, and press ENTER.

9. Select X, highlight A6..A9, and press ENTER.

10. Select B to establish hatch-mark patterns, highlight G1..G4, and press ENTER.

11. Save the graph by selecting Save, typing **PIE1**, and pressing ENTER.

12. Select Quit to return to READY mode.

    You now have two 1-2-3 .PIC files on your disk that you can print with PrintGraph or your add-in.

13. Select Range Erase, highlight G1..G4 and press ENTER since the hatch pattern codes are not needed anymore.

You can add the graphs to your add-in display with these steps:

1. Move the cell pointer to A11.

2. If you are using Allways again, invoke it. Activate the add-in's menu.

3. Select Graph Add.

4. With WYSIWYG you must select PIC then BAR1.PIC and with Allways you can select BAR1.PIC as your next step.

5. Specify the range A11..D26 and press ENTER.

    The bar graph now appears on your WYSIWYG screen as in Figure 12-11.

6. Select Graph Add.

7. With WYSIWYG select PIC and select PIE1.PIC. With Allways highlight PIE1.PIC and press ENTER.

8. Select the range E10..I27 and press ENTER.

Figure 12-11. *Adding a bar graph*

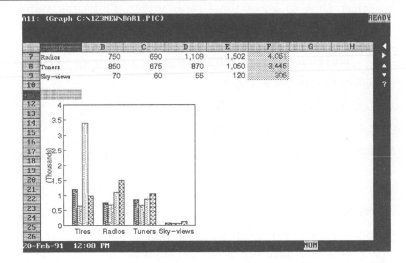

The two graphs display on the worksheet and can be printed. Figure 12-12 shows the WYSIWYG sheet with two graphs added. If the Display mode is set to text (Display Graphs No in Allways) the graph will not display.

Printing Graphs

Printing a graph with WYSIWYG or Allways is no different from printing a worksheet that contains text. You will use the same menu selections to specify the range of the worksheet that contains a graph. You can also make other menu selections to change settings if desired. When you are ready to print the graph, select Go from the Print menu.

Using the Auditor Add-In with Release 2.3

Release 2.3 provides an auditor add-in that allows you to take a closeup look at worksheet formulas or look for conditions that might cause

Figure 12-12.   *Two graphs added*

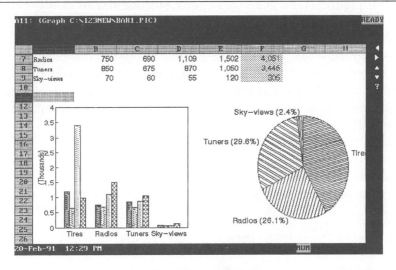

problems. You can have the add-in search for cells that depend on a specific cell, alerting you to which results will be affected if you change a cell. You can also have the add-in see which cells are used to compute a specific formula, identify the order of recalculation, or show you all the cells with circular references. You can highlight cells that meet the condition you selected, list them on the worksheet, or examine them one-by-one with a trace feature.

You can access the features of the Auditor add-in after attaching and invoking it. First you will detach WYSIWYG and free the memory that it is using. Follow these steps to try Auditor with the worksheet used earlier in the chapter:

1. Press ALT-F10 and select Detach, highlight WYSIWYG, and press ENTER.

2. Select Attach, highlight AUDITOR.ADN, and press ENTER.

3. Select ALT-F8 as the hot key for a quick way to invoke it later.

4. Invoke the add-in by selecting Invoke, highlighting AUDITOR, and pressing ENTER.

A dialog box and menu for the Auditor are presented on your screen, as shown in Figure 12-13. The dialog box enables you to select the Audit Range (controlling which cells are in the range examined by the add-in) and the Audit Mode (which controls the ways that you receive the information from the add-in). The default settings encompass the entire spreadsheet and use highlighting to mark the cells that meet the desired condition. The menu at the top allows you to decide whether you want to look at formulas or see which cells are used to create the result provided by a formula.

The Options selection in the menu allows you to make the same settings selections shown in the dialog box. Table 12-1 describes each of the tasks that the Auditor can perform in more detail.

Try the following sequence:

1. Select Precedents, then highlight F6 and press ENTER. With the default setting of Highlight the cells used to compute this result, B6, C6, D6, and E6 will be highlighted.

2. Select Quit to return to 1-2-3 for a better look at the highlighted cells.

3. Press ALT-F8, the hot key that you assigned, to invoke the Auditor again.

4. To remove the highlighting, select Options Reset Highlight.

Figure 12-13.   *The Auditor menu*

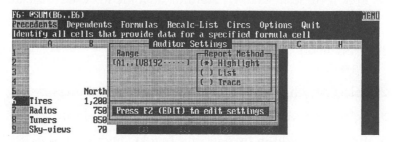

Table 12-1. Auditor tasks

Option	Indicates
Precedents	Data used to compute the result indicated
Dependents	Formulas that depend on the cell specified
Formulas	All the formula in the range specified, including external link formulas
Recalc-List	The order in which formulas on the worksheet are recalculated
Circ	Formulas that contain circular references

12

5. Select List from the Options menu, then select Quit.

6. Select Precedents, highlight F6 and press ENTER to specify the precedents source cell.

7. Move the cell pointer to A12 and press ENTER to indicate this location as the beginning of the list. Figure 12-14 shows the list beginning in A12. The Auditor will feel free to use all the cells down to A8192. If you have formulas beneath the cell specified, you will want to select a range rather than a single cell address to restrict the cells that can be used for the list. If you select a range that is too small, the Auditor will write as much as possible, then present an error message telling you that the Output Range is full.

Review

- WYSIWYG and Allways allow you to significantly enhance the appearance of printed output.

- As a first step you must attach WYSIWYG or Allways by pressing ALT-F10 and selecting Attach from the menu for the Add-In Manager. You can assign Allways to one of the hot keys (ALT-F7 through ALT-F10). You do not need to assign WYSIWYG to a hot key.

Figure 12-14.   *The list of precedents is shown as A12..A16*

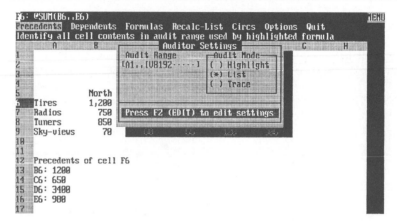

- To invoke Allways once it is attached, press the hot key assigned or press ALT-F10 and select Invoke from the menu. To invoke WYSIWYG, press : from READY mode.

- Selecting Quit or 1-2-3 in Allways returns you to 1-2-3. You can also leave the add-in by pressing ESC when the ALLWAYS mode indicator is on the screen.

- You can change the appearance of the worksheet with WYSI-WYG and Allways with the many format options. A graph can be displayed in any range of the worksheet if you have a 1-2-3 graphic image file stored on disk.

- Column widths and row heights can also be changed with WYSIWYG or Allways. When you return to 1-2-3, changes made with Allways will not be apparent on your 1-2-3 screen. Changing column widths in WYSIWYG also changes the column widths in 1-2-3.

- Saving a 1-2-3 file will save your modifications, making them available again the next time you load the spreadsheet and invoke WYSIWYG or Allways.

- Printing with Allways or WYSIWYG prints your formatted worksheet data and any graphs displayed on the worksheet. Printing in 1-2-3 does not print graphs or the add-in's formatting.

12

Commands and Keys

Entry	Action
AA	Add-In Attach loads an add-in to memory
AC	Add-In Clear unloads all add-ins from memory
AD	Add-In Detach unloads an add-in from memory
AI	Add-In Invoke starts a loaded add-in
AQ	Add-In Quit leaves the Add-In Manager menu

Allways and WYSIWYG Commands

Entry	Action
Q or 1	Quit or 1-2-3 returns you to 1-2-3
FB	Format Bold applies boldface to the selected range
FF	Format Font allows you to select a font for a specific range (Format Font Use in Allways)
FL	Format Lines adds lines or an outline around cells
FR	Format Reset eliminates formatting
FS	Format Shade adds light, dark, or black shading
FU	Format Underline adds or clears single or double underlining
FFR	Format Font Replace replaces a font in the font set
GA	Graph Add adds a graph to a range on the worksheet
GR	Graph Remove removes a graph from the worksheet
PG	Print Go starts printing
PLM	Print Layout Margins allows you to change any of the page margins (Layout Margins in Allways)
PLP	Print Layout Page-Size sets the dimensions of a printed page (Layout Page-Size in Allways)

Entry	Action
PR	Print Range clears or sets the print range
PS	Print Settings allows you to specify the number of copies and a range of pages to print
WCR	Worksheet Column Reset-Width reestablishes the global column width to the global column width used by 1-2-3
WCS	Worksheet Column Set-Width alters the column width

A

Installing 1-2-3 and WYSIWYG

This appendix is an introduction to installing Lotus 1-2-3 on your system. It will cover installation of 1-2-3 and its accessory programs on various types of equipment. You will find detailed instructions to ensure that the installation process proceeds smoothly.

If your copy of 1-2-3 has already been installed by your computer dealer or someone else, you do not need to read this appendix. If your copy of 1-2-3 is still covered in shrink wrap, you will need to install the package. In that case you will find this appendix to be a valuable reference for the steps that you must take. It will also provide some information on various equipment options to help you make intelligent selections during the installation process.

Before beginning with specifics, this appendix will introduce the hardware options and the various system components. You cannot install 1-2-3 if you do not have at least some general knowledge about the system you will be using. In order for the Install program to configure your copy of 1-2-3 to run with your specific hardware components, you must be able to tell the program what those components are.

Your Equipment

1-2-3 is designed to run on a personal computer or on one of the newer 80286- or 80386-based machines such as an AT or a PS/2 from IBM (or a compatible) computer. Because the compatible market is constantly changing, you will need to check with your dealer for the most up-to-date list of certified compatibles. In case of doubt, have the dealer demonstrate 1-2-3 on the machine you are considering. Throughout this appendix, the assumption is made that you have an IBM PC, XT, AT, or PS/2.

Minimum Configuration

The minimum system configuration required for the different releases of 1-2-3 is listed in Table A-1. An optimal configuration for your application may require more equipment. Notice the differences in memory and disk drive support among the different versions. All of the releases can use a hard disk, although you must continue to use the System disk with Release 1A. Using a hard disk to store the 1-2-3 program files prevents you from frequently having to change disks and improves the speed with which 1-2-3 performs the tasks you direct.

In order to use 1-2-3 add-ins, you will need to supplement minimal 1-2-3 requirements. For example, Allways and WYSIWYG only run on a computer with a hard disk. They need an additional 128K of RAM and 1MB (1 megabyte or one million bytes) on the hard disk.

Adding Memory

The models you create are limited by the amount of memory on your system. Operating 1-2-3 at the lowest memory level possible, you can use all of the package features but you are restricted in the size of your data files, the size of your spreadsheet applications, and the number of files you have in memory. If you plan to build large models, you will want to consider expanding the memory of your machine. Network and TSR software can still be used with 1-2-3, but those other programs further

Table A-1. *Minimum Configuration*

Release 1A	Release 2	Release 2.2	Release 2.3
IBM PC, XT, AT, PS/2 or compatible	IBM PC, XT, AT, PS/2 or compatible	IBM PC, XT, AT, PS/2 or compatible	IBM PC, XT, AT, PS/2 or compatible
Keyboard	Keyboard	Keyboard	Keyboard
192K RAM	256K RAM	384K RAM	320K RAM
2 double-sided/ double-density (DSDD) disks or 1 hard disk and 1 DSDD disk	1 DSDD disk or 1 hard disk	1 DSDD disk or 1 hard disk with 1,700,000 bytes free	1 hard disk with 1.7MB-6MB bytes free
Monochrome or color monitor	Monochrome or color monitor	Monochrome or color monitor	Monochrome or color monitor

limit the size of your worksheets. If you are using add-ins with 1-2-3, you may want to disable Undo so that your worksheets do not run out of memory.

With Release 2, you also have the option of expanding memory beyond the standard 640K. To do this, select a card that conforms to the Lotus/Intel/Microsoft Expanded Memory Specification 2.2, such as the AboveBoard card. With these cards, 1-2-3 can use up to 4MB of memory (approximately 4,000,000 characters) above the 640K memory limit. This expanded memory will allow you to build large data files and spreadsheets with the 1-2-3 program. You will need to run the expanded-memory management software that comes with your card before 1-2-3 can access this additional memory.

Releases 2 and higher also support the addition of a math coprocessor. The 8087, the 80387, and the 80287 coprocessor chips are supported and are automatically recognized once they are installed. Spreadsheet models with a significant number of calculations are calculated much faster with one of these chips added to the motherboard of your machine.

Keyboards

You will begin using the keyboard in this appendix as you work with the Install program. Any directions given will refer to key names on the regular or enhanced keyboard. The enhanced keyboard offers a second set of movement keys as well as the numeric keypad so that you can use the numeric keypad for numbers while you use the second set of movement keys for moving in 1-2-3. Pressing the key labeled NUM LOCK toggles the numeric keypad between movement keys and number keys. Other keyboard types usually have the same keys, but you must look for where these keys are located.

Monitors

Monitors can be described using two features. The first feature varies depending on whether the monitor can display multiple colors. Monitors come in two basic varieties, color and monochrome. Monochrome implies one color. This may be white, green, or amber on black. Normally a monochrome monitor will display only text, although you can add cards such as an Enhanced Graphics Adapter (EGA), or a Hercules card. Even with the graphics adapter, a monochrome monitor will display one-color graphs. A color monitor can display graphs in color as well as use color for highlighting some of the 1-2-3 screens. For example, it can use red for the error indicator and blue to highlight menu choices.

The second feature of a monitor is the resolution, or how many dots of light your monitor can display across the screen—the more dots your monitor uses to fill the screen, the sharper the images it displays. There are three basic types of monitors: CGA (Color Graphics Adapter), EGA (Enhanced Graphics Adapter), and VGA (Video Graphics Adapter). When you install 1-2-3 you will have to select the type of display you want based on the monitor's resolution and manufacturer.

Printers

If you have both a dot-matrix and a letter-quality printer, you may want to use the letter-quality device for text and use the dot-matrix device to print graphics. If you have both a dot-matrix printer and a laser printer, you can use the dot-matrix for draft copies and the laser for the final output. On a network you may have a variety of output devices from which to select, including a plotter for graphics and a laser printer for professional-looking text and graphics output.

To connect any of these printers to your system, you will also need a cable and an available port. It is possible to connect printers to both parallel and serial ports as long as they are compatible, but there are some special settings if you use a serial connection. First, you must set the printer's baud rate to control the speed of data transfer. At any baud rate except 110 you should also set 1 stop bit, 8 data bits, and no parity. With a speed of 110 there should be 2 stop bits. Once the program is loaded, use the Worksheet Global Default Printer Interface command and select the baud rate that matches your printer's rate. This is done by typing **/WGDPI**, pointing to the baud rate you need, and pressing ENTER. This change is saved with the Worksheet Global Default Update command. If you are purchasing your system at the same time as you acquire 1-2-3, your dealer will usually assist you with this installation.

A plotter provides another option for producing graphs. With most devices you can use either paper or transparencies in your plotter with the appropriate pens to create the display medium of your choice. Since 1-2-3 supports only a limited number of plotters, you will want to ensure that the one you purchase is on the acceptable list; otherwise, it may not function with 1-2-3.

Adding Disk Drives

1-2-3 offers several possibilities for storing the 1-2-3 programs and your data. You can store the 1-2-3 programs on your hard disk and use a hard disk or a floppy disk to store your data. Hard disks offer the advantage of storing large amounts of information. A hard disk that holds 100MB of information is equivalent to 278 floppy disks. Your computer may have one or two disk drives. When two disks are next to each other, the one to the left or above the other is usually referred to as drive A. The one to the right or below the other is usually referred to as drive B. If your computer only has one drive, it is drive A. Before you can store data on a floppy disk, the disk must be prepared. Use the FORMAT command described in your operating system manual or review the section "Formatting Disks" in Chapter 4 before storing data on floppy disks.

Another possibility for releases before 2.3 is running 1-2-3 using floppy disks. You can use one or two drives with 1-2-3. If you only use one disk, you will find that the required disk swapping is quite cumbersome. Data cannot be stored on the System disk containing the program and Help files, and so you will find yourself changing disks frequently.

Although releases before 2.3 can run solely on floppy disks, the best configuration for using 1-2-3 is to have a hard disk drive along with a floppy disk drive so that you can load all the 1-2-3 programs on the hard disk and have the flexibility of storing data files on either the hard disk or a floppy disk. You will then be able to switch from 1-2-3 to Translate or PrintGraph without having to search for the proper disk, since all three programs will be on your hard disk. Also, with a hard disk you will be able to store files that exceed a floppy disk's capacity.

The Operating System

The operating system is the control program that resides in the memory of your computer regardless of the software you are working with. It controls the interface between the various devices and establishes the format for data storage on disk. The different releases of 1-2-3 are compatible with different versions of the DOS operating system. Since DOS is absolutely essential to using your computer and its software, make sure you have a version of DOS that is compatible with your release of 1-2-3.

Release 1A of 1-2-3 was designed to run under DOS 1.1 or higher. Most other releases can use DOS release 2.0 or greater although your machine might require a higher DOS version to function properly. This may seem a bit confusing, but your dealer can advise you based on your configuration.

Noting Your Equipment

You are now ready to proceed with the steps needed to install your 1-2-3 disks. First, however, make a note of your hardware configuration. Figure A-1 provides a convenient form for doing this. You will want this information available when you use 1-2-3's Install program.

Installing 1-2-3

Installing Release 2.3 of 1-2-3 registers your disks with your name and company, copies files to the hard disk, and tailors your 1-2-3 disks to run

Figure A-1. *Configuration worksheet*

Hardware

Computer manufacturer _____

Computer model _____

Graphics card _____

Monitor _____

RAM _____

Printer manufacturer/model _____

Printer interface (serial or parallel) _____

Plotter model _____

Plotter interface (serial or parallel) _____

Disk drives—number and type
(hard vs. floppy) _____

Software

DOS version number _____

Lotus 1-2-3 version _____

with your specific hardware configuration. You can redo steps of this process later if you change your hardware configuration to include new items, such as a different printer or monitor.

When you purchase 1-2-3, the package you receive contains an envelope with several diskettes, depending on the disk size. These disks contain all of the program files that run 1-2-3 and its accessories. You will use these disks as you follow the steps to install 1-2-3 on your computer. These instructions assume DOS is already installed on your system. If this is not the case, install DOS before you install 1-2-3.

Follow these steps for installation:

1. Start DOS in your system without a disk in drive A. This will make your system boot from DOS on your drive C.

2. Enter the date and time if you do not have a clock card. The date format you should use is 12-15-91 for a date of December 15, 1991. Press ENTER after supplying the date. Enter the time in the form HH:MM. If the time is 1:30 P.M., for example, type **13:30** and press ENTER. If there is a clock card in your system, you do not have to enter the date or time.

3. To start the Install program, insert the Install disk into drive A. Type **A:** and press ENTER to make the drive current. (If you need to use drive B to install 1-2-3, insert the disk in drive B and type **B:**.) Then type **INSTALL** and press ENTER to start the installation program. Press ENTER after viewing the opening screen.

4. Install prompts you to register your name and the company's name. In the first line, enter your name. In the second line, enter your company name. If you do not have a company name to supply, reenter your name. Then press INS to finalize the entries. The Install program prompts for a confirmation, which you can supply by typing a **Y** and pressing ENTER.

5. Install prompts for the programs you want to transfer to your hard disk. This lets you select the parts of the 1-2-3 programs and accessory programs you want to install. Initially all of the programs are selected, which takes about 6MB of disk space. You can press F1 and PGDN to see the disk space requirements for each program. The program files on the disk are compressed so you must use Install to transfer these programs to your hard disk. You can add programs later by running Install again from drive A or B. To include or remove a program to be transferred to your hard disk, use the arrow keys to highlight a program and press the SPACEBAR. Press ENTER when the programs you want are selected.

6. Next, 1-2-3 prompts the disk drive 1-2-3 will use and displays C. If you want to use 1-2-3 on a hard disk other than drive C, enter the drive letter. Press ENTER to accept the default or your new entry.

If the disk you select does not have enough room, the Install program will display an error message. You can press ESC to leave Install or press ENTER to return to the screen that asks you to specify a new drive. If you return to that screen from there you can also press ESC to return to the screen that asks you to select which programs to transfer to your hard disk.

7. The program now prompts for the directory that 1-2-3 will use. Either use 1-2-3's suggested directory of \123R23, or supply a subdirectory name. Subdirectories have the same name conventions as filenames; they are limited to eight characters. Press ENTER to finalize the entry and continue with the next step.

    a. If the directory you chose does not exist, the installation program displays a confirmation box, prompting you to type a **Y** to continue and create the subdirectory, or an **N** to return to the previous screen to select a new directory. Then press ENTER to return to the previous screen or to advance to the next installation step.

    b. If you provide an existing empty directory, Install immediately starts copying files to that directory on the hard disk.

    c. If the directory exists and contains files, and you are installing the 1-2-3 program files, press ENTER after reading the message and specify a new directory since 1-2-3 program files cannot be installed in a directory that contains other files. If you are not installing the main 1-2-3 program, however, your add-ins will successfully be copied to this directory.

8. After you select a directory, 1-2-3 starts copying files from the Install disk. The Install program will prompt for the next disk it needs when it has finished copying files to your hard disk. For each of the disks that the installation program requests, insert the disk in drive A (or B) and press ENTER. Make sure to insert the disk fully into the disk drive and close the disk drive door. Also, do not remove a disk from the disk drive until the installation program prompts for the next disk.

9. Once Install has finished copying files to your hard drive, it displays the second part of the installation process: describing the equipment you will use. Press ENTER to continue.

10. The next screen (Figure A-2) lets you choose Select Your Equipment, Change Selected Equipment, Specify WYSIWYG Options, or End Install. Since you are installing 1-2-3 for the first time, press ENTER to choose Select Your Equipment. Later, if you use the Install program again, you will use the Change Selected Equipment option. At the end of the installation process, you may use the last option, End Install Program, to return to the operating system prompt.

11. Next, Install displays a screen describing what it has identified as the correct screen display. For most monitors, it is correct. Press ENTER to display the screen listing the available screen displays (see Figure A-3). Unless you know that the suggestion is incorrect, press ENTER to accept the suggestion. If the suggestion is wrong, highlight the correct display and press ENTER. Some monitor selections have a second menu that offers additional options for the resolution 1-2-3 will use when displaying your screen. The options may include available colors and the number of lines

Figure A-2. *Choosing Select Your Equipment from the Main Menu*

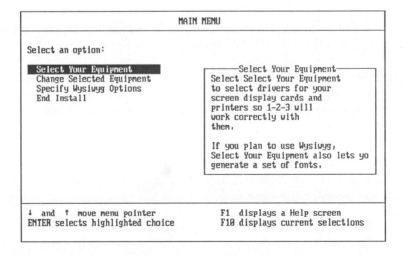

1-2-3 uses. For example, 1-2-3 can display with 25 or 43 lines for an Enhanced Graphics Array monitor.

12. Install next wants to know if you will use a text printer. This enables 1-2-3 to include correct printer codes in the information sent to the printer. Unless you do not have a printer, select Yes. Then select the printer manufacturer or one your printer is compatible with. The Install program will prompt for additional information about the printer model. Highlight the option that is appropriate for your printer and press ENTER.

    Then you can select Yes and press ENTER to select another text printer (and repeat the printer manufacturer and model selections) or select No and press ENTER to finish selecting text printers.

13. Next, you can select the graphics printer for printing graphs and worksheets with WYSIWYG. Select No and press ENTER if your printer cannot print graphics or select Yes and press ENTER if it can. If you select Yes, select a printer manufacturer and model

Figure A-3.   *Available screen displays*

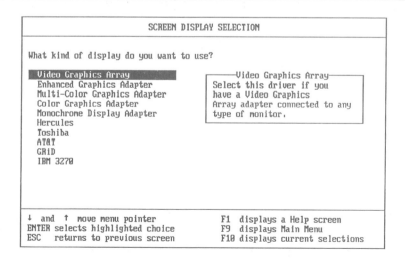

from the lists Install displays. After selecting a graphics printer, Install asks if you want to select another one. You can highlight No and press ENTER to finish selecting graphics printers or highlight Yes, press ENTER, and repeat the printer manufacturer and model selections.

14. After the printers are selected, the Install program asks if you want to change the name of the driver set. The driver set contains information about the screen display, printer, and other information that 1-2-3 uses to execute. If you select No, the installation program names it 123.SET. If you select Yes, you must provide a filename of up to eight characters and use .SET for the filename extension.

    You can see the selections this driver set uses at any time during the Install program by pressing F10, which creates a display like the one in Figure A-4.

15. If you are installing WYSIWYG, Install prompts you to select the fonts you want to generate. Press ENTER after reading the message

Figure A-4.   *Install listing current selections*

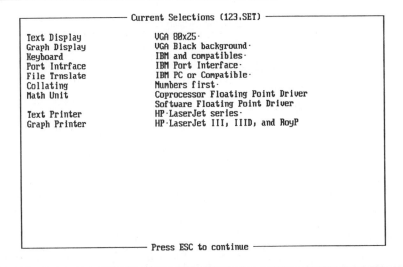

about selecting Basic, Medium, or Extended for the fonts. High-light one of the options and press ENTER. Install will start building the fonts for you. Once the fonts are generated, press any key to leave Install. You are now ready to run 1-2-3.

If you are not installing WYSIWYG, you will see a screen that the installation is complete. At this point, you can press ENTER to return to the DOS prompt. With 1-2-3 installed, you can start 1-2-3 by typing **123** and pressing ENTER.

Using Install After Installing 1-2-3

Once you have installed 1-2-3, you may continue to use the Install program. You may need to change the hardware configuration to include another printer or screen display, in which case you will use the Install program to add more than one driver. You may also want to change the sort order 1-2-3 uses for the Data Sort command.

In Release 2.3, using Install to change 1-2-3 settings requires that you start Install from the directory containing the 1-2-3 program files on your hard disk. You will only start Install from the floppy disk when you want to add 1-2-3 or its accessory programs to your hard disk. In other releases, you will start Install to change a driver set from the drive and directory where your 1-2-3 files are located.

Configuring More Than One Driver

If you use your Lotus software on more than one computer or if you frequently alter the configuration of your system, you will want more than one driver set. This will allow you to switch from one device to another without having to change the installation parameters each time.

If you use more than one driver set, pick a meaningful driver name for each, such as 2MONITOR, PLOTTER, or HOME. You can use up to eight characters for the first part of the name. You must avoid the following symbols: , . ; : / ? * ^ + = < > [ ] \ '. Install adds a .SET extension to the filename, as in COLOR.SET.

Use the Select Your Equipment option to create each driver set. Save each driver set under a different name. If you want to use different drivers with the files in different drives or directories, you may want to store each multiple driver set on a separate disk or in a different directory. To use a driver set other than 123.SET, specify the driver set when you start 1-2-3, as in 123 C:\BUDGET\HOME.SET.

Modifying the Current Driver

To modify the existing 1-2-3 driver sets, select Change Selected Equipment. To select a driver set to change, select Make Another Driver Set Current and supply a driver set filename.

If you do not select a driver set filename, Install uses 123.SET. Then select Modify the Current Driver Set. This displays a screen like the one in Figure A-5. As the figure indicates, 1-2-3 uses separate drivers for the text screen and the graph screen. Install selected the graph screen driver and text screen driver based on the selection you made for the screen display. This screen also includes other options that you did not select when you created the driver set, but you can change these now.

Figure A-5. *Install menu for modifying current driver set*

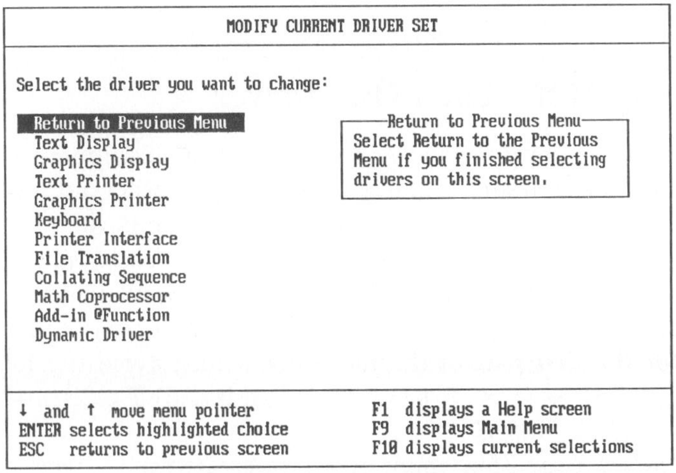

```
┌──────────────────────────────────────────────────────────────────────┐
│                         MODIFY CURRENT DRIVER SET                      │
│                                                                        │
│     Select the driver you want to change:                              │
│                                                                        │
│     ▐Return to Previous Menu▌       ┌─Return to Previous Menu─┐         │
│      Text Display                   │Select Return to the Previous      │
│      Graphics Display               │Menu if you finished selecting     │
│      Text Printer                   │drivers on this screen.            │
│      Graphics Printer               └──────────────────────────┘        │
│      Keyboard                                                          │
│      Printer Interface                                                 │
│      File Translation                                                  │
│      Collating Sequence                                                │
│      Math Coprocessor                                                  │
│      Add-in @Function                                                  │
│      Dynamic Driver                                                    │
│                                                                        │
│   ↓ and ↑ move menu pointer        F1  displays a Help screen          │
│   ENTER selects highlighted choice F9  displays Main Menu              │
│   ESC   returns to previous screen F10 displays current selections     │
└──────────────────────────────────────────────────────────────────────┘
```

One of these changes is choosing which mouse button is used as ENTER. You may select Switch Mouse Buttons and select Right (for holding the mouse in your left hand) or Left (if you will be holding the mouse in your right).

Changing the Display

The display driver may need to be changed if you want to change the initial display driver or you want to use different drivers for graphs and text. Several of the monitors can use more than one display driver. For example, if you are using a monitor with a VGA display, you may want to see how your graphs will look to someone with an EGA monitor. To change a display driver, select Text Display or Graph Display. The Install program lists the possible selections with a triangle next to the display driver that is currently selected. When you select a different driver, Install replaces the current selection with the new selection.

Changing the Printer

The printer driver may need to be changed if you change the printer or you want to add another one. 1-2-3 allows up to four text printer drivers and twelve graphics print drivers. To add or change a printer driver from the screen in Figure A-5, select Text Printer or Graphics Printer. The Install program lists the possible printer manufacturers with a triangle next to the printer manufacturer that you have selected. To add another printer driver, select the printer driver you want to add. Then make the additional menu selections appropriate for the printer. This selects the printer driver that you added as the secondary printer driver. To remove a printer driver, select Text Printer or Graphics Printer and press DEL after highlighting the manufacturer and the model.

To select a printer driver for 1-2-3, use the Worksheet Global Default Printer Name command. Then type the number that represents the selected driver. To select a printer driver for PrintGraph, use the Settings Hardware Printer command and select the printer driver from the list that PrintGraph displays. Notice that some printer selections made in Install have two or more selections in PrintGraph because some printers have multiple density or color selections for printing.

Changing the Sort Order

The Collating Sequence option allows you to change the collating sequence for the existing driver set. Install provides three options: ASCII,

Figure A-6.   *HELP screen illustrating different sort options*

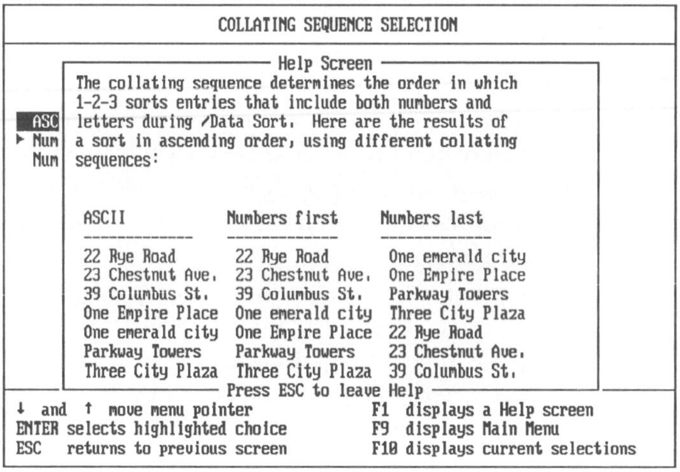

```
┌─────────────────────────────────────────────────────────────────┐
│                    COLLATING SEQUENCE SELECTION                   │
│         ┌──────────────── Help Screen ───────────────┐           │
│         │ The collating sequence determines the order in which │  │
│         │ 1-2-3 sorts entries that include both numbers and    │  │
│     ▓ASC│ letters during /Data Sort. Here are the results of   │  │
│     ▶ Num│ a sort in ascending order, using different collating │ │
│     Num │ sequences:                                           │  │
│         │                                                       │  │
│         │                                                       │  │
│         │ ASCII            Numbers first    Numbers last        │  │
│         │ ───────────      ───────────      ───────────         │  │
│         │ 22 Rye Road      22 Rye Road      One emerald city    │  │
│         │ 23 Chestnut Ave. 23 Chestnut Ave. One Empire Place    │  │
│         │ 39 Columbus St.  39 Columbus St.  Parkway Towers      │  │
│         │ One Empire Place One emerald city Three City Plaza    │  │
│         │ One emerald city One Empire Place 22 Rye Road         │  │
│         │ Parkway Towers   Parkway Towers   23 Chestnut Ave.    │  │
│         │ Three City Plaza Three City Plaza 39 Columbus St.     │  │
│         └───────────────── Press ESC to leave Help ──────────── ┘ │
│ ↓ and ↑  move menu pointer            F1  displays a Help screen  │
│ ENTER selects highlighted choice      F9  displays Main Menu      │
│ ESC   returns to previous screen      F10 displays current selections │
└─────────────────────────────────────────────────────────────────┘
```

Numbers first, and Numbers last. If you are not familiar with sorting sequences, look at the Install HELP screen shown in Figure A-6 for a sample of the three options. The sort order for each option is as follows:

- ASCII: Blank cells, followed by labels and values in ASCII order. Capitalization will affect the sort order with this choice. This selection also makes @functions case-sensitive and can have serious implications for formulas containing string functions that are used in computations or for the criteria area with Data Query commands.

- Numbers last: Blank cells, label entries with letters in alphabetical order, label entries beginning with numbers in numeric sequence, labels beginning with special characters, and then values.

- Numbers first: Blank cells, labels beginning with numbers in numeric sequence, labels beginning with letters in alphabetical order, labels beginning with special characters, and then values.

To change the collating sequence, select Collating from the menu and then select the sort order you want from the submenu.

Saving the Driver Files

Once you have changed your driver file's display, printer, and sort configurations, you need to save them so that the driver file will contain your new selections. To save the driver file, select Return to Previous Menu and then select Save the Current Driver Set. When 1-2-3 displays the filename, edit it if you want the new settings saved with a different filename. When the filename is correct, press ENTER to save the updated changes. When the new driver set file is saved, you are instructed to press F9 to return to the last menu or press ENTER to leave Install. After pressing ENTER, you must select Yes to confirm that you want to leave Install. If WYSIWYG is installed and you change the printer or display in a driver set, you will have to generate fonts. The menu selections and process are identical to installing fonts when you install WYSIWYG.

Changing Other Configuration Parameters

Most of the hardware configuration options are specified in the installation process. However, two additional options that could require frequent change are changed directly from 1-2-3. One is the disk drive assignment for data files, and the other is the printer settings. The disk drive assignment can be changed from the default drive of C:\123R23 to another drive. The command to do this within 1-2-3 is Worksheet Global Default Directory. Printer settings can be changed with Worksheet Global Default Printer. The changes made with this command can be saved with Worksheet Global Default Update.

Installing Other Releases of 1-2-3

If you are installing a prior release of 1-2-3, the steps you perform are different. In Releases 2.2 and 2.01, you must run a program called INIT to register your System disk before you copy the 1-2-3 files onto floppy backup disks or to your hard disk. After the disks are registered, you can use the DOS COPY command to copy them to floppy or hard disks. Before you start 1-2-3, you must run the Install program on the same disk as your

1-2-3 program files and select the equipment you are using. Select First-Time Installation to tell 1-2-3 the type of equipment you are using. These selections are very similar to the ones described in this appendix in steps 12 through 15.

If you are installing Allways, which is included with Release 2.2, you must install it separately using the menu driven AWSETUP program. You will need to select First-Time Installation and enter the display and printer you are using so AWSETUP copies the appropriate files to your hard disk.

Index

 **Expand** *Your Skill Even More*

with help from our expert authors. Now that you've gained greater skills with **1-2-3 Release 2.3 Made Easy***, let us suggest the following related titles that will help you use your computer to full advantage.*

WordPerfect® 5.1: The Complete Reference
by Karen L. Acerson

Every WordPerfect® 5.1 user will want to have this fabulous reference handy. Commonly referred to as the "WordPerfect Bible," Acerson's book covers every WordPerfect 5.1 feature, message, and menu item from A–Z. Each topic includes keystrokes, tips and hints, and several applications where the features can be used. Also included are chapters on installation, WordPerfect basics to help you get started, desktop publishing with WordPerfect, and details on integrating WordPerfect with other programs.
$24.95p ISBN: 0-07-881634-3, 1327 pp., 7 3/8 X 9 1/4

WordPerfect® 5.1 Made Easy
by Mella Mincberg

Mincberg, the author of two previous editions of *WordPerfect® Made Easy* that met with great success, has now published a volume on WordPerfect® Release 5.1. Follow these hands-on lessons and practical applications and you'll soon be producing reports, and other professional-looking documents. Learn to use all the improved WordPerfect 5.1 capabilities inicluding desktop publishing features, mail-merge features, the ability to create better tables and handle complex equations. Mincberg also covers WordPerfect 5.0.
$19.95p ISBN: 0-07-881625-4, 1071 pp., 7 3/8 X 9 1/4, Covers Releases 5.0 and 5.1

Simply DOS
by Kris Jamsa

Here's the ideal book for everyone who needs to learn the basics of DOS. DOS expert Kris Jamsa makes learning DOS simple, short, and painless. Clear, step-by-step instructions introduce the most essential DOS commands that you need for everyday DOS tasks. All versions of DOS are covered. Filled with helpful illustrations and examples, you'll find a great bonus that makes this book even easier to use—it has a special binding that lays flat when you open to any chosen page.
$14.95p, ISBN: 0-07-881715-3, 200 pp., 5 7/8 X 8 3/4

DOS: The Complete Reference, Second Edition
by Kris Jamsa

Every PC-DOS and MS-DOS user will find essential information — from an overview of the disk operating system to a reference for advanced programming and disk management techniques—in this updated and revised edition of the outstanding bestseller. Each chapter begins with a discussion of specific applications followed by a list of related commands.
$29.95p, ISBN: 0-07-881497-9, 1278 pp., 7 3/8 X 9 1/4, Covers MS-DOS/PC-DOS Versions Through 3.3

The PC User's Guide
by Nick Anis and Craig Menefee

The PC User's Guide offers comprehensive readable documentation for your IBM PC or PC compatible computer. The book begins by acquainting you with personal computer hardware and how to set it up, before delving into operating system software, applications software, and storage media. You'll also learn about servicing your computer system, optimizing its performance, and adding to or upgrading it. From unpacking to tweaking, from BASIC to BIOS, *The PC User's Guide* is your one-stop source for answers and information.
$29.95p ISBN: 0-07-881670-X, 700 pp., 7 3/8 X 9 1/4, Dvorak*Osborne/McGraw-Hill

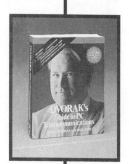

Dvorak's Guide to PC Telecommunications
by John C. Dvorak and Nick Anis

Telecommunications just got SIMPLE—all you need is your computer, a modem, and this exciting book and disk package. Internationally renowned John C. Dvorak, the world's most widely read computer columnist joins forces with programming wiz and author, Nick Anis, to present the most compelling reason for discovering telecommunications. Packaged with this comprehensive guide are two disks jam-packed with reliable, easy-to-use utilities, interactive tutorials, communications software, and special discounts from the major on-line services.
$49.95p ISBN: 0-07-881551-7, 1053 pp., 7 3/8 X 9 1/4, Dvorak*Osborne/McGraw-Hill

Computer Professional's Dictionary
by Allen Wyatt

For the largest selection of technical terms, concise definitions, and the latest computer jargon, this is the resource to choose. Written with the experienced computer user in mind, over 3,000 terms from "Abbreviated addressing" to "Zmodem" are included covering virtually every aspect of computing. You can quickly locate the meaning or use of a particular word, acronym, or abbreviation. Wyatt gives all programmers, MIS managers, and computer experts a dictionary that truly enlightens.
$19.95, ISBN: 0-07-881705-6, 350 pp. 7 3/8 X 9 1/4

▶ _____Osborne **McGraw-Hill** ■ **Available at local book and computer stores.**

Essential 1-2-3 Release 2.3 Commands

Worksheet Commands

Alters format of all worksheet cells

Alters width of all worksheet columns

Sets recalculation to automatic

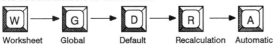

Sets recalculation to manual

Inserts rows or columns in worksheet

Deletes worksheet rows or columns

Alters width of a single column

Hides a worksheet column

Alters width of a range of columns

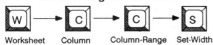

Erases worksheet even if worksheet has not been saved

Records keystrokes in a worksheet range

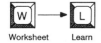

Worksheet Commands

Continued

Sets and clears worksheet titles

Sets and clears worksheet windows

Adds page break at the cell pointer location

Range Commands

Assigns format to a range

Changes label alignment of a range of labels

Erases contents of a range

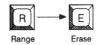

Creates and deletes range names

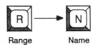

Names entry in worksheet cell to the cell immediately to its right

Alters orientation of a range of entries

Searches for an entry in a range

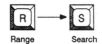

Copy Command

Copies worksheet entries

Copy

Move Command

Moves worksheet entries

Move

File Commands

Retrieves file from disk

File   Retrieve

Cancels save request

File   Save   Cancel

Tells 1-2-3 to replace disk file with current contents of memory

File   Save   Replace

Creates .WK1 file and .BAK file

File   Save   Backup

Combines information from disk with the current worksheet

File   Combine

Erases a file on disk

File   Erase

Creates list of files in the current directory

File   List

Changes current directory

File   Directory

Refreshes links to external files

File   Admin   Link-Refresh

Quit Command

Quits 1-2-3 even if the worksheet hasn't been saved

Quit   Yes   Yes

System Command

Temporarily exits to the operating system

System

Print Commands

Directs print output to printer

Print   Printer

Establishes range for printing

Print   Printer   Range

Advances one line

Print   Printer   Line

Advances one page

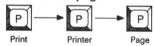

Print   Printer   Page

Enters a header line

Print   Printer   Options   Header

Enters a footer line

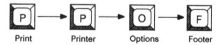

Print   Printer   Options   Footer

Directs print output to a disk file

Print   File

Directs print output to the printer through a background file

Print   Background

Essential 1-2-3 Release 2.3 Commands

Print Commands

Continued

Directs print output to a disk file with printer codes

Sets top, bottom, right and left margins

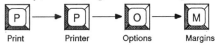

Establishes border rows or columns

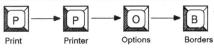

Enters a setup string to control print output

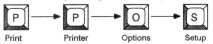

Sets page length

Provides access to other print settings

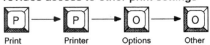

Quits the Print Options menu

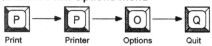

Clears print settings

Zeroes line count and tells 1-2-3 you're starting a new page

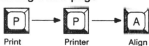

Starts printing

Graph Commands

Selects a graph type

Sets the X graph range

Sets the A graph range

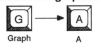

Sets the B graph range

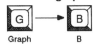

Sets the C graph range

Sets the D graph range

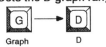

Sets the E graph range

Sets the F graph range

Views the graph

Saves the graph image file

Establishes legends for each graph data range

Creates graph titles

Graph Commands

Continued

Establishes and clears grid lines

Sets display to color

Sets display to black and white

Creates and uses graph names

Sets all graph ranges with one command

Data Commands

Generates series of evenly spaced numbers

Specifies range for sorting

Specifies main sort key

Specifies secondary sort key

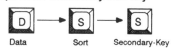

Sorts Data

Data Commands

Continued

Specifies input range for query

Tells 1-2-3 which record to use

Specifies output range for query

Highlights matching records

Extracts matching records

Add-In Commands

Loads an Add-In program into memory

Removes an Add-In program from memory

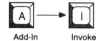

Activates an attached Add-In program

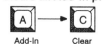

Clears all Add-In programs from memory

Quits the Add-In menu

Osborne McGraw-Hill

Computer Books

(800) 227-0900

— Tear off for Bookmark

▼

You're important to us...

We'd like to know what you're interested in, what kinds of books you're looking for, and what you thought about this book in particular.

Please fill out the attached card and mail it in. We'll do our best to keep you informed about Osborne's newest books and special offers.

► *YES, SEND ME A FREE COLOR CATALOG*
of all Osborne/McGraw-Hill computer books.

Name:_____Title:_____

Company:_____

Address:_____

City:_____State:_____Zip:_____

I'M PARTICULARLY INTERESTED IN THE FOLLOWING*(Check all that apply)*

I use this software:
❏ Lotus 1-2-3
❏ Quattro
❏ dBASE
❏ WordPerfect
❏ Microsoft Word
❏ WordStar
❏ Others_____

I use this operating system:
❏ DOS
❏ OS/2
❏ UNIX
❏ Macintosh
❏ Others_____

I rate this book:
❏ Excellent   ❏ Good   ❏ Poor

I program in:
❏ C
❏ PASCAL
❏ BASIC
❏ Others_____

I chose this book because...
❏ Recognized author's name
❏ Osborne/McGraw-Hill's reputation
❏ Read book review
❏ Read Osborne catalog
❏ Saw advertisement in _____
❏ Found while browsing in store
❏ Found/recommended in library
❏ Required textbook
❏ Price
❏ Other_____

Comments_____

_____

Topics I would like to see covered in future books by Osborne/McGraw-Hill

include:_____

_____

BUSINESS REPLY MAIL

First Class   Permit NO. 3111   Berkeley, CA

Postage will be paid by addressee

Osborne McGraw-Hill

2600 Tenth Street

Berkeley, California 94710–9938

Osborne **McGraw-Hill**

Computer

Books

(800) 227-0900